THE HIDDEN TRADITION

The
Hidden Tradition

WOMEN'S SPIRITUAL WRITINGS REDISCOVERED

An Anthology

Collected and Edited by
Lavinia Byrne

Crossroad · New York

1991

The Crossroad Publishing Company
370 Lexington Avenue, New York, NY 10017

Introductory matter and compilation © Lavinia Byrne 1991

Printed in the United States of America

Library of Congress Cataloging-in-Publication Data

The Hidden Tradition : women's spiritual writings
  rediscovered : an anthology / collected and edited by
  Lavinia Byrne.
        p.   cm.
  Previously published in U.K. : London : SPCK, 1991.
  Includes bibliographical references.
  ISBN 0-8245-1108-5
  1. Women—Religious life.   2. Christian life.
I. Byrne, Lavinia, 1947—
BV4527.H53   1991
248'.082—dc20   91-28835
                                                      CIP

In honour of
my mother
Edith Marion Josephe Byrne, née Macsherry
1909–

Grand'mère
Valérie Marie-Louise Macsherry, née Aubril
1876–1974

my own mothers in the Faith and in fact

Contents

Acknowledgements

Many women have collaborated with me in the preparation of this book. I want to thank Hannah Ward and Jennifer Wild who helped me to prepare the manuscript for publication and the many librarians, especially in convents, who patiently gave me access to their collections.

Thanks must also go to Major Genty Fairbank from the Salvation Army's Heritage Centre and archives, to Gordon Taylor, the author of *Companion to the Song Book of the Salvation Army* and to Jo Farrow from the Home Service of the Society of Friends. Elisabeth Jupp from the library at Heythrop College has been a mine of information and given me great encouragement and help. Ideas about material for inclusion in the text have also come thick and fast from Revd Pamela Maggs, Dr Jane Tillier and Angela Tilby.

Thanks must also go to my colleagues at the Institute of Spirituality, Heythrop College and to Judith Longman at SPCK. Her editorial advice has been invaluable to me.

I am grateful to the following for permission to reproduce copyright material:

Basil Blackwell for the extracts from *Maude Royden: A Life* by Sheila Fletcher.

Cistercian Publications, Kalamazoo, MI, for extracts from *Peace Weavers* edited by John Nichols and Lillian Thomas Shanks.

HarperCollins Publishers for the extracts from *Prayer* by Olive Wyon.

Cambridge University Press for the extracts from *Women Writers of the Middle Ages* by Peter Dronke and *I Believe* by Kathleen Lonsdale.

Darton, Longman and Todd for the extracts from *Till God Will* edited by M. Emmanuel Orchard.

William Heinemann for the extracts from *My Commonplace Book* by Mary Stocks.

David Higham Associates, London, and Watkins/Loomis Agency, Inc., New York, for extracts from the works of Dorothy L. Sayers.

ICS Publications, Washington, DC, for the extracts from *The Collected Works of St Teresa of Avila* translated by Kieran Kavanaugh and Otilio Rodriguez, © Washington Province of Discalced Carmelites 1976.

Longman for the extracts from *The Collected Papers of Evelyn Underhill* edited by Lucy Menzies.

Mary M. Martin for the extracts from the work of Helen Waddell.

Oxford University Press for the extract from *The Women's Movement in the Church of England* by Brian Heeny.

Oxford University Press, New York, for the extracts from *Medieval Women's Visionary Literature* edited by Elizabeth Alvida Petroff.

Paulist Press, Mahwah, NJ, for the extracts from *Francis de Sales, Jane de Chantal: Letters of Spiritual Direction* selected and introduced by Wendy M. Wright and Joseph Power, © the authors 1988; *Hadewijch: The Complete Works* translated by Mother Columba Hart OSB, © The Missionary Society of St Paul the Apostle in the State of New York 1980; *Julian of Norwich: Showings* translated by Edmund Colledge OSA and James Walsh SJ, © The Missionary Society of St Paul the Apostle in the State of New York 1978; and *Shakers: Two Centuries of Spiritual Reflection* by Robley Edward Wilson, © Robley Edward Wilson 1983.

Pitman Publishing for the extracts from *The Future of Religion* by Kathleen Bliss.

The Quaker Home Service for the extracts from *Tradition and Experience* by Richenda C. Scott and *Christian Faith and Practice in the Experience of the Society of Friends*.

SCM Press for the extracts from *The Service and Status of Women in the Churches* by Kathleen Bliss.

Tessa Sayle Agency for the extracts from *Concerning the Inner Life with the House of the Soul* by Evelyn Underhill.

Serenity Press, Oregon, for the extracts from *Daily Readings from Quaker Writings Ancient and Modern* edited by Linda Hill Renfer.

Simon & Schuster, Inc., New York, for the extracts from *Women of Spirit* edited by Rosemary Radford Ruether and Eleanor McLaughlin, © Rosemary Radford Ruether and Eleanor McLaughlin 1979.

Unwin Hyman Ltd for the extracts from *We Believe in God* edited by Rupert E. Davies.

The University of Georgia Press for the extracts from *Medieval Women Writers* edited by Katharina M. Wilson.

A. P. Watt Ltd on behalf of the Roman Catholic Diocese of Birmingham for the extract from *The Light and the Rainbow* by Hilda Graef.

For complete publication details see the source notes and the Bibliography. I have made every effort to trace and acknowledge copyright holders of the material in this anthology; information on any omissions should be communicated to the publishers, who will make full acknowledgement in future editions.

Introduction

The only reference given under the letter 'w' was to wealth. I was standing in a library holding an eminent contemporary history of the first twelve centuries of the Christian spiritual tradition. As I flicked idly through the chapter headings and then began a more thorough search of its pages, my spirits sank. The index of people and places contained not so much as a single reference to women. And when I turned to the subject index the word 'wealth' jumped out of the page at me.

At that moment the idea for this book was born.

Women have been writing authoritatively about their experience of God and of organized religion for centuries. An anthology of their writings would bring their thinking into the light. It would enable present-day women to place themselves in a wider context and see themselves as part of a long, if hidden, tradition. And so I began to read and to search and to listen to the voices I discovered.

At first I thought I had a scheme for organizing the material I would find. My intention was to group it in clusters using headings from the Magnificat as chapter headings. But as I read I had to abandon that idea. What emerged was that the most persuasive writing dictated my themes to me. Women in the tradition have written most powerfully when their theme has been their experience of the divine indwelling, of the person of Jesus, of call, the Christian life, prayer, mission and ministry, desire and of the Virgin Mary.

Each of the chapters in this book contains material grouped according to these highly traditional and totally timeless themes. The chapter headings tell their own story. The words 'the divine infilling' are taken from the writings of a Quaker woman, Joan Mary Fry. 'Gradually', she notices, 'as mind, soul and even body grow still, sinking deeper and deeper into the life of God, the pettinesses, the tangles, the failures of the outer life begin to be seen in their true proportions, and the sense of the divine infilling, uplifting, redeeming Love becomes real and illuminating.' What I notice as I read a passage like this is that the writer is talking about something she has herself experienced. So much so that she searches for words and piles them up on top of each other to make her point: 'infilling, uplifting, redeeming, illuminating'.

These are all present participles, a part of speech which recurs commonly in the pages of this book because of the ease with which it allows an experience to be re-lived. It neither condemns it to the past nor nails it exclusively to one set of events.

The heading of the second chapter, which collects material women have written about the person of Jesus, is taken from the writings of the twentieth-century Roman Catholic mystic, Caryll Houselander. 'If Christ is growing in us, if we are at peace, recollected, because we know that however insignificant our life seems to be, from it he is forming himself; if we go with eager wills, "in haste" to wherever our circumstances compel us, because we believe that he desires to be in that place, we shall find that we are driven more and more to act on the impulse of his love.' The theological insight is formidable. Much of the material in this chapter is concerned with what Lady Hosie called 'the courtesy of Christ to women', the fact that, as Dorothy L. Sayers saw, 'nobody could possibly guess from the words and deeds of Jesus that there was anything "funny" about women's nature'. But beyond the treatment meted out to people by Jesus during his preaching, healing and teaching ministry and in the events of his passion, lies our experience of the risen Christ. In reflecting upon this as an experience of transformation, Caryll Houselander gives us a task: 'It seems that this is Christ's favourite way of being recognized, that he prefers to be known, not by his own human features, but by the quickening of his own life in the heart, which is the response to his coming.' It is not incidental that the gospel story she is reflecting upon in this extract is that of the Visitation, the story of the embrace of Mary and Elizabeth and their two unborn children.

I hesitated over the title to chapter three. The chapter is about call and vocation. Would I choose Frances Willard's 'What wouldst thou have me to do?' with its strong scriptural overtones, or the more robust text from Elsie Chamberlain's contribution to the collection *We Believe in God*? In the event the robust text won. There is a real urgency to these texts; they testify so strongly to the fact that God has called women, God does call women, that the inferences are plain for all to see. If Gamaliel's law has in some strange and unspoken way been being applied to the active life of women in the Church's service, so that it has been admitted to be of God by default, as it were, the time has now come to take a more positive stand. In this way ministry itself will be transformed and become more whole, with women and men, ordained and lay people building up the kingdom together.

Caryll Houselander's poem 'A Prayer to Creatures' supplied me with my next chapter heading. The chapter is about the life of Christbearing women, the ordinary, everyday ways in which we are the body of Christ in the world: 'when the flame is lit, the wax is consumed quickly'. The light which is burning so strongly in our world at the moment was described in wonderfully enthusiastic terms by Evangeline Booth: 'The change that has come to women is a change, not in environment merely, not in wealth and habits merely, but in the very mind, the very being of the race itself. The forces of prejudice, of selfishness, of ignorance, which have arrested the progress and curtailed the influence of womankind for centuries, are receding from the foreground of the future.' The prejudice, selfishness and ignorance of patriarchy, which has had such a strong grip on the hearts and minds of all men and women for so many centuries are being eroded. And as we begin to witness this erosion in our own times, the testimony of these women from history who have been wrestling with the spiritual implications of prejudice has an added poignancy. Feminism may have given us a more sophisticated vocabulary for describing the experience of pain but these women certainly had an equally powerful taste of it.

Chapter five is about prayer. Again I was presented with a wealth of choice. The language which women use when they describe the experience of encounter with God is the language of love. Increasingly too it is the language of recognition as they begin to find themselves mirrored in the divine. In personal prayer women find an access to God which is not mediated by book or priest or sacrament. For this reason I have chosen a beautiful line from another Quaker, Caroline E. Stephen, who writes out of a tradition which is informed by the certainty of the presence of God to every individual – as well as to the society or company of friends who meet for prayer. 'It is out of the depths of this stillness that there do arise at times spoken words which, springing from the very source of prayer, have something of the power of prayer – something of its quickening and melting and purifying effect. Such words as these have at least as much power as silence to gather into stillness.' Quickening, melting, purifying. Once again Caroline E. Stephen – in common with the other women in this chapter – is writing of something she knows about and struggles to put into words.

One of the most moving testimonies in chapter six is given us by Evangeline Booth. Writing about the courage of Salvation Army women officers, she claims, 'Death and danger had not been the only trial of these women's faith. They had faced dirt, they had handled disease, they had not flinched before uttermost degradation, they had not been dismayed by the most awful defacements of God's image, imprinted on our race; there is no depth of misery, of despair, of iniquity that is concealed from the steady eyes of the women of the Salvation Army.' Her judicious choice of the adjective 'steady' speaks volumes. Any care and constancy and patience and steadfastness any of us has ever received at the hands of a woman is somehow recalled and contained in that one word. The esteem and respect in which Salvation Army officers are held and the work they do restoring the 'defacements of God's image' must, in some sense, be linked to the fact that they have always taken the replication of the divine image in women so seriously. That kind of integrity brings its own rewards and the confidence and joy of the Salvation Army women's texts tell their own story. But there are other traditions too and the active mission and ministry of women in other parts of God's Church is a more complicated story. Moreover it is an unfinished story and our own joy is that the tale has yet fully to be told.

In her quest for union with God Catherine of Siena wrote: 'O eternal Trinity, fire and abyss of charity, dissolve this very day the cloud of my body! I am driven to desire, in the knowledge of yourself that you have given me in your truth, to leave behind the weight of this body of mine and give my life for the glory and praise of your name.' Many other women are driven to desire too and chapter seven tries to demonstrate this desire in its many contexts. Above all it seeks to legitimize the experience of desire; we all have it and are asking questions about what to do with it, about focusing our choices and finding the will of God through the grace of discernment. With Catherine of Siena we are able to say, 'You have gifted me with power from yourself, eternal Father, and my understanding with your wisdom – such wisdom as is proper to your only-begotten Son; and the Holy Spirit, who proceeds from you and from your Son, has given me a will and so I am able to love.'

The first of the Christbearing women, Mary the mother of Jesus, is honoured in the texts of my final chapter. For the title I turned to a Victorian hymn. Christian Burke wrote:

> Since the day the blessed Mother
> Thee, the world's redeemer, bore,
> Thou hast crowned us with an honour
> Women never knew before;
> And that we may bear it meetly
> We must seek thine aid the more.

Whatever is written about Mary is also written indirectly about all women. That is why it is intriguing to notice what the Churches do with the mother of Jesus. For the women in this chapter she is a friend and an ally. My own desire is that she should become so for more women, because she has something to say to our own times.

In preparing this book I have discovered that women have been making theology and describing their living knowledge of the power and presence of God for centuries. This collection records the voices of over ninety of these women yet it is necessarily incomplete. Any selection of documents is inevitably unsatisfactory; many passages which are firm favourites for other people will have been omitted here. I cannot hope to please everyone. As it stands, however, this particular collection reveals something of the resolution with which women have clung to the integrity of their own insights down the ages. It records something that is essential and mainstream to the story of Christianity in its worldwide growth and spread. But equally it demonstrates what happens when mainstream Christianity becomes fragmented and new groups and new voices are heard, voices such as those of the Shakers which can no longer be contained within the body of believers. Above all it is evidence of the strength with which women respond to God and of the wealth of material that has been written by women. For this reason I have given bibliographical material in as much detail as possible so that more people can return to the sources I have used and draw strength from them as well.

In this way I hope the real significance of these texts will somehow emerge. At present I believe that they are important because they enable us to make contact with our origins and thus help us to feel less isolated. In the words of the woman in Jesus' parable, we can rejoice because that which was lost is found (Luke 15.9). Other women have lived through experiences which are familiar to many Christians at the present time. Their testimonies remind us that they developed strategies for surviving and managed to do so.

There is another insight which is equally strategic but situated at the level of theological insight rather than of spiritual practice. In today's world human experience is valued as a locus for divine revelation. We believe in a God who reaches out to us and greets and welcomes us within the events and relationships of everyday life. When we grow as reflective and loving people we do so because we are open to the voice of God and the call of God within our own circumstances. The value of this insight is proving to be of inestimable importance to the Churches. Clerical voices are no longer the only ones which may proclaim the marvellous works of God. God speaks to and is made known to lay men and women as well.

As a consequence of this insight we have begun to revel in the richness of our own vocation and identity as the beloved of God. Lay people have begun to claim and demonstrate the full meaning of the 'universal call to holiness' announced by the Roman Catholic Church's Second Vatican Council. But now we face another change of focus and direction. The insight is valid, God does communicate with us through our own experience. But equally God is greater than anything we personally can know or say in the divine name. Where our own experience is the only basis for making theology, there are no external points of reference or of balance. Of course 'my story' is valuable, but so too is 'our story' – and this is what this book attempts to tell. That is why I believe its appearance is particularly timely now. We live in an age when many women are tempted to discount the tradition precisely because they experience it as an exclusively male tradition. This book tells a different story. It restores women to their rightful place within the Christian tradition by dedicating space exclusively to their insights.

The story they tell needs minimum interpretation, maximum attention. It has enormous wisdom to feed into a tradition which is discredited where it excludes the voices and authority of women.

My hope is that this book will be well read and, above all, enjoyed. Use it to pray with. Use it as a starting point for your own theological reflection. Write down your own thoughts and prayers. Be inspired by what you read and share it with your friends.

In this way the lost tradition will gain new vitality and life as it inspires contemporary women and men in their own search for God.

Lavinia Byrne IBVM
25 March 1990
Feast of the Annunciation

1
The Divine infilling

The story Mary Ward narrates so simply at the beginning of this chapter places her among the ranks of the women mystics. There have been many of these down the ages, women who have recognized the divine presence and found themselves mirrored and imaged within it. What is extraordinary is the broad range of denominations these women represent. God has been seeking women out and finding them within their own life situations, whatever their denominational divide. So the Quaker, Joan Mary Fry, will speak of 'the divine infilling' and the Catholic, Angela of Foligno, will speak of her certainty at 'possessing God'.

The encounter with God is an encounter which has its own integrity. It happens, it is. At times it will be accompanied by a call, but this is not always necessarily the case. The testimony of the women who described their experience of God in the texts I have chosen here tells us this experience does not have to be mediated. In Julian of Norwich's words, 'Greatly ought we to rejoice that God dwells in our soul; and greatly ought we to rejoice that our soul dwells in God.' The language these women use is about dwelling and abiding and enclosure. The image they use most frequently is about sight, about the vision of God. Hadewijch, the Beguine from Brabant, puts it most compellingly: 'I remained to gaze fixedly upon my delightful sweet Love.' The image has its other side though, because sometimes the experience of God is an experience of darkness, of something closer to absence than to presence. While the Roman Catholic nun, Lucy Christine, talks about light which penetrates water and water which absorbs it, a powerful image of the attraction we have for God and God has for us, nevertheless the medieval mystic, Angela of Foligno, saw God 'darkly'. She goes on to say, 'This darkness was the greatest blessing that could be imagined.'

Heartening words to Madame Acarie, the French woman whose husband tried so hard to understand what was happening to his wife when she was 'rapt up to the heights' and yet, when he failed to do so, resorted to humiliating her in public. The testimony of married women is important in itself. It serves to remind us that God is a God of desires, a God of revelation who desires to be known – and known by married and single women as well as by nuns. In the 1937 Swarthmore lecture organized by the Society of Friends, Caroline C. Graveson wrote of this desire, reminding her audience that 'God is in all beauty' and going on to add that this could even be seen in 'a child's knitted frock'. The true contemplative will look upon the world with the gaze of God and find the divine image and the divine infilling all around her.

When the Free Church woman Hatty Baker writes about the 'denial of the existence of a soul in women' and its logical outcome, she identifies this as 'the denial of the out-pouring of the Holy Spirit'. None of the women in this chapter was prepared to deny the experience and understanding of God which was given to them by 'the mirror of eternity'. When Clare of Assisi used those words she went on to add to the woman to whom she was writing, 'Transform your whole being into the image of the Godhead Itself, through contemplation.' This contemplation of the divine infilling will lead many women to prayer, to transformation, even to the extent of 'becoming a perfect image of God' as Elizabeth of the Trinity perceived. The image into which women gaze when they look upon God becomes an image in which they can recognize and find themselves.

Evelyn Underhill, the great Anglican commentator on mysticism, sees a consequence of this. She writes of the uniqueness of each individual's relationship with God and yet reminds us that 'even the most hidden life is never lived for itself alone'. Contemplation and awareness of one's real identity before God leads us into relationship with other people, not away from it. From the hidden life she lived in her Carmelite convent, Thérèse of Lisieux had discovered this as well, 'that love is the vocation which includes all others'. Her Spanish predecessor, Teresa of Avila, saw it this way: the gift brought about by recognition of the divine infilling is the gift of truth. 'The soul cannot possibly do other than believe.' Contemplation, transformation, love and truth. These are the marks of the divine infilling.

He was very near me and within me, which I never perceived him to be before. I was moved to ask him with great confidence and humility what I came to know, to wit, what he was. I said, My God, what art thou? I saw him immediately and very clearly go into my heart, and little and little hide himself in it, and there I perceive him still to be in the same manner, my meditation being ended almost an hour since. I endeavoured to go forward according to the points of the meditation, but could not. He held my heart, I could not work. . . .

Mary Ward

Till God Will: Mary Ward through her Writings. Ed. M. Emmanuel Orchard I B V M (London, Darton, Longman and Todd, 1985), p. 46.

The Divine Infilling

Greatly ought we to rejoice that God dwells in our soul; and more greatly ought we to rejoice that our soul dwells in God. Our soul is created to be God's dwelling place, and the dwelling of our soul is God, who is uncreated. It is a great understanding to see and know inwardly that God, who is our Creator, dwells in our soul, and it is a far greater understanding to see and know inwardly that our soul, which is created, dwells in God in substance, of which substance, through God, we are what we are.

And I saw no difference between God and our substance, but, as it were, all God; and still my understanding accepted that our substance is in God, that is to say that God is God, and our substance is a creature in God. For the almighty truth of the Trinity is our Father, for he made us and keeps us in him. And the deep wisdom of the Trinity is our Mother, in whom we are enclosed. And the high goodness of the Trinity is our Lord, and in him we are enclosed and he in us. We are enclosed in the Father, and we are enclosed in the Son, and we are enclosed in the Holy Spirit. And the Father is enclosed in us, almighty, all wisdom and all goodness, one God, one Lord.

Julian of Norwich

Julian of Norwich *Showings*. Classics of Western Spirituality. Tr. and introd. Edmund Colledge OSA and James Walsh SJ (London, SPCK; Mahwah, NJ, Paulist Press, 1979), p. 285.

Think rather of the high noon of summer, or of the stillness of a snow-covered country, how the heat or lightness everywhere gives an intense sense of overflowing and abounding life, making a quietness of rapture rather than of fear. Such, only of a deeper and far more intimate kind, is the atmosphere of waiting souls. It may be that words will spring out of those depths, it may be that vocal prayer or praise shall flow forth at the bidding of him whose presence makes worship a communion, but whether there be speech or silence matters not. Gradually, as mind, soul and even body grow still, sinking deeper and deeper into the life of God, the pettinesses, the tangles, the failures of the outer life begin to be seen in their true proportions, and the sense of the divine infilling, uplifting, redeeming Love becomes real and illuminating. Things are seen and known that are hidden to the ordinary faculties. This state is not merely one of quiescence; the soul is alive, active, vigorous, yet so still that it hardly knows how intense is its own vital action.

Joan Mary Fry

Joan Mary Fry, *The Communion of Life*. Swarthmore Lecture, 1910 (London, Headley Brothers, 1910), pp. 53–4.

In case you think there is little gain to be derived from practising vocal prayer perfectly, I must tell you that, while you are repeating the Paternoster or some other vocal prayer, it is quite possible for the Lord to grant you perfect contemplation. In this way His Majesty shows that he is listening to the person who is addressing him, and that, in his greatness, he is addressing her, by suspending the understanding, putting a stop to all thought, and, as we say, taking the words out of her mouth so that even if she wishes to speak she cannot do so, or at any rate not without great difficulty.

Such a person understands that, without any sound of words, she is being taught by this Divine Master, who is suspending her faculties, which, if they were to work, would be causing her harm rather than profit. The faculties rejoice without knowing how they rejoice; the soul is enkindled in love without understanding how it loves; it knows it is rejoicing in the object of its love, yet it does not know how it is rejoicing in it. It is well aware that this is not a joy which can be attained by the understanding; the will embraces it, without understanding how; but, in so far as it can understand anything, it perceives that this is a blessing which could not be gained by the merits of all the trials suffered on earth put together. It is a gift of the Lord of earth and heaven, who gives it like the God he is. This, daughters, is perfect contemplation.

Teresa of Avila

Teresa of Jesus, *The Complete Works* vol. 2. Tr. and ed. E. Allison Peers (London and New York, Sheed and Ward, 1946), p. 104.

To most of us God is an experience before he is a concept, a presence in and with us, till we gradually realize that it is in this presence that we live and move and have our being. We may try to describe him as the Absolute, the Unconditional, the ground of being, the Ultimate Reality, as the Bishop of Woolwich does in his brave attempt to help men escape from crude and childish images, but these terms also are mental images, even if somewhat hazy ones, because we have no adequate content of meaning with which to fill them. No one can know what God is, or frame an all-embracing idea of him. In this lies the truth of the via negativa. How can the finite grasp Infinity? But we can come to discern the action of God upon us, and the possibility of a communion with him. Then we move beyond the sphere of the abstract, for one cannot commune with an abstraction or pray to the ground of oneself. Dr Robinson himself says: 'I pray to God as Father . . . The only God who meets my need as a Christian is "the God of Abraham, Isaac and Jacob", the God and Father of our Lord Jesus Christ' . . . We are plunged into a personal relationship with something not ourselves, but which includes the element of personality – the personality not of God, which may lead us again into anthropomorphism, but personality in God. As we apprehend something of the majesty and wonder and incomprehensibility of the infinite and absolute we find, paradoxically, that this is also something, someone, near and close. I use the term someone with hesitation because to many it seems at once to conjure up some divine potentate, creating the world by his mere command, aloof from strife and suffering – a supreme being, who is nevertheless an object like other objects, which God as the unconditional can surely never be. What I mean by 'someone' is the personal element at the heart of reality, with whom we can have relationship, which includes purpose and will and love and grace that seeks and responds to the love and truth in the human being. At the risk of being accused of suggesting God as 'out there' or 'up there', I would suggest that this creative love and purpose is not exhausted by the universe we know, is infinitely beyond as well as within the world. But he is in it, in all the agony of creation and creative effort, in the long, terrible patience of natural evolution, in the struggling human being and the tragedy and comedy of human life.

Richenda Scott

Richenda C. Scott, *Tradition and Experience*. Swarthmore Lecture, 1964 (London, George Allen and Unwin, 1964), pp. 46–7.

Beware also, daughters, of certain kinds of humility which the devil inculcates in us and which make us very uneasy about the gravity of our past sins. There are many ways in which he is accustomed to depress us so that in time we withdraw from Communion and give up our private prayer, because the devil suggests to us that we are not worthy to engage in it. When we come to the most holy sacrament, we spend the time during which we ought to be receiving grace in wondering whether we are properly prepared or not. The thing gets to such a pass that the soul can be made to believe that, through being what it is, it has been forsaken by God, and thus it almost doubts his mercy. Everything such a person does appears to her to be dangerous, and all the service she renders, however good it may be, seems to her fruitless. She loses confidence and sits with her hands in her lap because she thinks she can do nothing well and that what is good in others is wrong in herself.

Pay great attention, daughters, to this point which I shall now make, because sometimes thinking yourself so wicked may be humility and virtue and at other times a very great temptation. I have had experience of this, so I know it is true. Humility, however deep it be, neither disquiets nor troubles nor disturbs the soul; it is accompanied by peace, joy and tranquillity.

Teresa of Avila

Teresa of Jesus, *The Complete Works* vol. 2. Tr. and ed. E. Allison Peers (London and New York, Sheed and Ward, 1946), p. 169.

'The logical basis of male ascendency is the resolute denial of the existence of a soul in women', Miss C. Hamilton recently wrote. It may be, it often is, sub-conscious, but male ascendency is a striking feature of the ever man-filled pulpit, and although one hardly goes as far as to declare its logical basis to be the denial of the existence of a soul in woman, yet it does seem as if it led to the denial of the out-pouring of the Holy Spirit – with all his accompanying gift of prayer, and prophesying (preaching) to women.

I went recently to the Recognition Service of a new minister in the town where I was staying. In the evening, after an afternoon sermon, preached by a man, and a sumptuous tea prepared by and presided over by the ladies of the congregation, eight men-ministers, representing the various churches in town and district, ascended the platform. We had to listen to speeches from all of them! I thought I should like to have heard two or three women, to balance so much male wisdom and superiority. But had one hinted such a thought, what blank surprise would have overspread the ministerial countenances. 'Women?' I imagined them questioning, 'what do we want women on the platform for? Their place' – wave of the ministerial hand – 'their place is looking after the teapots, cutting the bread and butter, sitting here before us, listening to our speeches and laughing at our stories' (and oh some of them were such stale old chestnuts buried and apparently exhumed for Recognition and such like services!).

Hatty Baker

Hatty Baker, *Women in the Ministry* (London, C. W. Daniel,1911), pp. 48–9.

Later, one Easter Sunday, I had gone to God; and he embraced me in my interior senses and took me away in spirit. He brought me before the Countenance of the Holy Spirit, who possesses the Father and the Son in one Essence. And from the total Being of that Countenance I received all understanding, and thus I read all my judgments. A voice issued from this Countenance resounded so fearfully that it made itself heard above everything. And it said to me: 'Behold, ancient one, you have called me and sought me, what and who I, Love, am, myriads of years before the birth of man! See and receive my Spirit! With regard to all things, know what I, Love, am in them! And when you fully bring me yourself, as pure humanity in myself, through all the ways of perfect Love, you shall have fruition of me as the Love who I am. Until that day, you shall love what I, Love, am. And then you will be love, as I am Love. And you shall not live less than what I, Love, am, from that day until the death that will make you alive. In my unity, you have received me and I have received you. Go forth, and live what I am; and return bringing me full divinity, and have fruition of me as who I am.'

Then I returned to myself, and I understood all I have just said; and I remained to gaze fixedly upon my delightful sweet Love.

Hadewijch

Hadewijch, *The Complete Works*. Classics of Western Spirituality. Tr. and introd. Mother Columba Hart o s b (London, S PCK; Mahwah, NJ, Paulist Press, 1980), p. 272.

I saw my soul under the image of a very limpid stretch of water and above that water God appeared like an incomparable Star, whose light was more brilliant than that of the sun and gentler than that of the moon. Not only did the light irradiate all the surface of the water, but the water itself was so transparent that the rays of this light penetrated into its very depths. And these depths seemed to be inlaid with precious stones, which glittered through the water under the rays of the mysterious Star. With what ardour the light penetrated the water; with what love the water absorbed the light, I cannot find words to say! God made me understand that the fusion of these two elements was only an imperfect figure of the union which exists between him and my soul, when with him.

Lucy Christine

Lucy Christine in *An Anthology of Mysticism*. Ed. Paul de Jaegher s j (London, Burns, Oates and Washbourne, 1935), p. 251.

I first found myself within reach of a Friends' meeting (1872), and, somewhat to my surprise, cordially made welcome to attend it. The invitation came at a moment of need, for I was beginning to feel with dismay that I might not much longer be able conscientiously to continue to join in the Church of England service; not for want of appreciation of its unrivalled richness and beauty, but from doubts of the truth of its doctrines, combined with a growing recognition that to me it was as the armour of Saul in its elaboration, and in the sustained pitch of religious fervour for which it was meant to provide an utterance . . . On one never-to-be-forgotten Sunday morning, I found myself one of a small company of silent worshippers who were content to sit down together without words, that each one might feel after and draw near to the Divine Presence, unhindered at least, if not helped, by any human utterance. Utterance I knew was free, should the words be given; and, before the meeting was over, a sentence or two were uttered in great simplicity by an old and apparently un-taught man, rising in his place amongst the rest of us. I did not pay much attention to the words he spoke, and I have no recollection of their purport. My whole soul was filled with the unutterable peace of the undisturbed opportunity for communion with God, with the sense that at last I had found a place where I might, without the faintest suspicion of insincerity, join with others in simply seeking his pres-ence. To sit down in silence could at the least pledge me to nothing; it might open to me (as it did that morning) the very gate of heaven. And, since that day, now more than seventeen years ago, Friends' meetings have indeed been to me the greatest of outward helps to a fuller entrance into the spirit from which they have sprung; the place of the most soul-subduing, faith-restoring, strengthening, and peaceful com-munion, in feeding upon the bread of life, that I have ever known.

Caroline E. Stephen

Caroline E. Stephen, *Quaker Strongholds.* (1890), pp. 11–13. Quoted in *Christian Faith and Practice in the Experience of the Society of Friends* (London Yearly Meeting of the Religious Society of Friends, 1960), no. 80.

Let thy will be in every way fulfilled in me, and may it never please thy Majesty that a gift so precious as thy love be given to people who serve thee solely to obtain consolations.

It must be carefully noted – and I say this because I know it by experience – that the soul which begins to walk resolutely in this way of mental prayer can persuade itself to set little store by consolations and tenderness in devotion, and neither to be elated when the Lord gives them nor disconsolate when he withholds them, has already travelled a great part of its journey. However often it may stumble, it need not fear a relapse, for its building has been begun on a firm foundation. Yes, love for God does not consist in shedding tears, in enjoying those consolations and that tenderness which for the most part we desire and in which we find comfort, but in serving him with righteousness, fortitude of soul and humility. The other seems to me to be receiving rather than giving anything.

As for poor women like myself, who are weak and lack fortitude, I think it fitting that we should be led by means of favours: this is the way in which God is leading me now, so that I may be able to suffer certain trials which it has pleased His Majesty to give me. But when I hear servants of God, men of weight, learning and intelligence, making such a fuss because God is not giving them devotion, it revolts me to listen to them.

Teresa of Avila

Teresa of Jesus, *The Complete Works* vol. 1. Tr. and ed. E. Allison Peers (London and New York, Sheed and Ward, 1946), p. 68.

There was a time, we read, when my soul was exalted to behold God with so much clearness that never before had I beheld him so distinctly. But love did I not see here so fully; rather did I lose that which before I had and was left without love. Afterwards did I see him darkly, and this darkness was the greatest blessing that could be imagined and no thought could conceive aught that would equal this.

Then was there given unto the soul an assured faith, a firm and certain hope, wherein I felt so sure of God that all fear left me. For by that blessing which came with the darkness I did collect my thoughts and was made so sure of God that I can never again doubt but that I do of a certainty possess him.

Angela of Foligno

Angela of Foligno in Lucy Menzies, ed., *Mirror of the Holy* (Oxford, Mowbray, 1928), p. 138.

But now her husband, hearing on all sides that his wife was gifted with extraordinary graces, began again to seek for suitable books for her to read. Some one told him that Angela of Foligno had been led by the same extraordinary way and so he got her *Consolations* translated into French. But Mme Acarie could not at that time read anything; at the first word of any devotional book her spirit was rapt up to the heights and she was left without human understanding. Her husband could not grasp that. He had taken a great deal of trouble to get this book translated for his wife and now she would not read it! To be just to him, it was a little hard.

He began to get annoyed; to talk about his wife's inconvenient habits. He told her firmly that other young ladies – those who were, moreover, greatly thought of in the town! – did not practise their religion that way. They went quietly to church, had no extraordinary experiences, and troubled no one. Then he complained to the parish priest; and however much we try to sympathize with him, here he alienates our sympathy. One day he was specially insistent that his wife and all the household should go to church. They went obediently, suspecting nothing. But when the priest went up to the pulpit, he launched out into a violent diatribe against those women who indulged in strange experiences, who, under pretext of devotion failed to fulfil their duty to their husbands and households.

Madame Acarie *(as related by Lucy Menzies)*
Lucy Menzies, ed., *Mirror of the Holy* (Oxford, Mowbray, 1928), p. 235.

I saw the crucified Lord coming down to me in a great light, and for this, by the impetus of the mind that would fain go forth to meet its Creator, the body was constrained to rise. Then from the marks of his most sacred wounds, I saw five blood-red rays coming down upon me, which were directed towards the hands and feet and heart of my body. Wherefore, perceiving the mystery I straightway exclaimed: Ah, Lord my God, I beseech thee, let not the marks appear outwardly on my body! Then while I was yet speaking, before the rays reached me, they changed their blood-red colour to splendour and in the semblance of pure light they came to the five places in my body. So great is the pain that I endure sensibly in all those five places but especially within my heart, that, unless the Lord works a new miracle, it seems not possible to me that the life of my body can stay with such agony and that it will not end in a few days.

Catherine of Siena
Catherine of Siena in Lucy Menzies, ed., *Mirror of the Holy* (Oxford, Mowbray, 1928), p. 138.

Place your mind before the mirror of eternity!
Place your soul in the brilliance of glory!
Place your heart in the figure of the divine substance!
And transform your whole being into the image of the Godhead
Itself

through contemplation!
So that you too may feel what his friends feel
  as they taste the hidden sweetness
  which God himself has reserved
  from the beginning
  for those who love him.

Clare of Assisi

Francis and Clare: the Complete Works. Classics of Western Spirituality. Tr. and introd. Regis J. Armstrong OFM Cap. and Ignatius Brady OFM (London, SPCK; Mahwah, NJ, Paulist Press, 1982), p. 200.

First, we are led to consider the position of the house. However interesting and important its peculiarities may seem to the tenant, it is not as a matter of fact an unusually picturesque and interesting mansion made to an original design, and set in its own grounds with no other building in sight. Christian spirituality knows nothing of this sort of individualism. It insists that we do not inhabit detached residences, but are parts of a vast spiritual organism; that even the most hidden life is never lived for itself alone. Our soul's house forms part of the vast City of God. Though it may not be an important mansion with a frontage on the main street, nevertheless it shares all the obligations and advantages of belonging to the city as a whole. It gets its water from the main, and its light from the general supply. The way we maintain and use it must have reference to our civic responsibilities.

It is true that God creates souls in a marvellous liberty and variety. The ideals of the building-estate tell us nothing about the kingdom of heaven. It is true also, that the furnishing of our rooms and cultivation of our garden is largely left to our personal industry and good taste. Still, in a general way, we must fall in with the city's plan; and consider, when we hang some new and startling curtains, how they will look from the street. However intense the personal life of each soul may be, that personal life has got out of proportion, if it makes us forget our municipal obligations and advantages; for our true significance is more than personal, it is bound up with the fact of our status as members of a supernatural society. So into all the affairs of the little house there should enter a certain sense of the city, and beyond this of the infinite world in which the city stands: some awe-struck memory of our double situation, at once so homely and so mysterious. We must each maintain unimpaired our unique relation with God; yet without forgetting our intimate contact with the rest of the city, or the mesh of invisible life which binds all the inhabitants in one.

For it is on the unchanging life of God, as on a rock, that the whole

17

city is founded. That august and cherishing Spirit is the atmosphere which bathes it, and fills each room of every little house – quickening, feeding and sustaining. He is the one reality which makes us real; and, equally, the other houses too. 'If I am not in thee,' said St Augustine, 'then I am not at all.' We are often urged to think of the spiritual life as a personal adventure, a ceaseless hustle forward; with all its meaning condensed in the 'perfection' of the last stage. But though progress, or rather growth, is truly in it, such growth in so far as it is real can only arise from, and be conditioned by, a far more fundamental relation – the growing soul's abidingness in God.

Evelyn Underhill

Evelyn Underhill, *Concerning the Inner Life with the House of the Soul* (London, Methuen, 1947), pp. 66–7.

'The kingdom of God is within you.' God has just invited us to 'live on in him', to live already, spiritually, in his heritage of glory; now he reveals to us that we need not go outside ourselves to find him: 'The kingdom of God is within you.' St John of the Cross tells us that 'it is in the substance of the soul, which is inaccessible to both the devil and the world, that God gives himself to us; then all the movements of the soul become divine, and, though they are from God, they are equally from us, because our Lord elicits them in us and with us.' The same saint says elsewhere that God is the 'centre of the soul'. If we know and love God with our whole strength, and find in him our whole joy, we have reached the deepest centre of our being where he is accessible to us. Before arriving at this stage we do already live in God who is the centre of our being but we do not live in our deepest centre since we can go further.

As it is love that unites us to God, the more intense our love the deeper we enter into God, and become centred in him. When we possess one degree of love, we are already in our centre, but when this loves attains its perfection we will have penetrated into our deepest centre. There we will be transformed to the extent of becoming a perfect image of God.

Elizabeth of the Trinity

Elizabeth of the Trinity, *Spiritual Writings*. Ed. M. M. Philipon OP (London, Geoffrey Chapman, 1962), p. 142.

The time spent in prayer may last, and does last, for some hours; for, once the two faculties have begun to grow inebriated with the taste of this divine wine, they are very ready to lose themselves in order to gain the more, and so they keep company with the will and all three rejoice together. But this state in which they are completely lost – is, as I say, of brief duration, although the faculties do not recover to such an extent as not to be for some hours, as it were, in disorder, God, from time to time, gathering them once more to himself.

Let us now come to the most intimate part of what the soul experiences in this condition. The persons who much speak of it are those who know it, for it cannot be understood, still less described. As I was about to write of this (I had just communicated and had been experiencing this very prayer of which I am writing), I was wondering what it is the soul does during that time, when the Lord said these words to me: 'It dies to itself wholly, daughter, in order that it may fix itself more and more upon me; it is no longer itself that lives, but I. As it cannot comprehend what it understands, it is an understanding which understands not.' One who has experienced this will understand something of it; it cannot be more clearly expressed, since all that comes to pass in this state is so obscure. I can only say that the soul feels close to God and that there abides within it such a certainty that it cannot possibly do other than believe.

Teresa of Avila

Teresa of Jesus, *The Complete Works* vol. 1. Tr. and ed. E. Allison Peers (London and New York, Sheed and Ward, 1946), pp. 110–11.

Those who have any experience of real prayer know full well that in the pause of the soul before God, after it has uttered its complaint, made known its desires, or sought guidance in perplexity, there comes the clearer vision of duty, and the still small voice of guidance is heard, rectifying the judgement, strengthening the resolve, and consoling the spirit; they know that an influence external to us yet within us, deals with us, speaks with us, in fire. Prayer cannot be truly called commission, if the only voice heard be the voice of the pleader.

Josephine Butler

Joseph Williamson, *Josephine Butler – the Forgotten Saint* (Leighton Buzzard, The Faith Press, 1977), p. 93.

Woman, bearer; Woman, teacher;
Overflowing love and labour,
Service of the tireless mother
    Filling all the earth; –
Now her mind awakening, searching,
Sees a fair world young and growing,
Sees at last our real religion –
    Built on Birth.

Birth, and the Growth of the Soul; –
The Soul, in the body established,
In the ever-new beauty of childhood,
In the wonder of opening power,
Still learning, improving, achieving,
In hope, new knowledge, and light,
Sure faith in the world's fresh Spring, –
Together we live, we grow,
On the earth that we love and know –
    Birth, and the Growth of the Soul.

Charlotte Perkins Gilman

Charlotte Perkins Gilman, *His Religion and Hers: a Study of the Fathers and the Work of Our Mothers* (New York, Century, 1923), pp. vii–viii. Quoted in Rosemary Radford Ruether, *Womenguides* (Boston, Beacon Press, 1985), pp. 224–5.

There is a daily round for beauty as well as for goodness, a world of flowers and books and cinemas and clothes and manners as well as of mountains and masterpieces. God is in all beauty, not only in the natural beauty of earth and sky, but in all fitness of language and rhythm, whether it describe a heavenly vision or a street fight, a Hamlet or a Falstaff, a philosophy or a joke; in all fitness of line and colour and shade, whether seen in the Sistine Madonna or a child's knitted frock: in all fitness of sound and beat and measure, whether the result be Bach's Passion music or a nursery jingle. The quantity of God, so to speak, varies in the different examples, but his quality of beauty in fitness remains the same.

Caroline C. Graveson

Caroline C. Graveson, *Religion and Culture* (Swarthmore Lecture 1937), pp. 24–5. Quoted in *Christian Faith and Practice in the Experience of the Society of Friends* (London Yearly Meeting of the Religious Society of Friends 1960), no. 463.

It is of great importance, then, that the director should be a prudent man – of sound understanding, I mean – and also an experienced one; if he is a learned man as well, that is a very great advantage. But if all these three qualities cannot be found in the same man, the first two are the more important, for it is always possible to find learned men to consult when necessary. I mean that learning is of little benefit to beginners, except in men of prayer. I do not mean that beginners should have no communication with learned men, for I should prefer spirituality to be unaccompanied by prayer than not to be founded upon the truth. Learning is a great thing, for it teaches those of us who have little knowledge, and gives us light, so that, when we are faced with the truth of holy scripture, we act as we should. From foolish devotions may God deliver us!

I want to explain myself further, for I seem to be getting involved in a great many subjects. I have always had this failing – that I cannot explain myself, as I have said, except at the cost of many words. A nun begins to practise prayer: if her director is a simpleton and gets the idea into his head, he will give her to understand that it is better for her to obey him than her superior, and he will do this without any evil intention, thinking he is right. Indeed, if he is not a religious, it will probably seem right to him. If he is dealing with a married woman, he will tell her it is better for her to be engaged in prayer when she has work to do in her home, although this may displease her husband: he cannot advise her about arranging her time and work so that every-thing is done as true Christianity demands. Not being enlightened himself, he cannot enlighten others, even if he tries. And although learning may not seem necessary for this, my opinion has always been, and always will be, that every Christian should try to consult some learned person, if he can, and the more learned this person, the better. Those who walk in the way of prayer have the greater need of learning; and the more spiritual they are, the greater is their need.

Teresa of Avila

Teresa of Jesus, *The Complete Works* vol. 1. Tr. and ed. E. Allison Peers (London and New York, Sheed and Ward, 1946), pp. 80–1.

2
If Christ is growing in us

Relationship is central to all belief and for Christian women, the relationship which Gospel women enjoyed with Jesus and which contemporary women may enjoy with the risen Christ is central to their self-perception and sense of identity. When a woman contemplates the words and deeds of Jesus, she discovers the freedom and love with which she is held in the divine esteem. Baptized into the fullness of the life of the risen Christ this freedom and love become her heritage. As Kathleen Bliss, the broadcaster, saw: 'she is a person in the true sense of the word and what she portrays is the mind of Christ.' Hers is a theological claim. Constance Coleman was making the same point when she noted 'Our Lord had no special attitude to women. He just treated them as human.'

When we listen to the voices of women recorded in this chapter, what do we discover? Firstly, with the novelist Dorothy L. Sayers, we are reminded that Jesus 'drove a coach and horses through a number of sacrosanct and hoary conventions'. As Maude Royden, the preacher, recognized, with him there was 'no limitation of sphere'. For this reason 'the glory of the coming of the Lord' whose 'truth is marching on' is greeted by Julia Ward Howe in a song of triumph. Her military language stands in contrast to the imagery chosen by Julian of Norwich. Her writings on Christ as the 'true Mother of life and of all things' have helped an enormous number of people realize that the preferred (masculine) metaphors of the tradition are not the only ones. Hatty Baker contributes to the same debate when she claims: 'We surely need a woman as well as a man to interpret the heart of our Mother-Father God.' The medieval visionary Marguerite d'Oingt put it even more graphically: 'When the hour of your delivery came you were placed on the hard bed of the cross. It is no surprise that your veins burst when in one day you gave birth to the whole world.'

This devotion to the person of Christ and what he represents is particularly clear in the hymns written by women. They return time and again to the theme of the cross where Christ laboured for our salvation. But equally it forms a strong feature of the writings of Caryll Houselander, the Roman Catholic mystic. She writes of 'the quickening of his own life in the heart', of recognizing the presence of Christ both in oneself and one's own reactions and as well in the people one meets. For Teresa of Avila this devotion becomes desire;

22

she wants to see 'the colour of his eyes'. For Evangeline Booth it is expressed in the love which brought the gospel women 'loyally and modestly and reverently to the silent tomb'.

If women came to the tomb as grieving, dispirited disciples, they were sent away from their encounter with the risen Christ as vibrant, transformed apostles. This is what women discover as they pray.

The very variety of the images and emotions with which these women write about their experience of the person of Christ reminds us that there is no such thing as a standardized or stereotypical reaction to the gospel. 'If Christ is growing in us', as Caryll Houselander saw, we will recognize Christ in a multitude of places and ways. And not only will we recognize Christ there, we will bring him with us too.

The people who hanged Christ, to do them justice, never accused him of being a bore – on the contrary; they thought him too dynamic to be safe. It has been left for later generations to muffle up that shattering personality and surround him with an atmosphere of tedium. We have very efficiently pared the claws of the Lion of Judah, certified him 'meek and mild', and recommended him as a fitting household pet for pale curates and pious old ladies. To those who knew him, however, he in no way suggested a milk-and-water person; they objected to him as a dangerous firebrand. True, he was tender to the unfortunate, patient with honest inquirers, and humble before heaven; but he insulted respectable clergymen by calling them hypocrites; he referred to King Herod as 'that fox'; he went to parties in disreputable company and was looked upon as a 'gluttonous man and a wine-bibber, a friend of publicans and sinners'; he assaulted indignant tradesmen and threw them and their belongings out of the Temple; he drove a coach-and-horses through a number of sacrosanct and hoary regulations; he cured diseases by any means that came handy, with a shocking casualness in the matter of other people's pigs and property; he showed no proper defense for wealth or social position; when confronted with neat dialectical traps, he displayed a paradoxical humour that affronted serious-minded people, and he retorted by asking disagreeably searching questions that could not be answered by rule of thumb. He was emphatically not a dull man in his human lifetime, and if he was God, there can be nothing dull about God either. But he had 'a daily beauty in his life that made us ugly,' and officialdom felt that the established order of things would be more secure without him. So they did away with God in the name of peace and quietness.

Dorothy L. Sayers

Dorothy L. Sayers, *Creed or Chaos* (New York, Harcourt Brace, 1949), pp. 5–6. Quoted in Rosamond Kent Sprague, *A Matter of Eternity: Selections from the Writings of Dorothy L. Sayers* (London and Oxford, Mowbray, 1973), pp. 16–17.

Though I saw that he was speaking to me, and though I was looking upon the great beauty of his, and experiencing the sweetness with which he uttered those words – sometimes stern words – with that most lovely and divine mouth, and though, too, I was extremely desirous of observing the colour of his eyes, or his height, so that I should be able to describe it, I have never been sufficiently worthy to see this, nor has it been of any use for me to attempt to do so; if I tried, I lost the vision altogether. Though I sometimes see him looking at me compassionately, his gaze has such power that my soul cannot endure it and remains in so sublime a rapture that it loses this beauteous vision in order to have the greater fruition of it all. So there is no question here of wanting to see the vision. It is clear that the Lord wants of us only humility and shame, our acceptance of what is given us and our praise of its Giver.

Teresa of Avila

Teresa of Jesus, *The Complete Works* vol. 1. Tr. and ed. E. Allison Peers (London and New York, Sheed and Ward, 1946), pp. 187–8. Quoted in *Medieval Religious Women* vol. 2: *Peace Weavers*, ed. John A. Nichols and Lillian Thomas Shanks (Kalamazoo, MI, Cistercian Publications, 1987), p. 326.

It is part of the amazing originality of Christ that there is to be found in his teaching no word whatever which suggests a difference in the spiritual ideals, the spheres, or the potentialities of men and women. There is no classification of virtues assigning some to men . . . and others to women. There is no limitation of sphere . . . If the words of Christ were isolated from their context and read to one to whom the gospels were not familiar it would be absolutely impossible for him to guess whether any special word or phrase was addressed to a woman or to a man.

Maude Royden

Maude Royden, *The Church and Women* (1924), p. 167. Quoted in Sheila Fletcher, *Maude Royden: A Life* (Oxford, Basil Blackwell, 1989), p. 3.

Jesus said to the two Marys: 'All hail! And they came and held him by the feet, and worshipped him. Then said Jesus unto them, Be not afraid: go, tell my brethren that they go into Galilee, and there shall they see me' (Matt. 28.9, 10). There are two or three points in this beautiful narrative to which we wish to call the attention of our readers.

First, it was the first announcement of the glorious news to a lost world and a company of forsaking disciples. Second, it was as public as the nature of the case demanded; and intended ultimately to be published to the ends of the earth. Third, Mary was expressly commissioned to reveal the fact to the apostles; and thus she literally became their teacher on that memorable occasion. Oh, glorious privilege, to be allowed to herald the glad tidings of a Saviour risen! How could it be that our Lord chose a woman to this honour? Well, one reason might be that the male disciples were all missing at the time. They all forsook him, and fled. But woman was there, as she had ever been, ready to minister to her risen, as to her dying Lord.

> Not she with traitorous lips her Saviour stung,
> Not she denied him with unholy tongue;
> She, whilst apostles shrunk, could danger brave;
> Last at the cross, and earliest at the grave.

But, surely, if the dignity of our Lord or his message were likely to be imperilled by committing this sacred trust to a woman, he who was guarded by legions of angels could have commanded another messenger; but, as if intent on doing her honour, and rewarding her unwavering fidelity, he reveals himself first to her; and, as an evidence that he had taken out of the way the curse under which she had so long groaned, nailing it to his cross, he makes her who had been first in the transgression first also in the glorious knowledge of complete redemption.

Catherine Booth

Catherine Booth, *Female Ministry: an Address by Mrs General Booth* (London, Salvation Army Book Department, 1909), pp. 22–3.

I, poor woman, was so bold in my prayer that I impudently took corrupt Christianity into the arms of my soul and lifted it in lamentation. Our Lord said:

> Leave it! It is too heavy for you.
> No, sweet Lord!
> I will lift it up and carry it before your feet,
> with your own arms
> with which you bore it on the cross!
> And God granted me, poor wretch, my will
> that I might find rest.

When poor Christianity came before our Lord, she was like a maiden. I looked at her and saw also that our Lord looked at her. And I was very ashamed. Then our Lord said: behold, is it fitting for me to love this maid in my eternal infinite wedding bed and to draw her to me in my imperial arms and to look at her with my divine eyes, since she is half-blind in her knowledge and crippled in her hands, which hardly do any good works? She also limps in the feet of her desire, for she rarely and then indolently thinks of me. Her skin is also filthy, for she is unclean and unchaste. Then the poor soul spoke: what advice can one give her? And our Lord said: I will wash her in my own blood and I will protect all the blessed who are truly innocent and take them intimately to me in a blessed death.

Mechthild of Magdeburg

Mechthild of Magdeburg, *The Flowing Light of the Godhead*, 6,5; 6,21. Tr. Joan Howard. Quoted in *Medieval Women Writers*, ed. Katharina M. Wilson (Manchester University Press 1984), pp. 170–1.

As to the first, I saw and understood that the high might of the Trinity is our Father, and the deep wisdom of the Trinity is our Mother, and the great love of the Trinity is our Lord; and all these we have in nature and in our substantial creation. And furthermore I saw that the second person, who is our Mother, substantially the same beloved person, has now become our mother sensually, because we are double by God's creating, that is to say substantial and sensual. Our substance is the higher part, which we have in our Father, God almighty; and the second person of the Trinity is our Mother in nature and in our substantial creation in whom we are founded and rooted, and he is our Mother of mercy in taking our sensuality. And so our Mother is working on us in various ways, in whom our parts are kept undivided; for in our Mother Christ we profit and increase, and in mercy he reforms and restores us, and by the power of his Passion, his death and his Resurrection he unites us to our substance. So our Mother works in mercy on all his beloved children who are docile and obedient to him, and grace works with mercy, and especially in two properties, as it was shown, which working belongs to the third person, the Holy Spirit. He works, rewarding and giving. Rewarding is a gift for our confidence which the Lord makes to those who have laboured and giving is a courteous act which he does freely, by grace, fulfilling and surpassing all that creatures deserve.

Thus in our Father, God almighty, we have our being, and in our Mother of mercy we have our reforming and our restoring, in whom our parts are united and all made perfect man, and through the rewards and the gifts of grace of the Holy Spirit we are fulfilled. And our substance is in our Father, God almighty, and our substance is in our Mother, God all wisdom, and our substance is in our Lord God, the Holy Spirit, all goodness, for our substance is whole in each person of the Trinity, who is one God. And our sensuality is only in the second person, Christ Jesus, in whom is the Father and the Holy Spirit; and in him and by him we are powerfully taken out of hell and out of the wretchedness on earth, and gloriously brought up into heaven, and blessedly united to our substance, increased in riches and nobility by all the power of Christ and by the grace and operation of the Holy Spirit.

Julian of Norwich

Julian of Norwich, *Showings*. Classics of Western Spirituality. Tr. and intro. Edmund Colledge OSA and James Walsh SJ (London, SPCK; Mahwah, NJ, 1978), pp. 294–5.

When once I had seen the great beauty of the Lord, I saw no one who by comparison with him seemed acceptable to me or on whom my thoughts wished to dwell. For if I merely turn the eyes of my mind to the image of him which I have within my soul, I find I have such freedom that from that time forward everything I see appears nauseating to me by comparison with the excellences and glories which I have seen in this Lord. Nor is there any knowledge or any kind of consolation to which I can attach the slightest esteem by comparison with that which it causes me to hear a single word coming from that Divine mouth – and more wonderful still is it when I hear many. And, unless for my sins the Lord allows this memory to fade, I consider it impossible for me to be so deeply absorbed in anything that I do not regain my freedom when I turn once more in thought, even for a moment, to this Lord.

This has happened to me with some of my confessors, for I always have a great affection for those who direct my soul, looking upon them as so truly in the place of God that I always like to follow their advice more than anything else. As I was feeling perfectly safe, therefore, I would show myself pleasant to them. But they, being God-fearing and God-serving men, were afraid that I might in some way become attached to them and drawn towards them – in a spiritual sense, of course – by the bonds of affection; so they would treat me quite unpleasantly. This happened after I became accustomed to obeying them; before that I had had no such affection for them. I used to laugh to myself when I saw how mistaken they were.

Teresa of Avila

Teresa of Jesus, *The Complete Works* vol. 1. Tr. and ed. E. Allison Peers (London and New York, Sheed and Ward, 1946), pp. 262–3.

Our Lord prayed that his people might be one 'that the world may believe'. Would the fuller ministry of women hasten revival? Yes, because we are standing for the ultimate spiritual equality, not merely of women alongside men, but of all human souls in the sight of God. You may know the story of the Eton boy who, when asked to comment on our Lord's attitude to women, could think of nothing to say, until he wrote: 'Our Lord commended the action of the poor widow who threw her two children into the treasury!' But no wonder he was hard put to it, for in one sense our Lord had no special attitude to women. He just treated them as human beings. 'Neither male nor female, neither Jew nor Greek, neither bond nor free', there is the Magna Carta of the spiritual rights, not of women alone, but of humanity, and all three clauses hang together. Our faith in the supreme worth of every individual soul, in the supremacy of the spiritual over the material, in the superiority of the whole armour of God over the arm of flesh – here lies not only the justification for the ministry of women, but also the eternal foundations of democracy, the true guarantee of freedom, and the only avenue to lasting peace.

Constance Coleman

Constance Coleman, 'Women's Kingdom' in *Women in the Pulpit*. Ed. D. P. Thompson (London, James Clarke, n.d.), p. 109.

It is true that Jesus said greatly comforting things to women. He called a girl of twelve 'Little darling', according to our new commentators, when he took her small hand and drew her back from death. He speaks to and of mothers and widows. He made no jokes about a mother-in-law, but raised one from her fever, and she ministered in the way that the mothers-in-law I know minister, even when dwelling in 'other people's houses'.

I am not sure that the most beautiful story in the whole Testament is not that of the old woman, bowed these eighteen years in spirit and body, with no beauty surely on her face, and probably neither rich nor clever; yet one who had come to the place where she could meet with God. He had to 'call' her, for she would not think that a young man of three-and-thirty could seek out herself. But she was in need; and that was sufficient for the Good Shepherd.

The courtesy of Christ to women goes far deeper than race or appearance; and with that he has raised the nature of his fellow-men. Indeed, when I have heard good men tell an audience of women that they ought to be 'grateful' to Jesus, for he has 'raised the status of woman', I shrink, surprised at their blindness. It is just a century since slavery was abolished in the British Empire. Would we wish for our own sakes to go back to it, even if we could? Do we not pray to be delivered from the burden of knowing that some of our labour here is still semi-slavery? When we freed the slaves, we ourselves were freed just as much as they.

Lady Hosie

Lady Hosie, 'Christ and Women' in *Women in the Pulpit*. Ed. D. P. Thompson (London, James Clarke, n.d.), p. 109.

1 Loving Shepherd of thy sheep,
   Keep me, Lord, in safety keep;
Nothing can thy power withstand,
   None can pluck me from thy hand.

2 Loving Shepherd, thou didst give
   Thine own life that I might live;
May I love thee day by day,
   Gladly thy sweet will obey.

3 Loving Shepherd, ever near,
   Teach me still thy voice to hear;
Suffer not my step to stray
   From the strait and narrow way.

4 Where thou leadest may I go,
   Walking in thy steps below;
Then before thy Father's throne,
   Jesu, claim me for thine own.

Jane Elizabeth Leeson

Jane Elizabeth Leeson in *The Westminster Hymnal* (London, Burns, Oates and Washbourne, 1953), no. 178.

Yet again: I once heard a man say deliberately that because Jesus Christ came as a man, his must be the higher sex. Suppose a class in grammar were asked to parse God.

God? Proper noun. Number? The scholar might be in some doubt whether to put singular or plural. Gender? This would be un-hesitatingly dubbed masculine. And how many masters would do other than let it pass?

Where does it say anywhere Christ was made a man? I find it written, 'Neither is the woman without the man, nor the man without the woman, in the Lord' (1 Cor. 11.12). We suffer in the English language from a paucity of words. We require a word which includes man and woman. It is clumsy to say humanity whenever we mean the two sexes.

Our ancient fathers were more careful than we in their choice of expressions. They never wrote Christ was made a man. They said 'homo non vir', i.e., human nature. Christ was made humanity. Note the creed in the Communion service, 'Christ was incarnate by the Holy Ghost of the Virgin Mary, and was made', not a man, but 'man'.

It is impossible to think truly of God without seeing womanly-manly attributes. Our Father-Mother God. 'Like as a father pitieth' – true, but also 'Like as a hen gathereth' – 'Like as a mother-bird protected' (the feminine gender is used in this beautiful similitude of Isaiah's). There must be behind the universe, in and through the universe, a heart like a woman's, tender, pitiful, compassionate, faithful, loving to the end, to death, and we need – we surely need a woman as well as a man to interpret the heart of our Mother-Father God.

Hatty Baker

Hatty Baker, *Women in the Ministry* (London, C. W. Daniel, 1911), pp. 46–7.

Any Christian attitude to women and to the relations of men and women, works itself out . . . in a continuing intricate dialogue between the Church and society in real life. Theology plays a part in this dialogue, calling the participants back to the sources of their faith in God and his Word, detecting and grappling with non-Christian conceptions, but it is not determinative. It has never been a theological statement of man-woman relationships which has convinced non-Christians that Christianity really has some positive saving message to mankind in its duality of male and female. The power comes from the recognition – in a world which empirically belongs to the male sex – of a phenomenon, the Christian woman. She may be as different as a Quaker, a Salvation Army lassie, a nun, a deaconess or a Christian mother: she has not a heightened femininity nor is she de-feminised, but the category of the feminine is transcended in her by that of the personal: she is a person in the true sense of the word and what she portrays is the mind of Christ. Such a woman may be seen only very rarely, but the point is that she is unmistakably a Christian type and she is the product of grace working through a Church always composed of sinners.

Kathleen Bliss

Kathleen Bliss, *The Service and Status of Women in the Churches* (London, SCM, 1952), p. 22.

If Christh is growing in us

For what we call the woman's movement is not social merely, not political merely, not economic merely. It is the direct fulfilment of the gospel of the Redeemer. It was Jesus who taught the world the full lesson of what is meant by chivalry to women. It was he who, at the well of Samaria, talked with an oft-divorced wife and told her of a God whom she could worship in spirit and in truth. It was he who, within the Temple itself, at Jerusalem, dared to defend a woman, taken in adultery, from her heartless persecutors by saying to man in his hypocrisy, 'He that is without sin among you, let him first cast a stone at her'. He it was who visited the little girl on her deathbed and, by the omnipotence of love, called her back to life again. He it was who likened his Church to a bride, and himself to the bridegroom, drawing from the life of women, their lamps, their pieces of silver for house-keeping, the very broom with which they sweep the house, his immortal parables.

Happy, then, is the woman who realizes, even in these days of enfranchisement, that her life, however abundant it may be, is still hidden in the Christ of God. For it is in Christ that woman is transformed and transfigured by a miracle of redemption. Accustomed to flattery, to ease and to affluence, she breaks her alabaster box of spikenard, very precious, and pours the ointment over his feet, so that the fragrance thereof fills the whole house where they are sitting. Indeed, the woman who had nought save penitence to bring him, shed her tears also over those same weary feet and wiped them with the hair of her head. Is it the women who go to church? It has not always been to so comfortable a place as church that women have trod the Via Dolorosa of a faith that nothing in heaven, nothing in hell itself could shake from its foundations. On that first Good Friday, when all the apostles had forsaken the crucified Christ and fled from the scene of his redeeming agony, it was the women who were last seen at the cross, watching him there; and on the morn of resurrection, when the night was still unlit by the first hint of the brightest dawn in history, the women were not afraid to risk the perils of those riotous streets and make their way, loyally and modestly and reverently, to the silent tomb. It was in the body of a woman that Christ was born; and the souls of women were the cradles of the Church.

Evangeline Booth

Evangeline Booth, *Woman* (New York, Fleming H. Revell, 1930), pp. 16–17.

For are you not my mother and more than my mother? The mother who bore me laboured in delivering me for one day or one night but you, my sweet and lovely Lord, laboured for me for more than thirty years. Ah . . . with what love you laboured for me and bore me through your whole life. But when the time approached for you to be delivered, your labour pains were so great that your holy sweat was like great drops of blood that came out from your body and fell on the earth . . . when the hour of your delivery came you were placed on the hard bed of the cross . . . and your nerves and all your veins were broken. And truly it is no surprise that your veins burst when in one day you gave birth to the whole world.

Marguerite d'Oingt

Marguerite d'Oingt in *Medieval Women's Visionary Literature*. Ed. Elizabeth Alvilda Petroff (Oxford University Press 1986), p. 279.

1   Beneath the cross of Jesus
      I fain would take my stand –
   The shadow of a mighty rock,
      Within a weary land;
   A home within the wilderness,
      A rest upon the way,
   From the burning of the noontide heat,
      And the burden of the day.

2   O safe and happy shelter,
      O refuge tried and sweet,
   O trysting-place where heaven's love
      And heaven's justice meet!
   As to the holy patriarch
      That wondrous dream was given,
   So seems my Saviour's cross to me,
      A ladder up to heaven.

3   Upon that cross of Jesus
      Mine eyes at times can see
   The very dying form of one
      Who suffered there for me;
   And from my smitten heart with tears
      Two wonders I confess – like this.
   The wonders of his glorious love,
      And my own worthlessness.

4   I take, O cross, thy shadow,
      For my abiding-place!
   I ask no other sunshine than
      The sunshine of his face;
   Content to let the world go by,

If Christ is growing in us

To know no gain or loss –
My sinful self my only shame,
My glory all – the cross.

Elizabeth Clephane

Elizabeth Clephane in *The Baptist Hymn Book* (London, Psalms and Hymns Trust, 1962), no. 427.

And we have all this bliss by mercy and by grace, and this kind of bliss we never could have had and known, unless that property of goodness which is in God had been opposed, through which we have this bliss. For wickedness has been suffered to rise in opposition to that goodness; and the goodness of mercy and grace opposed that wickedness, and turned everything to goodness and honour for all who will be saved. For this is that property in God which opposes good to evil. So Jesus Christ, who opposes good to evil, is our true Mother. We have our being from him, where the foundation of motherhood begins, with all the sweet protection of love which endlessly follows.

As truly as God is our Father, so truly God is our Mother, and he revealed that in everything, and especially in these sweet words where he says: I am he; that is to say: I am he, the power and goodness of fatherhood; I am he, the wisdom and the lovingness of motherhood; I am he, the light and the grace which is all blessed love; I am he, the Trinity; I am he, the unity; I am he, the great supreme goodness of every kind of thing; I am he who makes you to love; I am he who makes you to long; I am he, the endless fulfilling of all true desires. For where the soul is highest, noblest, most honourable, still it is lowest, meekest and mildest.

And from this foundation in substance we have all the powers of our sensuality by the gift of nature, and by the help and the furthering of mercy and grace, without which we cannot profit. Our great Father, almighty God, who is being, knows us and loved us before time began. Out of this knowledge, in his most wonderful deep love, by the prescient eternal counsel of all the blessed Trinity, he wanted the second person to become our Mother, our brother and our saviour. From this it follows that as truly as God is our Father, so truly is God our Mother. Our Father wills, our Mother works, our good Lord the Holy Spirit confirms. And therefore it is our part to love our God in whom we have our being, reverently thanking and praising him for our creation, mightily praying to our Mother for mercy and pity, and to our Lord the Holy Spirit for help and grace. For in these three is all our life: nature, mercy and grace, of which we have mildness, patience and pity, and hatred of sin and wickedness; for the virtues must of themselves hate sin and wickedness.

And so Jesus is our true Mother in nature by our first creation, and

33

he is our true Mother in grace by his taking our created nature. All the lovely works and all the sweet loving offices of beloved motherhood are appropriated to the second person, for in him we have this godly will, whole and safe forever, both in nature and in grace, from his own goodness proper to him.

I understand three ways of contemplating motherhood in God. The first is the foundation of our nature's creation; the second is his taking of our nature, where the motherhood of grace begins; the third is the motherhood at work. And in that, by the same grace, everything is penetrated, in length and in breadth, in height and in depth without end; and it is all one love.

Julian of Norwich

Julian of Norwich, *Showings*. Classics of Western Spirituality. Tr. and introd. Edmund Colledge OSA and James Walsh SJ (London, SPCK; Mahwah, NJ, Paulist Press, 1978), pp. 295–6.

When picturing Christ in the way I have mentioned, and sometimes even when reading, I used unexpectedly to experience a consciousness of the presence of God, of such a kind that I could not possibly doubt that he was within me or that I was wholly engulfed in him. This was in no sense a vision: I believe it is called mystical theology. The soul is suspended in such a way that it seems to be completely outside itself. The will loves; the memory, I think, is almost lost; while the understanding, I believe, though it is not lost, does not reason – I mean that it does not work, but is amazed at the extent of all it can understand; for God wills it to realize that it understands nothing of what His Majesty represents to it.

Previously to this, I had experienced a tenderness in devotion, some part of which, I think, can be obtained by one's own efforts. This is a favour neither wholly of sense nor wholly of spirit, but entirely the gift of God. It seems, however, that we can do a great deal towards the obtaining of it by reflecting on our lowliness and our ingratitude to God, on the great things that he has done for us, on his Passion, with its grievous pains, and on his life, which was so full of afflictions. We can also do much by rejoicing in the contemplation of his works, his greatness, his love for us, and a great deal more. Anyone really anxious to make progress often lights upon such things as these, though he may not be going about looking for them. If to this there be added a little love, the soul is comforted, the heart melts and tears begin to flow: sometimes we seem to produce these tears by force; at other times the Lord seems to be drawing them from us and we cannot resist him. For the trifling pains we have taken His Majesty appears to be requiting us with the great gift of the comfort which comes to a soul

34

from seeing that it is weeping for so great a Lord; and I do not wonder at this, for it has ample reason to be comforted. For here it finds encouragement, and here it finds joy.

Teresa of Avila

Teresa of Jesus, *The Complete Works* vol. 1. Tr. and ed. E. Allison Peers (London and New York, Sheed and Ward, 1946), p. 58.

By the discovery of God . . . I do not mean anything mysterious, or mystical, or unattainable. I simply mean becoming acquainted with him as one becomes acquainted with a human friend; that is, finding out what is his nature, and his character, and coming to understand his ways . . . My own experience has been something like this. My knowledge of God, beginning on a very low plane, and in the midst of the greatest darkness and ignorance, advanced slowly through many stages, and with a vast amount of useless conflict and wrestling, to the place where I learned at last that Christ was the 'express image' of God, and where I became, therefore, in a measure acquainted with him, and discovered to my amazement and delight his utter unselfishness, and saw that it was safe to trust him. And from this time all my doubts and questionings have been slowly but surely disappearing in the blaze of this magnificent knowledge.

Hannah Whitall Smith

Hannah Whitall Smith, *The Unselfishness of God* (1903), 14, 18–19. Quoted in *Christian Faith and Practice in the Experience of the Society of Friends* (London Yearly Meeting of the Religious Society of Friends 1960), no. 77.

The demand for temperance of soul, for an acknowledgement of the sacred character of the normal, is based on that fact – the central Christian fact – of the humble entrance of God into our common human life. The supernatural can and does seek and find us, in and through our daily normal experience: the invisible in the visible. There is no need to be peculiar in order to find God. The Magi were taught by the heavens to follow a star; and it brought them, not to a paralysing disclosure of the Transcendent, but to a little boy on his mother's knee.

So too we observe how moderate, humble, attuned to the scale of our daily life are all the crucial events of the New Testament. Seen from the outside, none could have guessed their shattering and transfiguring power. The apocalyptists looked for a superhuman being 'coming in the clouds' – they could not escape from the idea of the abnormal – but the real events which transformed the spiritual history of man were startling only in their simplicity. The quiet routine of a childhood and working life in Nazareth; the wandering ministry of teaching and compassion, with the least possible stress laid on supernatural powers; the homely little triumph of Palm Sunday; the pitiful sufferings of an arrest and execution too commonplace to disturb the city's life. Christ never based his claim on strangeness: it is by what he is, rather than by what he does, that he awes, attracts, amazes.

In spite of its contrasts between the stern and tender, how steadily temperate and central in its emphasis is all his teaching: full of the colour and quality of real life free from the merely startling, ever keeping close to our normal experience. Sowing, reaping, bread-making, keeping sheep; in these the secrets of the kingdom are hid.

Evelyn Underhill

Evelyn Underhill, *Concerning the Inner Life of the House of the Soul* (London, Methuen, 1947), pp. 90–1.

On Calvary, on the altar, Christ makes himself not invulnerable but vulnerable. He lays himself bare to the hand of friend and enemy alike. On the cross he was one great wound from head to foot, the nerves that should be hidden were exposed, the body was rent and open; the tenderest touch of his mother's hand would have inflicted the keenest agony, for those nerves and muscles which should be covered lay exposed and bare. As so it must always be in proportion as we love. It is an inevitable result of love upon this earth that, in loving, we give to the beloved the power of paining us; and the greater our love the greater also the corresponding power. For to love is, as it were, to lay heart and soul open to our friend; it is to strip ourselves, not only of all artificial armour, but even of the covering that Nature herself provides for the feelings and the heart. And this is the love that Christ has for all men: the best and the worst have power to wound because he gives it to them by the mere fact of his love. We cannot love as he did, and therefore we cannot, even were we willing, become vulnerable as he was, for the one is in proportion to the other. He loved all, we love only a few; he loved intensely and continuously, we love only feebly and by fits and starts. But in every mass we have a reminder of that love deeper than we can comprehend . . .

Maude Petre

Maude D. Petre, 'Devotional Essays' in *The Method of Theology* (London, Catholic Truth Society, 1902), pp. 26–7.

The mother can give her child to suck of her milk, but our precious Mother Jesus can feed us with himself, and does, most courteously and most tenderly, with the blessed sacrament, which is the precious food of true life; and with all the sweet sacraments he sustains us most mercifully and graciously, and so he meant in these blessed words, where he said: I am he whom Holy Church preaches and teaches to you. That is to say: All the health and life of the sacraments, all the power and the grace of my word, all the goodness which is ordained in Holy Church for you, I am he.

The mother can lay her child tenderly to her breast, but our tender Mother Jesus can lead us easily into his blessed breast through his sweet open side, and show us there a part of the godhead and of the joys of heaven, with inner certainty of endless bliss. And that he revealed in the tenth revelation, giving us the same understanding in these sweet words which he says: See, how I love you, looking into his blessed side, rejoicing.

This fair lovely word 'mother' is so sweet and so kind in itself that it cannot truly be said of anyone or to anyone except of him and to him who is the true Mother of life and of all things. To the property of motherhood belong nature, love, wisdom and knowledge, and this is God. For though it may be so that our bodily bringing to birth is only little, humble and simple in comparison with our spiritual bringing to birth, still it is he who does it in the creatures by whom it is done. The kind, loving mother who knows and sees the need of her child guards it very tenderly, as the nature and condition of motherhood will have. And always as the child grows in age and in stature, she acts differently, but she does not change her love. And when it is even older, she allows it to be chastised to destroy its faults, so as to make the child receive virtues and grace. This work, with everything which is lovely and good, our Lord performs in those by whom it is done. So he is our Mother in nature by the operation of grace in the lower part, for love of the higher part. And he wants us to know it, for he wants to have all our love attached to him; and in this I saw that every debt which we owe by God's command to fatherhood and motherhood is fulfilled in truly loving God, which blessed love Christ works in us. And this was revealed in everything, and especially in the great bounteous words when he says: I am he whom you love.

Julian of Norwich

Julian of Norwich, *Showings*. Classics of Western Spirituality. Tr. and introd. Edmund Colledge O S A and James Walsh S J (London, SPCK; Mahwah, NJ, Paulist Press, 1978), pp. 298–9.

Men and women still feel, in a way they cannot explain, that in the sacrifice of the cross something has happened to them, has been done for them. It is nothing so simple as averting the wrath of a just and outraged God through the sacrifice offered in appeasement on behalf of sinful man. As we grope for understanding, do we find that the conquest of sin at the unconscious as well as the conscious depths did achieve something for the human race, did break a bond that held human nature in its grip, so that the way is opened for a fresh approach to God and to the whole universe in which our existence is set? In the words of the dying prayer of St Margaret, Queen of Scots, in 1093, do we find here the realization of Christ, by his death, has given life to the world? In these realms we are the limits of thought, and the meaning, though it may be pulsatingly real in experience, eludes definition.

Richenda C. Scott

Richenda C. Scott, *Tradition and Experience*. Swarthmore Lecture, 1964 (London, George Allen and Unwin, 1964), pp. 68–9.

1 At the name of Jesus
    Every knee shall bow,
Every tongue confess him
    King of Glory now;
'Tis the Father's pleasure
    We should call him Lord,
Who from the beginning
    Was the mighty Word.

2 At his voice creation
    Sprang at once to sight,
All the angel faces,
    All the hosts of light,
Thrones and dominations,
    Stars upon their way,
All the heavenly orders
    In their great array.

3 Humbled for a season,
    To receive a name
From the lips of sinners
    Unto whom he came,
Faithfully he bore it
    Spotless to the last,
Brought it back victorious
    When from death he passed.

4 Bore it up triumphant
    With its human light,

If Christ is growing in us

Through all ranks of creatures
  To the central height,
To the throne of Godhead,
  To the Father's breast;
Filled it with glory
  Of that perfect rest.

5 In your hearts enthrone him;
  There let him subdue
All that is not holy,
  All that is not true;
Crown him as your captain
  In temptation's hour;
Let his will enfold you
  In its light and power.

Caroline Maria Noel

Caroline Maria Noel in *The Song Book of the Salvation Army* (London, 1986 edn).

So in Jesus of Nazareth we find a man, subject to all the disabilities and curtailments imposed by his finitude, including the facing and battling with the temptations of his human selfhood. There is all the power he could wield as the political and social revolutionary leader, able to satisfy the needs and desires of his people at the material level, or to restore the glory of the Kingdom of David by freeing his nation, which he loved so deeply, from the Roman yoke; there is the sudden, dramatic act which would focus all eyes upon him, and lend him a supernatural prestige and potency to use in furtherance of the divine ends. Each one has a powerful emotional pull, each calls for a moment of decision at cost of mind and will and spiritual energy; otherwise the story of the temptation holds no significance. He emerges from those weeks of wrestling, his vision of God clarified and deepened, his whole being open and receptive in his longing to do the will of the Father. All his attention is focused in expectancy to respond to the least impulsion of that will, all his strength is poured out in the love and service of the people around him, in the longing that they may come to share with him, by discovering for themselves, the freedom and joy of the eternal kingdom in which he dwells. So the larger life, the infinite creative power and love and beauty of God could flow into and fill the person and being of the man Jesus, and radiate from him in a way never possible before or since, in a unique act of God in time. In Jesus of Nazareth is found the utmost expression of the infinite and eternal reality of God that is possible within the limits of a human personality, so that Jesus, reaching out to take that life within his own, could declare in and from his manhood: 'He that hath seen me hath seen the Father.'

The vision and existence of God in Christ as something passionately real, not just a phrase in a creed, strains and tears at the muscles of thought as we strive to apprehend it.

Richenda C. Scott

Richenda C. Scott, *Tradition and Experiences*. Swarthmore Lecture, 1964 (London, George Allen and Unwin, 1964), pp. 60–1.

It's very early, and nobody's awake; it's been raining and the light is in the drops on the plane tree, and the birds are talking. There's a faint light in the sky, as if the world wasn't sure yet that the grave would even open, and yet in its blind heart knew that it would. My darling, something I read the other day about Christ begging the others in the Garden to sit up with him, and to pray lest they enter into temptation – 'The spirit indeed is willing' – and that he knew he was himself in extreme temptation, made the whole agony different. You know how I have harped on one's reluctance to suffer. I believe that cry, 'Let this cup pass from me', was the last knife-edge pinnacle of human dread of anguish at Calvary, even more that physical. I think we harp far too much on Christ's Godhead, make things too easy for him that way. I believe in the Incarnation, but I believe that it was a real incarnation – that the temptations to shortcuts in the wilderness were real temptations, that he was in a sense walking in the world with bandaged eyes, like the rest of us, and that he had to spend those long nights praying, to feel for the hand of God to guide him.

Helen Waddell

Dame Felicitas Corrigan, *Helen Waddell* (London, Gollancz, 1986), p. 322. Letter to her sister, Meg, Easter Saturday, 1942.

Women, rouse yourselves! The tocsin of reason resounds through the whole universe: recognize your rights. The powerful empire of nature is no longer surrounded by prejudices, fanaticism, superstition and lies. The flame of truth has banished the clouds of stupidity and encroachment. Enslaved man doubled his efforts and still had need of yours to cast off his chains. Now that he is free he has become unjust towards his companion.

O women, women, when will you stop being so blind? What advantages have you gained from the revolution? A more marked distrust, a more conspicuous disdain. Throughout centuries of corruption you have reigned only over men's weakness. Your empire is now in ruins – what is left to you? Only the conviction of men's injustices. Only your claim for patrimony, based on nature's wise decrees. What is there to fear from entering into such a fine enterprise? The praise of the Lawmaker at the wedding of Cana?

Olympe de Gourges

Olympe de Gourges, *The Rights of Women* (Paris 1791). Tr. Val Stephenson (London, Pythia Press, 1989), p. 13.

Thank God the day is dawning with respect to this subject. Women are studying and investigating for themselves. They are claiming to be recognized as responsible beings, answerable to God for their convictions of duty; and, urged by the divine Spirit, they are overstepping those unscriptural barriers which the Church has so long reared against its performance.

Whether the Church will allow women to speak in her assemblies can only be a question of time; common sense, public opinion, and the blessed results of female agency will force her to give us an honest and impartial rendering of the solitary text on which she grounds her prohibitions. Then, when the true light shines, and God's words take the place of man's traditions, the Doctor of Divinity who shall teach that Paul commands woman to be silent when God's Spirit urges her to speak, will be regarded much the same as we should regard an astronomer who should teach that the sun is the earth's satellite.

Another argument urged against female preaching is, that it is unnecessary; that there is plenty of scope for her efforts in private, in visiting the sick and poor, and working for the temporalities of the Church. Doubtless, woman ought to be thankful for any sphere for benefiting her race and glorifying God. But we cannot be blind to the supreme selfishness of making her so welcome to the hidden toil and self-sacrifice, the hewing of wood and the drawing of water, the watching and waiting, the reproach and persecution attaching to her Master's service, without allowing her a title of the honour which he has attached to the ministration of his gospel. Here, again, man's theory and God's order are at variance. God says: 'Them that honour me I will honour'. Our Lord links the joy with the suffering, the glory with the shame, the exaltation with the humiliation, the crown with the cross, the finding of life with the losing of it. Nor did he manifest any such horror at female publicity in his cause as many of his professed people appear to entertain in these days. We have no

41

intimation of his reproving the Samaritan woman for her public proclamation of him to her countrymen; nor of his rebuking the women who followed him amidst a taunting mob on his way to the cross. And yet, surely, privacy was their proper sphere. On one occasion he did say, with reference to a woman: 'Verily, I say unto you, wheresoever this gospel shall be preached in the whole world, there shall also this, that this woman hath done, be told for a memorial of her' (Matthew 26.12; see also Luke 7.37–50).

As to the obligation devolving on woman to labour for her Master, I presume there will be no controversy. The particular sphere in which each individual shall do this must be dictated by the teachings of the Holy Spirit and the gifts with which God has endowed her. If she have the necessary gifts, and feels herself called by the Spirit to preach, there is not a single word in the whole Book of God to restrain her, but many, very many, to urge and encourage her. God says she SHALL do so; and Paul prescribed the manner in which she shall do it; and Phoebe, Junio, Philip's four daughters, and many other women actually did preach and speak in the primitive churches.

Catherine Booth

Catherine Booth, *Female Ministry: an Address by Mrs General Booth* (London, Salvation Army Book Department, 1909), pp. 18–19.

1 Mine eyes have seen the glory of the coming of the Lord;
  He is trampling out of the vintage where the grapes of wrath are
      stored;
  He hath loosed the fateful lightening of his terrible swift sword,
    His truth is marching on.

          Glory, glory, hallelujah!
          Glory, glory, hallelujah!
          Glory, glory, hallelujah!
          His truth is marching on.

2 I have seen him in the watch-fires of a hundred circling camps;
  They have builded him an altar in the evening dews and
      damps;
  I have read his righteous sentence by the dim and flaring
      lamps;
    His day is marching on.

3 He has sounded forth the trumpet that shall never call retreat;
  He is sifting out the hearts of men before his judgment seat;
  O be swift, my soul, to answer him, be jubilant my feet!
    Our God is marching on.

4 In the beauty of the lilies Christ was born across the sea,
   With a glory in his Bosom that transfigures you and me;
   As he died to make men holy, let us live to make men free,
      While God is marching on.

Julia Ward Howe

Julia Ward Howe in *The Song Book of the Salvation Army* (London, 1986 edn).

On one occasion, when I was reciting the Hours with the community, my soul suddenly became recollected and seemed to me to become bright all over like a mirror: no part of it – back, sides, top or bottom – but was completely bright, and in the centre of it was a picture of Christ our Lord as I generally see him. I seemed to see him in every part of my soul as clearly as in a mirror, and this mirror – I cannot explain how – was wholly sculptured in the same Lord by a most loving communication which I shall never be able to describe. This, I know, was a vision which, whenever I recall it, and especially after Communion, is always of great profit to me. It was explained to me that, when a soul is in mortal sin, this mirror is covered with a thick mist and remains darkened so that the Lord cannot be pictured or seen in it, though he is always present with us and gives us our being; with heretics it is as if the mirror were broken, which is much worse than being dimmed. Seeing this is very different from describing it, for it cannot be properly explained. But it has helped me a great deal and has also caused me deep regrets at the many occasions when, through my faults, my soul has become darkened and so I have been unable to see the Lord.

This vision seems to me a very beneficial one for recollected persons, for it teaches them to think of the Lord as being in the very innermost part of their soul. This is a meditation which has a lasting effect, and, as I have said on other occasions, is much more fruitful than thinking of him as outside us, as certain books do which treat of prayer, telling us where we are to seek God.

Teresa of Avila

Teresa of Jesus, *The Complete Works* vol. 1. Tr. and ed. E. Allison Peers (London and New York, Sheed and Ward, 1946), p. 292.

If Christ is growing in us, if we are at peace, recollected, because we know that however insignificant our life seems to be, from it he is forming himself; if we go with eager wills, 'in haste', to wherever our circumstances compel us, because we believe that he desires to be in that place, we shall find that we are driven more and more to act on the impulse of his love.

And the answer we shall get from others to those impulses will be an awakening into life, or the leap into joy of the already wakened life within them.

It is not necessary at this stage of our contemplation to speak to others of the mystery of life growing in us. It is only necessary to give ourselves to that life, all that we are, to pray without ceasing, not by a continual effort to concentrate our minds but by a growing awareness that Christ is being formed in our lives from what we are. We must trust him for this, because it is not a time to see his face, we must possess him secretly and in darkness, as the earth possesses the seed. We must not try to force Christ's growth in us, but with a deep gratitude for the light burning secretly in our darkness, we must fold our concentrated love upon him like earth, surrounding, holding, and nourishing the seed.

We must be swift to obey the winged impulses of his love, in carrying him to wherever he longs to be; and those who recognize his presence will be stirred, like Elizabeth, with new life. They will know his presence, not by any special beauty or power shown by us, but in the way that the bud knows the presence of the light, by an unfolding in themselves, a putting forth of their own beauty.

It seems that this is Christ's favourite way of being recognized, that he prefers to be known not by his own human features, but by the quickening of his own life in the heart, which is the response to his coming.

Caryll Houselander

Caryll Houselander, *The Reed of God.* (London, Sheed and Ward, 1955), pp. 33–4.

Perhaps it is no wonder that the women were first at the cradle and last at the cross. They had never known a man like this man – there never has been such another. A prophet and teacher who never nagged at them, never flattered or coaxed or patronised who never made arch jokes about them, never treated them either as 'The women, God help us!' or 'The ladies, God bless them!'; who rebuked without querulousness and praised without condescension; who took their questions and arguments seriously; who never mapped out their sphere for them, never urged them to be feminine or jeered at them for being female; who had no axe to grind and no uneasy male dignity to defend; who took them as he found them and was completely unselfconscious. There is no act, no sermon, no parable in the whole

Gospel that borrows its pungency from female perversity; nobody could possibly guess from the words and deeds of Jesus that there was anything 'funny' about woman's nature.

Dorothy L. Sayers

Dorothy L. Sayers, *Are Women Human?* (Grand Rapids, MI, Eerdmans, 1971), p. 47.

3

An exciting, driving
sense of vocation

*While encounter with God has its own integrity, as is apparent in the
writings of the women in the first chapter, nevertheless an awareness
of the presence of God is often accompanied by an experience of call.
The only call story narrated about any woman in the scriptures is the
story of the call of Mary. The annunciation story places her at the
hinge between the Old Testament and the New. Equally the call
stories in this chapter place the women who heard them between a
covenant that was old, the covenant of their own experience of
baptism and one which was about to be, their own personal new
covenant. What they write is valuable because it reminds us that there
is a congruence between the two calls. As the Quaker Elizabeth Fox
Howard put it: 'Looking back over many years, I fancy my choice now
would be much the same.'*

*In this chapter we learn that God can speak to women and call them
to do great things in the divine service. So Isabella Gilmore, the
Anglican deaconess, hears a trumpet call to go and work in the Lord's
vineyard, Kathleen Lonsdale of the Society of Friends knows that she
must refuse to register for war duties and Hannah Whitall Smith,
another Quaker, hears God tell her to sit in her wheeled chair as she
prepares for death. Janet Erskine Stuart, the Roman Catholic who
learns she has a vocation to the religious life discovers this by a bed of
blue hyacinths in Regent's Park. Thérèse of Lisieux hears an equally
important call when 'Jesus, who became a child for love of me,
deigned to bring me forth from the swaddling clothes and imperfections of infancy'. Vocation is about growth and self-acceptance as
well as about the things to be done in God's service.*

*Other calls appear to offer nothing but conflict with the prevailing
establishment, whether secular or religious. A nineteenth-century
Quaker, Sarah Lynes Grubb relates that: 'In Bath I had to go to the
Pump Room and declare the truth to the gay people there.' And
Florence Booth of the Salvation Army takes a difficult stand in 1914
when she writes, 'I believe the rights and liberties of women stand
urgently in need of the whole hearted championship of our sex.' These
women are 'trumpets through which the divine admonition becomes
audible'. Hildegard, the mystic of Bingen, sums up the position: 'The
talk of the people I can easily bear, but not of those who wear clerical
garb, they bitterly oppress my spirit.' More philosophically we note*

that Edith Stein, who became a Carmelite nun after converting to Christianity, wrote: 'Life itself has made our existence problematic.'

As I read the texts I began to notice something else as well. These calls are not greeted naively. The women who receive them know that the divine call often leads to total misunderstanding. Instinctively they sense the possibility of this bitter oppression. It makes demands that seem overwhelming, so that some women who hear the call will rise like Elizabeth Collins, 'in fear and trembling'. Even Catherine Booth marvels, 'Who would ever have thought, twenty years ago, when I first raised my voice, a feeble, trembling woman . . . the hundreds of precious souls that would be given me?'

Such wrestling with the divine call is not just about misunderstanding and anxiety. God who calls us is a God of desire, a God who wants to be known. The Shaker eldress, Rebecca Jackson reminds us that the divine call is all about revelation – of the nature of God as well as one's own personal vocation. In a moment of despair she records: 'I was all alone, had nobody to tell my troubles to except the Lord . . . I throwed myself on the Lord. I saw that night, for the first time, a Mother in the Deity.' And Teresa of Avila notes: 'God converted the aridity of my soul into deepest tenderness.' This has to be one of the reasons why Elsie Chamberlain can write of 'an exciting, driving sense of vocation'. As Charlotte Elliott proclaims in song: 'Just as I am – I come.'

When I was about seven years old, I announced that my favourite text was 'Hitherto hath the Lord helped me'. The elders were amused, but I am not so sure that it was funny after all. The distance from one birthday to the next seems infinite to a small child, and 'the thoughts of youth are long long thoughts'. Looking back over many years, I fancy my choice now would be much the same. I am not prepared, here and now, to analyse and define the reasons, but I can only say that this quiet certainty has run all through my life, linking up babyhood and youth and middle age with the latest stretch of the road . . . and 'hitherto', though sometimes almost slipping through one's fingers, that golden thread has never wholly escaped my grasp.

Elizabeth Fox Howard

Elizabeth Fox Howard, *Midstream: a Record of Many Years* (1947), p. 1. Quoted in *Christian Faith and Practice in the Experience of the Society of Friends* (London Yearly Meeting of the Religious Society of Friends 1960), no. 97.

At school I sought the Lord, feeling his power in my heart operating against the evil propensities of my nature; yet to these corrupt inclinations I many, many times gave way; and for this I was brought under great condemnation, even as early as when nine years old . . . I went on sinning and repenting for years; still my love for good books increased, and for good people. We had few books. The bible and one or two Journals of Friends are all that I can recollect reading; and I really valued them as highly as I was capable of doing in this my childhood. When I grew to about thirteen years of age, I began to discover something about me, or in my mind, like the heavenly anointing for the ministry; for the Lord had revealed his word as a hammer and had broken the rock in pieces in my living experience; and I was contrited under a sense of power and love; saying even vocally when alone, 'Lord, make me a chosen vessel unto thee' . . . With respect to my first appearances (in ministry, when about seventeen years old) . . . I shrunk from it exceedingly; and often have I hesitated, and felt such a reluctance to it, that I have suffered the meeting to break up without my having made the sacrifice: yea, when the word of life in a few words was like a fire within me . . . It pleased the Lord to call me into a path much untrodden, in my early travels as a messenger of the gospel, having to go into markets and to declare the truth in the streets . . . No one knows the depth of my sufferings and the mortifying, yea, crucifying of my own will, which I had to endure in this service; yet I have to acknowledge to the sufficiency of divine grace herein . . . At Bath I had to go to the Pump Room and declare the truth to the gay people who resorted there. This was a time very relieving to my sorely exercised mind. In these days and years of my life I was seldom from under some heavy burden, so that I went greatly bowed down; sometimes ready to say, 'If it be thus with me, O thou who has given me a being, I pray thee take away my life from me' . . . In the year 1801, I wrote thus: 'O my heavenly Father, thou hast seen me in the depth of tribulation, in my many journeyings and travels . . . It was thy power which supported me when no flesh could help, when man could not comprehend the depth of mine exercise . . . Be thou only and for ever exalted in, by and through thy poor child, and let nothing be able to pluck me out of thy hand.'

Sarah Lynes Grubb

Sarah Lynes Grubb, *Letters* (1864) pp. 3, 4, 6, 7, 12–14. Quoted in *Christian Faith and Practice in the Experience of the Society of Friends* (London Yearly Meeting of the Religious Society of Friends 1960), no. 57.

But I – a poor woman, weak and frail from my infancy – have been compelled in a true and mysterious vision to write this letter. And lying in bed with a serious illness, I have written it by the command and assistance of God to present it to the prelates and masters who are sealed for God's service, that in it they might see who and what they are . . . And I heard a voice from heaven saying: Let no one despise these words, lest if anyone despise them, the vengeance of God fall upon him.

Hildegard of Bingen

Hildegard of Bingen in *Ep 31*: PL 197: 286c. Quoted in *Medieval Religious Women* vol. 2: *Peace Weavers*. Ed. John A. Nichols and Lillian Thomas Shanks (Kalamazoo, MI, Cistercian Publications, 1987), p. 103.

As I write that one word 'witness', it recalls to me a scene in a filthy street, one of our worst, a den of thieves, what a sister who takes our children from it to her country home calls 'a hell'. I came out of a house there . . . and saw, standing on the other side of the street, a deaconess leaning against the wall writing a note; a miserable starving child was clasping her dress; sitting on the pavement close to her was a wretched drunken woman; around us both were the usual hideous sounds in streets such as that; the sun was shining on her cross and on her blue dress; upon her face a look full of pity, of love, and of unspeakable peace. I longed just then to have someone to paint her, but as I raised my heart in thanksgiving for her and others whom God has sent us, the words, 'Ye shall be witnesses for me' came to me, and I realized, as I had never done before, the witness that one saintly soul walking humbly in love and good works, unseen by the world, gaining no praise of men, was for him amidst such surroundings. Surely as the years go on it shall tell, and though now the work seems slow, the day will come when we shall see that the message was not taken in vain or lived in vain amongst them.

Isabella Gilmore

Janet Grierson, *Isabella Gilmore* (London, SPCK, 1962), pp. 112–13.

I was still being tormented by this question of unfulfilled longings and it was a distraction in my prayer, when I decided to consult St Paul's epistles in the hopes of getting an answer. It was the twelfth and thirteenth chapters of First Corinthians that claimed my attention. The first of these told me that we can't all of us be apostles, all of us be prophets, all of us doctors and so on; the Church is composed of members which differ in their use; the eye is one thing and hand is another. It was a clear enough answer, but it didn't satisfy my aspirations, didn't set my heart at rest. The Magdalen, by stooping now and again into the empty tomb, was at last rewarded for her search; and I, by sinking down into the depths of my own nothingness, rose high enough to find what I wanted! Reading on to the end of the chapter, I met this comforting phrase: 'Prize the best gifts of heaven. Meanwhile I can shew you a way which is better than any other.'

What was it? The apostle goes on to explain that all the gifts of heaven, even the most perfect of them, without love, are absolutely nothing; charity is the best way of all, because it leads straight to God. Now I was at peace; when St Paul was talking about the different members of the mystical body I couldn't recognize myself in any of them; or rather I could recognize myself in all of them. But charity – that was the key to my vocation. If the Church was a body composed of different members, it couldn't lack the noblest of all; it must have a heart, and a heart burning with love. And I realized that this love was the true motive force which enabled the other members of the Church to act; if it ceased to function the apostles would forget to preach the gospel, the martyrs would refuse to shed their blood. Love, in fact, is the vocation which includes all others; it's a universe of its own, comprising all time and space – it's eternal. Beside myself with joy, I cried out: 'Jesus, my Love! I've found my vocation, and my vocation is love.' I had discovered where it is that I belong in the Church, the niche God has appointed for me. To be nothing else than love, deep down in the heart of Mother Church; that's to be everything at once – my dream wasn't a dream after all.

Thérèse of Lisieux

Thérèse of Lisieux, *Autobiography of a Saint.* Tr. Ronald Knox (London, Fontana, 1960), pp. 185–6.

Who would ever have thought, twenty years ago, when I first raised my voice, a feeble, trembling woman, one of the most timid and bashful the Lord ever saved, the hundreds of precious souls that would be given me? I only refer to myself because I know my own case better than that of another; but, let me ask you – supposing I had held back and been disobedient to the heavenly vision, what would God have said to me for the loss of all this fruit? Thank God, much of it is already gathered into heaven, people who have sent me word from their dying beds, that they blessed God they had ever heard my voice, saying that they should wait for me on the other side, prepared to lead me to the throne – what would have become of the fruit? I should not have had it anyway. They would never have become my crown of rejoicing in the day of the Lord. Oh, who can tell what God can do by any man or woman, however timid, however faint, if only fully given up to him. My brother, my sister, he holds you responsible. He holds you responsible, my sister – you, who wrote me about your difficulties and temptations in testifying of Jesus – he holds you responsible. What are you going to do? Ask yourself. It is coming. You believe it.

You say you do. Unless you are a confirmed hypocrite, you do – that you are going to stand before the throne of his glory.

Catherine Booth

Catherine Booth, *Papers of Aggressive Christianity* (Salvation Army 1980), pp. 13–14.

The other day, disputing with a father who loves you well, I could not make him think otherwise than that women are yet by nature full of fears and affections, more than men, which, with respect to him, is not so. It is true if we will not place our knowledge right, we shall be full of fears and affections. We shall fear that which is not to be feared, and, remaining in troubles, love and adhere to that which is not worthy of love. We know that God only is to be feared and he only is worthy of love. Remember then that he be the end of all your actions and therein you will find great satisfaction and think all things easy and possible.

For I do truly more esteem the perfection of this company than anything whatsoever in the world I can think of.

Mary Ward

Till God Will: Mary Ward through her Writings. Ed. M. Emmanuel Orchard I B V M (London, Darton, Longman and Todd, 1985), p. 60.

Believing, then, that at the door of womankind is laid so large a proportion of the world's undoing, it behoves every woman to bestir herself, and to see to it that our sex is relieved of so serious a stigma. If I am instrumental in helping one woman here to fully realize her responsiblity for the blessing of the world, to realize amongst other things that her tender, impressionable nature has been given her in order that it may be stirred to effort for the righting of what is wrong, and for the helping of those who suffer, I shall feel that it will have been well worth while to have occupied your time and attention.

I have no desire to make this Meeting an occasion for the advocacy of so-called Women's Rights. We do not meet here merely as women of the world, though it might have been very useful to do so, for I believe the rights and liberties of women stand urgently in need of the whole-hearted championship of our sex; and the fact that many, I might even say the generality of women, are so indifferent and apathetic in the matter, is a clear indication of their needy and limited condition. But we meet here to-day as Christian women, and I must assume that, as such, you accept the authoritative words: 'There is neither male nor female . . . in Christ Jesus'.

This statement presupposes:—

1. That in God's sight, the fact that we are women does not make us unfit nor incapable of performing the highest service in his kingdom.
2. That God's love and power and faithfulness are the same, whether he deals with women or with men.
3. That the responsibility we have as Christians for representing Christ to the world rests upon women equally with men.

What mighty channels for the outpouring of God's love upon the world would be represented here to-day if each woman before me were prepared to obey the heavenly vision!

Equality of sex is one of the principles upon which the Salvation Army stands, and it is from the application of this principle that the work about which I have been asked to speak to you has grown and developed.

Perhaps, just here, I ought to mention that to imagine that the work done by the women of the Salvation Army is exclusively in the interests of the outcast classes, is a mistake. Whilst our Women's Social Work is an important, interesting, and exceedingly fruitful branch of Salvation Army activity, it ranks, after all, as only one of many.

Indeed, I think that the raising of women to the same plane of service as that occupied by man, and the opening to her of a wider door of opportunity than she had hitherto enjoyed, is one of the greatest achievements of the Salvation Army.

Florence Booth

Florence Booth, *Mothers and the Empire* (Salvation Army Book Department 1914), pp. 42–3.

I may here note, that sitting in a Meeting at home under exercise, a few words presented to express, but for want of attending singly to the opening, I gave way to reasoning and putting off, which has too often been the case, until the meeting was nearly over; when this language was intelligibly spoken to my inward ear, if thou art not more faithful, thy gift shall be taken from thee. The language was awful; I was brought to see the deplorable situation I should be left in, if after receiving so precious a gift, I should neglect to reimprove it, and it should be taken away, and I left poor and distressed. I was led to cry for mercy and for strength to be more faithful; and in fear and trembling, I arose and expressed what was before me.

Elizabeth Collins

Handwritten memoir of Elizabeth Collins. Quoted in *Friendly Women* vol. 9, no. 3, p. 14.

An exciting, driving sense of vocation

I will say then to the women here one word. Dear women, I recall a scene; you will understand me. The night of the memorable debate in April, lasting many hours, there were meetings of women not far from the House of Commons, where I was in the Ladies' Gallery, and joined those meetings for a few minutes. It was a sight I shall never forget. At one meeting there were the poorest, most ragged and miserable women from the slums of Westminster on their knees before the God of Hosts with tears and groans pouring out the burden of their sad hearts. He alone knew what their burden was. There were women who had lost daughters; there were sad-hearted women; and side by side with these poor souls, dear to God as we are, there were ladies of high rank, in their splendid dresses – Christian women of the upper classes kneeling and also weeping. I thank God for this wonderful solidarity of the women of the world before God. Women are called to be a great power in the future, and by this terrible blow which fell upon us forcing us to leave our privacy and bind ourselves together with our less fortunate sisters, we have passed through an education – a noble education. God has prepared in us, in the women of the world, a force for all future causes which are great and just.

We shall not stop, our efforts will not cease when this particular struggle is at an end. God has called us out, and we must not go back from any warfare to which he will now call us in the future. We praise, we thank him for what he has done already for us, and for what he is going to do, for we shall one day have a complete victory. We can echo the words of that which is written: 'My soul doth magnify the Lord, and my spirit hath rejoiced in God my Saviour, for he hath regarded the low estate of his handmaidens.' And remember, women, if we are faithful unto death, henceforth all men shall call us blessed. Yes, generations to come, your children and your children's children will call you blessed, because you have laboured for purer morals and for juster laws.

Josephine Butler

Joseph Williamson, *Josephine Butler – the Forgotten Saint* (Leighton Buzzard, The Faith Press, 1977), p. 97.

Again: women who think and feel strongly are becoming impatient of the male-bias, male-ascendency, common (however sub-consciously) among ministers. There is need, therefore, of the woman to stand by the side of the man, that she may give her feminine, he is masculine, presentations of God, truth, holiness, purity. We may often hear it said of a particular church, or service, that 'the congregation consisted mainly of women', or 'the great percentage of the audience were men'. It were well to ponder the reason of the variation of tone in the case of each criticism. And male-bias, though often successfully disguised, is apparent when certain subjects – e.g., moral ones – are under discussion.

'Since by a woman sin came into the world', I once heard a Baptist minister somewhat brutally and narrowly exclaim, 'it is fitting that woman should bear a hand in working out redemption.' I mentioned this to a friend, and she told me that in her Church – Anglican – on the same morning, she had listened to a discourse on woman's subjection and how she was created to be a helpmeet for man. One Sunday lately, I went to a well-known Presbyterian church. The service and sermon might have been prepared wholly for men, although they represented a very inconsiderable part of the congregation; while the prayer contained appeals for young men in colleges, and even the Young Men's Christian Association was mentioned by name, but the Young Women's might not have existed as far as this preacher was concerned.

Hatty Baker

Hatty Baker, *Women in the Ministry* (London, C. W. Daniel, 1911), pp. 44–5.

. . . Because I believe in a God with a sense of humour (and not only because he created ducks), I believe he is lovingly amused at my impertinence – like parents with very small bumptious children – not angry about it.

Here is this speck of life in an immeasurable universe daring to try to say something about the value and purpose behind the immeasurableness. If I were a sinless creature, perhaps I would not dare to do it. Something of the egotism of my fallen state, as it is called, helps me. The fact that I am conceited and big-headed and self-centred makes me bold to talk about God – as if I knew, as if I were always there, as if his plan was laid before me. (Shades of Job and the questions that came to him – 'Where wast thou when I laid the foundations of the earth?')

But again my egotism asserts itself; in some sense the plan is laid before me. This is my belief that 'he who made the stars made me', and made me able to contemplate the stars, and made me able to decide that the stars can't contemplate me. I even have the effrontery to believe that he has called me to a particular job in life. I spent some time doing other things and trying to think that giving my spare time to God was really enough; but that didn't work. 'I fled him down the night and down the days', but always he was there. And I had to give in, and for me that meant going to school again to learn how to be a minister. And each tentative, somewhat doubtful step led on to another until the doubt about that particular issue dwindled away.

An exciting, driving sense of vocation

But there were new problems to be faced. Did I believe in a God who gave me an exciting, driving sense of vocation, and gave a lot of other people jobs – sometimes dull monotonous jobs? Where now is the centenarian's philosophy that everyone is first with God? This sort of favouritism might well be yet another divisive factor among the children of men, and break the rule of 'no favourites' that Jesus stressed. What was the vocation God offered, and did he only offer it to the few? And even if it was tremendously important to me, would it not seem more important to many people that there should be someone to un-stop their drains or price the goods in the super-market? I remembered that it was mostly in quite ordinary events shared by a lot of people that God had 'called' me. For instance, those sermons I heard that seemed to demand a response in service had been preached to a whole congregation. Oh vanity! I even ascertained later that the preacher had no conscious sense of directing his words to a particular person. (Indeed one learns early in the Ministry never to do this. It always misfires!) Of the people who heard these particular sermons, maybe many responded to God's call to the vocation; but if the whole congregation had volunteered for the Ministry, they might well have been suspected of mass hysteria: What is our vocation? Is it not to accept the privilege of being a child of God and work out his plan for us? I believe his plan is there – to accept or reject. But the God I believe in takes great trouble to veil what he wants, so that free will can be real. And just as children in one family may, or more probably may not, follow one profession or trade, so God's family needs many members following various professions, trades, 'jobs' – but all are called to be one family and share in the responsibility for all.

Elsie Chamberlain

Elsie Chamberlain, *We Believe in God*. Ed. Rupert E. Davies (London, George Allen and Unwin, 1968), pp. 58–9.

The night of Christmas 1886 was, it is true, decisive for my vocation, but to give it a more exact name I should call it the night of my conversion. On that blest night, of which it is written that it illumines God's own delights, Jesus, who became a child for love of me, deigned to bring me forth from the swaddling clothes and imperfections of infancy. He transformed me so utterly that I no longer recognized myself. But for this change, I should have had to remain many years longer in the world. St Teresa – who said to her daughters 'I want you in nothing to be women but in everything to equal strong men' – St Teresa would have been unwilling to acknowledge me as her child, if the Lord had not clad me in his divine strength, if he had not himself armed me for war.

I promise, Brother, to commend to Jesus quite specially the girl you speak of, who is finding obstacles in the way of her vocation. I sympathize sincerely in her trouble, knowing as from experience what an affliction it is to be unable to answer God's call at once. My wish for her is that she may not be forced to go to Rome as I was . . .

Thérèse of Lisieux

Thérèse of Lisieux, *Collected Letters* (London, Sheed and Ward, 1949), p. 259.

One morning, making my meditation coldly and not at all to my satisfaction, at the end of it I resolved to assist a person to be accepted in some convent, who much desired to become a nun but wanting a portion could not otherwise enter. And then going to dress myself according to the fashion of the country and other circumstances, whilst I adorned my head at the mirror, something very supernatural befell me, similar to that already related on the day of St Athanasius, but more singular and as it appears to me, with greater impetuosity, if there could be. I was abstracted out of my whole being and it was shown to me with clearness and inexpressible certainty that I was not to be of the Order of St Teresa, but some other thing was determined for me, without all comparision more to the glory of God than my entrance into that holy religious Order. I did not see what the assured good thing would be, but the glory of God which was to come through it, showed itself inexplicably and so abundantly as to fill my soul in such a way that I remained for a good space without feeling or hearing anything but the sound 'GLORY, GLORY, GLORY'. All appeared to last but a moment, even at those times when afterwards I made a computation and found it to have been about two hours.

On this occasion a good deal of time passed before I recovered, but returning to myself, I found my heart full of love for this thing, accompanied by such glory that not yet can I comprehend what it is.

Mary Ward

Till God Will: Mary Ward through her Writings. Ed. M. Emmanuel Orchard I B V M (London, Darton, Longman and Todd, 1985), p. 27.

1 Just as I am – without one plea,
But that thy blood was shed for me,
And that thou bid'st me come to thee,
O Lamb of God, I come.

2 Just as I am – and waiting not
To rid my soul of one dark blot,
To thee, whose blood can cleanse each spot,
    O Lamb of God, I come.

3 Just as I am – though tossed about
With many a conflict, many a doubt,
Fightings and fears within, without,
    O Lamb of God, I come.

4 Just as I am – poor, wretched, blind;
Sight, riches, healing of the mind,
Yea, all I need, in thee to find,
    O Lamb of God, I come.

5 Just as I am – thou wilt receive,
Wilt welcome, pardon, cleanse, relieve:
Because thy promise I believe,
    O Lamb of God, I come.

6 Just as I am – thy love unknown
Has broken every barrier down;
Now to be thine, yea, thine alone,
    O Lamb of God, I come.

7 Just as I am – of that free love
The breadth, length, depth, and height to prove,
Here for a season, then above,
    O Lamb of God, I come.

Charlotte Elliott

Charlotte Elliott in *The Baptist Hymn Book* (London, Psalms and Hymns Trust, 1962), no. 443.

While alone on my knees one sabbath, in the capital of the Crusade state Columbus, Ohio, as I lifted my heart to God crying, 'What wouldst thou have me to do?' there was borne in my mind, as I believe from loftier regions, this declaration, 'You are to speak for woman's ballot as a weapon for protection for her home.' Then for the first and only time in my life, there flashed through my brain a complete line of arguments and illustrations.

Frances Willard

Ray Stachey, *Frances Willard: Her Life and Work* (New York, Fleming H. Revell, 1913), p. 209. Quoted in *Women of Spirit*, ed. Rosemary Radford Ruether and Eleanor McLaughlin (New York, Simon Schuster, 1979), p. 235.

In 1835 I was in the west – I thought I would not mention this but I feel it a duty so to do – persecution was raging on every side. The Methodist ministers told the trustees not to let me speak in the church nor in any of the houses. And nobody must go to hear me – if they did, they should be turned out of the church. One of the trustees got up and said he would go 20 miles to hear me. So the minister turned him right out, and said he hoped he would never be taken in again.

They published me in three Quarterly Meetings – at Bush Hill, West Chester, and West Town. He said he would stop me. He would go as far as his horse would travel, and then he would write, where he could not go.

The friends stopped him in Downingtown and told him that they would stop him or me. So they took his horse, and told him they would take care of it, and him too, until he proved Rebecca Jackson to be the woman he said she was. They had sent to me before, desiring me to put the law in force, and defend my course. I told them that I understood my call, before I started, was to live the life that I preached, and if I did, they would say all manner of evil about me, for they had about Christ when he was on earth.

This great persecution throwed open doors before me. Even a wicked drunken man, when the members was afraid to let me speak in their houses and the people waiting to hear the word, he opened his house and said, 'Let her come into my house and preach. I don't belong to meeting'. So when the people heard, they came and told me. I went. The house was filled and all around the house and the road each way.

And at this time I had as much upon me as my soul and spirit was able to bear. I was all alone, and nobody to tell my troubles to except the Lord. When I got up to speak to the people, and seeing them on the fence, on the road, in the grass, my heart seemed to melt within. I throwed myself on the Lord. I saw that night, for the first time, a Mother in the Deity. This indeed was a new scene, a new doctrine to me. But I knowed when I got it, and I was obedient to the heavenly vision – as I see all that I hold forth, that is, with my spirit eye. And was I not glad when I found that I had a Mother! And that night she gave me a tongue to tell it! The spirit of weeping was upon me, and it fell on all the assembly. And though they never heard it before, I was made able by her Holy Spirit of Wisdom to make it so plain that a child could understand it.

Rebecca Jackson

Gifts of Power: the Writings of Rebecca Jackson, Black Visionary, Shaker Eldress. Ed. Jean McMahon Humez (Amhurst, MA, University of Massachusetts Press, 1981), pp. 71–2, 107–8. Quoted in Rosemary Radford Ruether, *Womenguides* (Boston, Beacon Press, 1985), pp. 150–2.

An exciting, driving sense of vocation

In the year 1142, when I was forty-two years and seven months old, it happened that a great light of brilliant fire came from the open heavens and overwhelmed all my mind, my heart, and my breast, not so much like a flickering flame, but rather like glowing heat, as the sun warms other things on which it sheds its rays. And suddenly I had the power of explaining scripture, not by a word-for-word interpretation, nor a division of syllables, or cases or tenses. From the time I was a little girl about five years old, I was conscious of a mysterious hidden power and experienced wonderful visions within myself, but told them to none except a few religious with whom I lived. And during that time until the grace of God wished them to be made known, I hid them under strict silence. These visions which I saw were not in sleep nor in dreams, nor in my imagination nor by bodily eyes or outward ears nor in a hidden place; but in watching, aware with the pure eyes of the mind and inner ear of the heart. But I received them while wide awake, according to the will of God. How this happened it is difficult for mortal men to understand.

Hildegard of Bingen

Hildegard of Bingen in P L 197:384. Quoted in *Medieval Religious Women* vol. 2: *Peace Weavers*, ed. John A. Nichols and Lillian Thomas Shanks (Kalamazoo, MI, Cistercian Publications, 1987), p. 94.

It must have been some time after she had begun to write visions that Elisabeth wrote the following letter to Hildegard. It is preserved in the third book of her visions, and also in the correspondence of Hildegard, together with the reply sent to it.

'What you said had been revealed to you concerning me, I now write to confirm; a cloud of distrust has come over my mind owing to the foolish sayings of some people who are ever talking of me; they are not true. The talk of the people I can easily bear, but not of those who wear clerical garb, they bitterly oppress my spirit. For goaded on, at whose instigation I know not, they ridicule the grace of God that is within me, and do not hesitate rashly to condemn what they do not understand. I hear that certain letters written in their spirit are circulating under my name. They accuse me of having prophesied concerning the Day of Judgment, which I surely never have presumed to do, as knowledge of its advent is denied to mortal man.' She goes on to explain how the angel of God had repeatedly appeared to her, saying that the time for contrition and repentance had come, and how she had spoken of this to others. But now a letter is circulated, full of threats against the abbot. In her distress she begs that Hildegard will accept this explanation, offer prayers in her behalf and write her some words of consolation.

In her reply to this letter Hildegard admits Elisabeth's power of prophecy. She also is a trumpet through which the blasts of divine admonition become audible.

Lina Eckenstein

Lina Eckenstein, *Women under Monasticism* (Cambridge University Press 1896), p. 282.

When I took the habit, the Lord at once showed me how great are his favours to those who use force with themselves in his service. No one realized that I had gone through all this; they all thought I had acted out of sheer desire. At the time my entrance into this new life gave me a joy so great that it has never failed me, even to this day, and God converted the aridity of my soul into the deepest tenderness. Everything connected with the religious life caused me delight; and it is a fact that sometimes, when I was spending time in sweeping floors which I had previously spent on my own indulgence and adornment, and realized that I was now free from all those things, there came to me a new joy, which amazed me, for I could not understand whence it arose. Whenever I recall this, there is nothing, however hard, which I would hesitate to undertake if it were proposed to me. For I know now, by experience of many kinds, that if I strengthen my purpose by resolving to do a thing for God's sake alone, it is his will that, from the very beginning, my soul shall be afraid, so that my merit may be the greater; and if I achieve my resolve, the greater my fear has been, the greater will be my reward, and the greater, too, will be my retrospective pleasure. Even in this life His Majesty rewards such an act in ways that can be understood only by one who has enjoyed them. This I know by experience, as I have said, in many very serious matters; and so, if I were a person who had to advise others, I would never recommend anyone, when a good inspiration comes to him again and again to hesitate to put it into practice because of fear; for if one lives a life of detachment for God's sake alone, there is no reason to be afraid of that things will turn out amiss, since he is all-powerful. May he be blessed for ever. Amen.

Teresa of Avila

Teresa of Jesus, *The Complete Works* vol. 1. Tr. and ed. E. Allison Peers (London and New York, Sheed and Ward, 1946), pp. 20–1.

In the year 1830, July, I was wakened by thunder and lightning at the break of day . . . I rose up and walked the floor back and forth wringing my hands and crying under great fear. I heard it said to me, 'This day thy soul is required of thee', and all my sins from my childhood rushed into my mind like an over swelling tide, and I expected every clap of thunder to launch my soul at the bar of God with all my sins that I had ever done. I have no language to describe my feelings . . . I then thought to attempt to pray to God to forgive me all my sins just as I was agoing to die – I thought it would be an insult to such a merciful God. And all this time it was thundering and lightning as if the heavens and earth were acoming together – so it seemed to me at that time. And I felt it was just that I should be damned for sinning against a just and holy God. I then felt a love mingled with sorrow toward an insulted God, whom I had sinned against all my days. While these thoughts with many more rolled against my troubled breast, they covered me with shame, fear, and confusion to think of living all my days in sin and then dying and being driven from the presence of a merciful and holy God. It was more than I could bear.

I then thought, 'I might as well go to hell off my knees acrying for mercy as anywhere else'. So I kneeled at the head of the garret stairs, which was the first impression, and down I kneeled and I cried and prayed to God with all my might and strength. The more I prayed, the worse I felt. My sins like a mountain reached to the skies, black as sack cloth of hair and the heavens was as brass against my prayers and everything above my head was of one solid blackness. And the fearful foreboding of my sudden destruction caused me to cry out in the bitterness of my soul, 'Lord, I never will rise from my knees till thou for Christ's sake has mercy on my poor sinking soul or sends me to hell'. For I felt as though my soul had come into the chamber of death. And in this moment of despair the cloud bursted, the heavens was clear, and the mountain was gone. My spirit was light, my heart was filled with love for God and all mankind. And the lightning, which was a moment ago the messenger of death, was now the messenger of peace, joy, and consolation. And I rose from my knees, ran down stairs, opened the door to let the lightning in the house, for it was like sheets of glory to my soul.

My brother came downstairs. I said, 'Oh, I have found the Lord'. 'Has thee?' he said. 'Oh, yes, yes, I have. Come and help me praise him.' 'Oh, yes, sister, I will. I am glad thee has found the Lord again.' And at every clap of thunder I leaped from the floor praising the God of my salvation. I opened all the windows in the house to let the lightning in for it was like streams of bright glory to my soul and in this happy state I praised the Lord for about an hour without ceasing. My brother then said, 'Sister, let us now return the Lord's thanks for what he has done for us'. 'Oh, yes, yes, my brother, we will.' And down we kneeled. My brother made a feeling prayer. When he closed, I lifted up my voice in prayer, in thanks to Almighty God who had heard my prayer for Christ's sake.

After I received the blessing of God, I had a great desire to read the bible. I am the only child of my mother that had not learning. And now, having the charge of my brother and his six children to see to, and my husband, and taking in sewing for a living, I saw no way that I could now get learning without my brother would give me one hour's lesson at night after supper or before he went to bed . . . And my brother so tired when he would come home that he had not power so to do, and it would grieve me. Then I would pray to God to give me power over my feelings that I might not think hard of my brother. Then I would be comforted . . . I felt hurt, when he refused me these little things. And at this time, I could not keep from crying. And these words were spoken in my heart, 'Be faithful, and the time shall come when you can write'. These words were spoken in my heart as though a tender father spoke them. My tears were gone in a moment.

One day I was sitting finishing a dress in haste and in prayer. This word was spoken in my mind, 'Who learned the first man on earth?' 'Why, God.' 'He is unchangeable, and if he learned the first man to read, he can learn you.' I laid down my dress, picked up my bible, ran upstairs, opened it, and kneeled down with it pressed to my breast, prayed earnestly to Almighty God if it was consisting to his holy will, to learn me to read his holy word. And when I looked on the word, I began to read. And when I found I was reading, I was frightened – then I could not read one word. I closed my eyes again in prayer and then opened my eyes, began to read. So I done, until I read the chapter. I came down. 'Samuel, I can read the bible.' 'Woman, you are agoing crazy!' 'Praise the God of heaven and of earth, I can read his holy word!' Down I sat and read through . . .

So I tried, took my bible daily and praying and read until I could read anywhere. The first chapter that I read I never could know it after that day. I only knowed it was in James, but what chapter I never can tell.

Rebecca Jackson

Gifts of Power: the Writings of Rebecca Jackson, Black Visionary, Shaker Eldress. Ed. Jean McMahon Humez (Amhurst, MA, University of Massachusetts Press, 1981), pp. 71–2, 107–8. Quoted in Rosemary Radford Ruether, *Womenguides* (Boston, Beacon Press, 1985), pp. 150–2.

I am seldom now in any part of London but our own districts on a Sunday, but whenever I am and I see the crowded churches, with hundreds and thousands of seemingly devout women worshippers, I wonder if they know the need; surely if Christ is real to them, if they believe in any way the message that it is for all, they must be longing to carry it; once the desire is there, once the word comes 'Lord here I am, send me', difficulties will vanish.

An exciting, driving sense of vocation

There are certain gifts natural and acquired, which are necessary if the work is to be done efficiently. We want women whose good natural capabilities have been improved by education, who can bring the habit of observation and the quickness of the cultivated eye and hand to the work, and whose health and strength are vigorous enough to meet the demands of a busy life. Women who realize that a gentle-woman can undertake the most menial duties, sweep a room, cook a meal, attend to a patient in the most loathesome state of neglect if need be, turn her hand to any work that meets her in the miserable rooms and degraded surroundings of the purlieurs of London, should her lot be cast there, and yet feel that she is in her right place, that such service is honourable and dignified beyond expression, for it is a humble following of him 'who came not to be ministered unto but to minister'. We want in fact the highest type of woman for the office.

Isabella Gilmore

Janet Grierson, *Isabella Gilmore* (London, SPCK, 1962), pp. 220–1.

When I was about fifteen years old, while living in the house of a relation of my mother, in great measure because the retirement was more to my taste, I had a religious vocation. This grace by the mercy of God has been so continuous that not for one moment since then have I had the least thought of embracing a contrary state. My parents, though otherwise extraordinary pious, would not for any consider-ation give their consent, for I was the eldest child and much loved, especially by my father. I was therefore obliged to remain in England six years and some months longer.

But, O Parent of parents, and Friend of all friends, thy intent in thus disposing was different from this; for here without entreaty thou tookest me into thy care, and by degrees led me from all else that at length I might see and settle my love in thee. What had I ever done to please thee? Or what was there in me wherewith to serve thee? Much less could I ever deserve to be chosen by thee. O happy begun freedom, the beginning of all my good, and more worth to me at that time than the whole world besides. Had I never since hindered thy will and working in me, what degrees of grace should I now have had. It is more than nineteen years since, and where as yet am I? My Jesus, forgive me, remember what thou hast done for me, and whither thou hast brought me, and for this excess of goodness and love let me no more hinder thy will in me.

Mary Ward

Till God Will: Mary Ward through her Writings. Ed. M. Emmanuel Orchard IBVM (London, Darton, Longman and Todd, 1985), pp. 9–10.

One day, it was May 6, 1882, when I was walking up through Regent's Park to the Helpers of the Holy Souls, I was thinking of religious life and saying to almighty God, 'O my God, I should like it very much, but you see it is impossible to think of it at present' – and then and there, standing by the side of a bed of blue hyacinths – *factum est ad me verbum Domini* and I saw it all.

When I went into the convent chapel, the blessed sacrament was exposed, and the nun who was on the prie-dieu was replaced by another as I came in. I asked as a sign that, if the 'word' was from God, he would put me on the prie-dieu instead of the nun who had just come, and almost immediately she left the prie-dieu and came to beg me to take it, saying she felt too ill to stay – so I did not doubt further.

Janet Erskine Stuart

Maud Monahan, *Janet Erskine Stuart* (London, Longmans, 1923), p. 42.

I went to early service alone, and to the 11 o'clock with the children; the preacher was a stranger; he gave out his text, 'Go work for me today in my vineyard'. To me it was a trumpet call; I never heard any of the sermon. I could hardly keep from off my knees until it was finished; it was just as if God's voice had called me, and the intense rest and joy were beyond all words; the village church, the big square pew, the children, the service going on was all like a dream, that call was the only real thing.

Isabella Gilmore

Janet Grierson, *Isabella Gilmore* (London, SPCK, 1962), pp. 47–8.

I have sometimes been asked what were my reasons for deciding on that refusal to register for war duties that sent me to Holloway Jail 22 years ago. I can only answer that my reason told me that I was a fool, that I was risking my job and my career, that an isolated example could do no good, that it was a futile gesture since even if I did register my three small children would exempt me. But reason was fighting a losing battle. I had wrestled in prayer and I knew beyond all doubt that I must refuse to register, that those who believed that war was the wrong way to fight evil must stand out against it however much they stood alone, and that I and mine must take the consequences. The 'and mine' made it more difficult, but I question whether children ever really suffer loss in the long run through having parents who are willing to stand by principles; many a soldier had to leave his family and thought it his duty to do so. When you have to make a vital decision about behaviour, you cannot sit on the fence. To decide to do nothing is still a decision, and it means that you remain on the station platform or the airstrip when the train or plane has left.

If we knew all the answers there would be no point in carrying out scientific research. Because we do not, it is stimulating, exciting, challenging. So too is the Christian life, lived experimentally. If we knew all the answers it would not be nearly such fun.

Kathleen Lonsdale

Kathleen Lonsdale, *I Believe* (Cambridge University Press 1964), pp. 54–5.

There comes before us a queenly figure amongst them – one Olympia, of Constantinople, who stands out of the page of history as one whom God had endowed with great gifts – beauty, wealth, position and great influence. She was a strength to St Chrysostom, and had been admitted to her office by his predecessor at a very early age, because of the beauty of her character. Letters of St Chrysostom to her are extant. There is a passage in one which comes home with as much force to the rich deaconess of these times as, no doubt, it did to her: 'If you give your wealth to those who need it not, you might with equal wisdom throw it into the sea. You have devoted your prosperity to God; well, then, you are God's steward. You cannot depose yourself from your responsibility of dispensing his wealth wisely for him.' Under this great Head Deaconess were forty women belonging to that one great church.

Isabella Gilmore

Janet Grierson, *Isabella Gilmore* (London, SPCK, 1962), p. 208.

A discerning young girl recently asked me, 'Why is it that at this time so much is being said, even by men, about the nature and vocation of women?' It is astonishing how this topic is constantly being taken up by various parties, and how differently it is being treated. Leading intellectuals are painting a shining ideal of feminine nature, and they are hoping that realization of this ideal will be the cure for all contemporary ailments and needs. At the same time, in the literature of the present and of the last decades, we see woman presented again and again as the demon of the abyss. A great responsibility is being laid upon us by both sides. We are being obliged to consider the significance of woman and her existence as a problem. We cannot evade the question as to what we are and what we should be. And it is not only the reflective intellect which faces us with this question; life itself has made our existence problematic.

An evolution which was sensed in advance by some, wanted and worked for by few, and one which surprised most people entirely, has torn women out of the well-enclosed realm of the home and out of a matter-of-course kind of life and has suddenly plunged them into the most manifold alien situations and undreamt of problems. We have been thrown into the river, and we must swim. But when our strength threatens to give out, we try to reach at least the shore for safety. We would like to think through the question of whether we should go on; and if we should go on, what we should do so that we will not drown. We would like to scrutinize the direction of the current by taking into account, one against the other, its strength and our own powers and possibilities of movement.

Edith Stein

The Collected Works of Edith Stein, Sister Benedicta of the Cross, Discalced Carmelite, vol. 2. Tr. Freda Mary Oben (Washington DC, ISC Publications, 1987), pp. 86–7.

We must be confident that there is still more 'life' to be 'lived' and yet more heights to be scaled. The tragedy of middle age is that, so often, men and women cease to press 'towards the goal of their high calling'. They cease learning, cease growing; they give up and resign from life. As wisdom dawns with age, we begin to measure our experiences not by what life gives to us, not by the things withheld from us, but by their power to help us to grow in spiritual wisdom.

Evelyn Sturge

Evelyn Sturge, *The Glory of Growing Old* (1950 edn), pp. 7–8. Quoted in *Christian Faith and Practice in the Experience of the Society of Friends* (London Yearly Meeting of the Religious Society of Friends 1960), no. 463.

Once my Divine Master sent me on his errands, and I knew his will was good, and was happy in trying to do it. And now he has shut me up to an invalid life, and tells me to sit in my wheeled chair, and to be content to let others do his errands and carry on his work, and I know his will is good just the same, and am happy in trying to accept it.

Hannah Whitall Smith

Hannah Whitall Smith, letter to a friend, written three days before she died. Quoted in *Christian Faith and Practice in the Experience of the Society of Friends* (London Yearly Meeting of the Religious Society of Friends 1960), no. 79.

4
When the flame is lit

When the call is heard and answered, what direction does the life of Christian women take? In Church circles we are so accustomed to being told the answer to this question by men that it is refreshing to discover that the women in this chapter can give no one single answer. In the face of the evidence our stereotypes crumple. Dorothy Day, the great American Roman Catholic lay woman, is quite unsentimental when she lists the tasks that come one's way: 'paper work, cleaning the house, cooking the meals, dealing with the innumerable visitors who come all through the day, answering the phone, keeping patience and acting intelligently'. The medieval mystic Margery Kempe has her own list: 'washing and wringing and drying' as she clears up after her incontinent husband and comments that she was 'kept to a great extent from contemplation'.

'The secular vocation is sacred.' 'The only Christian work is good work well done.' Dorothy L. Sayers' forthright claims need to be heard again today as clearly as when she first wrote them. The secular vocation brings colossal responsibilities without always offering the infrastructure of spiritual and emotional support the Church is able to give to those whose work is obviously Church work. Yet, with Olive Wyon, 'we must begin where we are' and then be 'on the alert, peacefully busy, but inwardly watching for signs of the will of God in the ordinary setting of our lives'. The place where God meets us is within our own setting. That is why Thérèse of Lisieux can talk about buying half a bottle of Tissérand water for two francs fifty and seven or eight nutcrackers in the same breath as she reflects upon the gospel story of Martha, Mary and Lazarus.

This is what so appeals to Evelyn Underhill and leads her to pray, 'Lay your sacred hands on all the common things and small interests of life.' Caryll Houselander puts her finger on it like this: 'When we think of Christ in the workman, we think of him in a special kind of workman who wears an open shirt and is assisted in carrying the burden of social injustice by a truly magnificent physique.' Not only do we have difficulty in accepting the ordinariness of our own lives, we also find it difficult to let Christ be ordinary. We are embarrassed because, in Houselander's poem, 'Despair' in the face of an old woman with her jug for a pint of beer 'troubles to curl her hair'. We are shocked when a benefactor is mistaken for what Dorothy Day calls 'a derelict woman'.

Does all this mean that the life of a good Christian woman has to be banal? The answer is clearly no. What the women in this chapter are *saying is encapsulated in Mary Ward's insight about sexual politics. The territory of men's work and women's work, men's proper sphere and women's proper sphere is not a morally neutral one. Somewhere an assumption is hovering and the priest who talks to Mary Ward gives the game away when he says that 'he would not for a thousand worlds be a woman, because he thought that a woman could not apprehend God'. As a seventeenth-century Englishwoman Mary Ward, 'answered nothing but only smiled, although I could have answered him by the experience I have of the contrary'. Three hundred years later Evangeline Booth writes that 'the women's movement is spreading, the exhilaration and invigoration of its spirit is in the very air we breathe, bracing the nerves, stimulating the will, and reinforcing the faculties'. Ours is a more political age. Women are actively engaged in commerce – 'still at the gate at midnight, seeing to the loading and unloading of merchandise' – in social work, in making community, in caring for the sick, the addicts, and their own children. It is all too easy to dismiss the work of women – either by ignoring it or by parodying those who do it. As Mary Stocks notes: 'Charis Frankenburg and I found ourselves described . . . as "the kind of idle women who visit matinées and sit with cigarettes between their painted lips".' On this occasion a sense of humour came to their rescue and they gained pleasure from the contrast between the description and their usual sense of themselves as 'rather dowdy social workers'.*

Where Mary Ward could smile and say nothing and the birth control pioneers could laugh, there is now a changed atmosphere. In the name of the gospel and all it teaches us to value, the flame has been lit and will not be extinguished. Kathleen Bliss's reminder is timely: 'Women have wielded influence with very great skill over the centuries and many prefer it to any form of responsibility which brings them out into the open. But the choice between influence and responsibility is one that women have to make, and Churches have to make in relation to women.'

Come let us pray
that the seed of our life's flowering,
falls not upon rock
falls not upon thorns
or the hard frost
or among weeds.
But that today's sorrow,
prepare the world's soil
and sift for sowing tomorrow.

When the flame is lit

I beseech you
be gentle.
Because, when the flame is lit,
the wax is consumed quickly.
When the leaf flowers
swift is the withering.
But if the seed falls
into the heart in fallow,
the passing loveliness,
the flicker of light,
will remain in the dark night,
to flower with eternal life.

Caryll Houselander

Caryll Houselander, 'A Prayer to Creatures' in *The Flowering Tree* (London, Sheed and Ward, 1945), pp. 108–9.

The official Church wastes time and energy, and, moreover, commits sacrilege, in demanding that secular workers should neglect their proper vocation in order to do Christian work – by which she means ecclesiastical work. The only Christian work is good work well done.

Dorothy L. Sayers

Dorothy L. Sayers, *Creed or Chaos* (New York, Harcourt, Brace, 1949), pp. 57–8. Quoted in Rosamond Kent Sprague, *A Matter of Eternity: Selections from the Writings of Dorothy L. Sayers* (London and Oxford, Mowbray, 1973), p. 105.

When a mother, a housewife, asks what she can do, one can only point to the way of St Thérèse, that little way, so much misunderstood and so much despised. She did all for the love of God, even to putting up with the irritation in herself caused by the proximity of a nervous nun. She began with working for peace in her own heart, and willing to love where love was difficult, and so she grew in love, and increased the sum total of love in the world, not to speak of peace.

Paper work, cleaning the house, cooking the meals, dealing with the innumerable visitors who come all through the day, answering the phone, keeping patience and acting intelligently, which is to find some meaning in all these encounters – these things too are the work of peace, and often seem like a very little way.

But as Pope John told the pilgrimage of women, Mothers for Peace, the seventy-five of us who went over to Rome to thank him for his encyclical *Pacem in Terris*, just the month before his death, 'the beginnings of peace are in your own hearts, in your families, school-rooms, offices, parishes, and neighbourhoods'.

It is working from the ground up, from the poverty of the stable, in work as at Nazareth, and also in going from town to town, as in the public life of Jesus two thousand years ago. And since a thousand years are as one day, and Christianity is but two days old, let us take heart and start now.

Dorothy Day

Dorothy Day, *On Pilgrimage: The Sixties* (New York, Curtis Books, 1972), pp. 258–9.

As a sculptor would cast into the breach any stone rather than that which he had wrought into a statue, so women, when the gulf opens between the nations, would cast in anything rather than the men they have made. 'No woman who is a woman,' writes Mrs Schreiner, 'says of a human body, "It is nothing."'' This phrase, like the whole chapter in which it appears, became a classic of the Woman's Movement. It was believed to express the true, the inevitable attitude of women as a sex, whether in or outside the progressive ranks. It was assumed to be so 'natural' to them, that to put power into their hands was to forge a weapon against war. It was not denied that they might feel that war might in some cases still be a national duty; but it was believed with conviction that women, from their very nature, would approach the question with an unspeakable reluctance, that war would appear to them in all its naked horror, shorn of glory, that they would be free from the 'war fever' to which men so easily fall victims.

In support of this view, it is to be borne in mind that women's internationalism has on the whole broken down less conspicuously than men's, two international congresses having been held since the war began, and both representing women. It is probably also true that among working people the desire for peace is still stronger among the women than the men.

Maude Royden

Maude Royden, 'War and the Woman's Movement' in *Towards a Lasting Settlement*. Ed. Charles Roden Buxton (London, George Allen and Unwin, 1915), p. 135.

Let me give one simple illustration of the difference between the right and the wrong kind of feminism. Let us take this terrible business – so distressing to the minds of bishops – of the women who go about in trousers. We are asked: 'Why do you want to go about in trousers? They are extremely unbecoming to most of you. You only do it to copy the men.' To this we may very properly reply: 'It is true that they are unbecoming. Even on men they are remarkably unattractive. But, as you men have discovered for yourselves, they are comfortable, they do not get in the way of one's activities like skirts and they protect the wearer from draughts about the ankles. As a human being, I like comfort and dislike draughts. If the trousers do not attract you, so much the worse; for the moment I do not want to attract you. I want to enjoy myself as a human being, and why not? As for copying you, certainly you thought of trousers first and to that extent we must copy you. But we are not such abandoned copy-cats as to attach these useful garments to our bodies with braces. There we draw the line. These machines of leather and elastic are unnecessary and unsuited to the female form. They are, moreover, hideous beyond description. And as for decency – of which you sometimes accuse the trousers – we at least can take our coats off without becoming the half-undressed, bedroom spectacle that a man presents in his shirt and braces.'

So that when we hear that women have once more laid hands upon something which was previously a man's sole privilege, I think we have to ask ourselves: is this trousers or is it braces? Is it something useful, convenient and suitable to a human being as such? Or is it merely something unnecessary to us, ugly, and adopted merely for the sake of collaring the other fellow's property? These jobs and professions, now. It is ridiculous to take on a man's job just in order to be able to say that 'a woman has done it – yah!' The only decent reason for tackling any job is that it is your job, and you want to do it.

Dorothy L. Sayers

Dorothy L. Sayers, *Are Women Human?* (Grand Rapids, MI, Eerdmans, 1971), pp. 22–3.

1 I sing a song of the saints of God,
      Patient and brave and true,
   Who toiled and fought and lived and died
      For the Lord they loved and knew.
   And one was a doctor, and one was a queen,
   And one was a shepherdess on the green;
   They were all of them saints of God; and I mean,
      God helping, to be one too.

2 They loved their Lord so good and dear,
 And his love made them strong;
 And they followed the right, for Jesus' sake,
 The whole of their good lives long.
 And one was a soldier, and one was a priest,
 And one was slain by a fierce wild beast:
 And there's not any reason, no, not the least,
 Why I shouldn't be one too.

3 They lived not only in ages past,
 There are hundreds of thousands still;
 The world is bright with the joyous saints
 Who love to do Jesus' will.
 You can meet them in school, or in lanes, or at sea,
 In church, or in trains, or in shops, or at tea,
 For the saints of God began just like me,
 And I mean to be one too.

Lesbia Scott

Lesbia Scott in *The Baptist Hymn Book* (London, Psalms and Hymns Trust, 1962), no. 259.

We must begin where we are. For many people the heavy responsibilities of home and family and earning a living absorb all their time and strength. Yet such a home – where love is – may be a light shining in a dark place, a silent witness to the reality and the love of God.

We must begin where we are, but once we have put ourselves and our lives into God's hands, to be used as he wills, and when and where, we must be on the alert, peacefully busy, but inwardly watching for signs of the will of God in the ordinary setting of our lives. To ears which have been trained to wait upon God in silence, and in the quietness of meditation and prayer, a very small incident, or a word, may prove to be a turning-point in our lives, and a new opening for his love to enter our world, to create and to redeem.

Olive Wyon

Olive Wyon, *Prayer* (London, Fontana Books, 1962).

There is, it sometimes seems, an excess of religious and social busyness these days, a round of committees and conferences and journeyings, of which the cost in 'peaceable wisdom' is not sufficiently counted. Sometimes we appear overmuch to count as merit our participation in these things . . . At least we ought to make sure that we sacrifice our leisure for something worthy. True leisureliness is a beautiful thing and may not lightly be given away. Indeed, it is one of the outstanding and most wonderful features of the life of Christ that, with all his work in preaching and healing and planning for the kingdom, he leaves behind this sense of leisure, of time in which to pray and meditate, to stand and stare at the cornfields and fishing boats, and to listen to the confidences of neighbours and passers-by . . .

Most of us need from time to time the experience of something spacious or space-making, when Time ceases to be the enemy, goad-in-hand, and becomes our friend. To read good literature, gaze on natural beauty, to follow cultivated pursuits until our spirits are refreshed and expanded, will not unfit us for the up and doing of life, whether of personal or church affairs. Rather will it help us to separate the essential from the unessential, to know where we are really needed and get a sense of proportion. We shall find ourselves giving the effect of leisure even in the midst of a full and busy life. People do not pour their joys or sorrows into the ears of those with an eye on the clock.

Caroline C. Graveson

Caroline C. Graveson, *Religion and Culture* (Swarthmore Lecture 1937), pp. 37–40. Quoted in *Christian Faith and Practice in the Experience of the Society of Friends* (London Yearly Meeting of the Religious Society of Friends 1960), no. 458.

The next act of faith is in Christ in other people.

It is very easy to believe in the indwelling presence of Christ in the souls of imaginary people; to believe in it in people whom we do not know; but it is very difficult to believe in it in the case of our own relations and our intimate friends.

Somehow it is difficult to believe that the Holy Spirit abides in people who are not picturesque. When we think of Christ in the workman, we think of him in a special kind of workman who wears an open shirt and is assisted in carrying the burden of social injustice by a truly magnificent physique. We do not think of him in the man who delivers the milk or calls to mend the pipes. We do not think of him in the porters in the apartment houses. Recently, in a big block, a frail little porter fell down dead. Everyone agreed that the heavy luggage he had been in the habit of carrying for the tenants was too much for him, though only after a post mortem was it realized. No one was struck by the idea that in this little man a scene from the Passion had been lived again; he had fallen under the weight of the cross.

It is easy to believe in Christ in the refugee when he is on the road, easy to believe when the refugee mother arrives at an English port, with a shawl round her head and a baby in her arms; but how hard to believe in the presence of God in the same refugees when they have got good work, are housed and fed, and possess hats and gloves.

Caryll Houselander

Caryll Houselander, *The Reed of God* (London, Sheed and Ward, 1955), p. 101.

Women are not human. They lie when they say they have human needs: warm and decent clothing; comfort in the bus; interests directed immediately to God and his universe, not intermediately through any child of man. They are far above man to inspire him, far beneath him to corrupt him; they have feminine minds and feminine natures, but their mind is not one with their nature like the minds of men; they have no human mind and no human nature. 'Blessed be God,' says the Jew, 'that hath not made me a woman.'

God, of course, may have his own opinion, but the Church is reluctant to endorse it. I think I have never heard a sermon preached on the story of Martha and Mary that did not attempt, somehow, somewhere, to explain away its text. Mary's, of course, was the better part – the Lord said so, and we must not precisely contradict him. But we will be careful not to despise Martha. No doubt, he approved of her too. We could not get on without her, and indeed (having paid lip-service to God's opinion) we must admit that we greatly prefer her. For Martha was doing a really feminine job, whereas Mary was just behaving like any other disciple, male or female; and that is a hard pill to swallow.

Dorothy L. Sayers

Dorothy L. Sayers, *Are Women Human?* (Grand Rapids, MI, Eerdmans, 1971), pp. 46–7.

It is true that although the principles of militarism and feminism are fundamentally opposed many people do not know it, and – since we are not a peculiarly logical race – many Englishmen and women who are genuinely shocked at Prussianism as expounded by Bernhardi and applied to Belgium, have themselves expatiated eloquently in the same vein when the question was of classes or sexes instead of nations. There are militarists who believe themselves feminist, and feminists who are undoubtedly militarist. And, after all, since we are most of us perfectly aware that 'logic is not a science but a dodge', we must beware of dismissing a paradox merely because it involves an apparent contradiction. When, however, the contradiction is real – when the opposition between two principles is fundamental – the human mind cannot for ever hold them both. One must drive out and destroy the other. Those feminists who had most closely thought out their position had already grasped the issue. When war broke out, and ordinary political activities were necessarily suspended, it seemed to them as inevitable that they should take up the task of combating the real enemy of women (and of civilization) – militarism – as it was that they should take their share in the relief of the physical miseries and material burdens of war. There was no question of opposition to the war itself within the great Suffrage organizations, since the vast majority of their members believed that war had been forced upon us and was, on our part, a battle against a militarist ideal. But there was a deep consciousness that the spirit of militarism is very hardly separated from the fact of war, and that this spirit is immovably opposed to the feminism which rests its whole claim on the supremacy of spiritual force. War, indeed, has its spiritual passion; but the fact that this must find its expression in the crudest forms of violence tends to exalt the latter at the expense of the former. Women can do no greater service to the world than to increase the healthy scepticism of violence as a method of imposing ideals which the history of religious persecution has already created.

War may claim for itself the power to destroy and to clear the ground. It can never construct or create. It is not the means by which ideals are imposed. There is ultimately no way of combating a wrong idea but the setting forth of a right one. Whether they are right who believe that moral force is 'the ultimate appeal' against which coercion is vain and violence merely a counsel of despair, or they who see in physical force the real basis of government, let time show. One thing at least is certain – that as the Woman's Movement embodies the one creed and 'militarism' the other, so these two must be in eternal opposition. The victory of one is the defeat of the other. Women, whatever other claim may be made for them, are not equal to men in their capacity to use force or their willingness to believe in it. For them, therefore, to ask for equal rights with men in a world governed by such force is frivolous. Their claim would not be granted, and if granted would not be valid. Like the negro vote in America, it would be a cheat and a delusion. But if moral power be the true basis of human relationship, then the Woman's Movement is on a sure foundation and moves to its inevitable triumph. Its victory will be an element in the making of permanent peace, not because women are less liable to 'war fever' than men, but because their claim and its fulfilment involves the assertion of that which war perpetually denies.

Maude Royden

Maude Royden, 'War and the Woman's Movement' in *Towards a Lasting Settlement*. Ed. Charles Roden Buxton (London, George Allen and Unwin, 1915), pp. 145–6.

Then the Pope began to speak and the words that fell from his lips seemed to be directed to us, to our group, speaking as he did about the 'Pilgrims for Peace' who came to him, and his gratitude for their gratitude and encouragement. The young woman who had helped us find our places was translating his words as fast as he spoke them and writing them down while two of us read over her shoulder. She kept beaming at us, and all those around us, seeing our buttons, large almost as saucers, bright blue and bearing the legend 'Mothers for Peace' in Italian, also smiled and indicating the Holy Father and us in turn, seemed to be letting us know that he was speaking to us especially.

It seemed too good to be true and if all those around us had not kept assuring us he was speaking to us, I would have considered it but a coincidence. Our messages had reached him we felt, impossible though it had seemed they would. I wrote these things in the post-script to my account in the last month's issue of the CW [Catholic Worker], but I am calling attention in more detail this month to our difficulties.

We were truly an ecumenical group made up as we were of all faiths, of believers and unbelievers, and I had no doubt but that a few of the women, perhaps one or two, were working with the communist peace groups too. This did not disturb me, though I would prefer that those of that political point of view were more open about it so that there were more chance of frank discussion about our oppositions and points of concordance. One can understand however the economical disadvantage, the loss of jobs, that such openness would lead to.

Dorothy Day

Dorothy Day, *On Pilgrimage: The Sixties* (New York, Curtis Books, 1972), pp. 144–7.

1 Take my life, and let it be
Consecrated, Lord, to thee:
Take my moments and my days,
Let them flow in ceaseless praise.

2 Take my hands, and let them move
At the impulse of thy love:
Take my feet, and let them be
Swift and beautiful for thee.

3 Take my voice, and let me sing,
Always, only, for my king:
Take my lips, and let them be
Filled with messages from thee.

When the flame is lit

4 Take my silver and my gold;
Not a mite would I withold:
Take my intellect, and use
Every power as thou shalt choose.

5 Take my will, and make it thine;
It shall be no longer mine:
Take my heart – it is thine own;
It shall be thy royal throne.

6 Take my love; my Lord, I pour
At thy feet its treasure-store:
Take myself, and I will be,
Ever, only, all for thee. Amen.

Frances Ridley Havergal

Frances Ridley Havergal in *The Baptist Hymn Book* (London, Psalms and Hymns Trust, 1962), no. 527.

I used to know (socially only) Christopher Cheshire, who was Warden of Liddon House once, and have been to tea there. I remember (I think in the twenties) being embarrassed because he hadn't warned me who was coming, and there was an elderly lady whom he addressed as 'Mam,' and I thought she must be his mother, and greeted her in the ordinary way and sat down by her and chatted, and it turned out gradually that she was Princess Louise (I think) to whom I should have curtsied and waited to be spoken to first, etc. I apologized afterwards to my host, who said cheerfully, 'That's the stuff to give 'em,' but of course it wasn't at all! I think he is now a Prebendary. I never knew Fr Underhill, though I met his sister Evelyn, who wasn't quite so good as her books.

Rose Macaulay

Rose Macaulay, *Letters to a Friend 1950–52* (London, Fontana, 1961), pp. 90–1.

And they drew nigh unto the village, whither they went: and he made as though he would have gone further. But they constrained him saying, Abide with us: for it is toward evening, and the day is far spent. And he went in to tarry with them.

Not when you stand by us as an explanation of life, but when you enter our life with all its homely limitations, as friend and guest. Come in to abide with us, accepting what we have to offer; when the mysterious pilgrim passing through the world who always seems to be going further than we are, towards a strange, unknown destination – turns a chance meeting into something far deeper and closer, something we can never describe and never forget.

But that will not happen unless I ask you for it, unless I open the door. Only my desire, constraining you will make you come in, abide with me, share my small premises, my humble life. The choice is left to me.

Lord! Give me courage and love to open the door and constrain you to enter, offer all my resources, whatever the disguise you come in, even before I fully recognise my guest.

Come in! Enter my small life!

Lay your sacred hands on all the common things and small interests of that life and bless and change them. Transfigure my small resources, make them sacred. And in them give me your very self.

When out of the heart of my own homely circumstances, you feed me – then my eyes are open to the presence I long for and can never understand.

Evelyn Underhill

Evelyn Underhill on Prayer, ed. Tony Castle (London, Marshall Pickering, 1989), pp. 41–2.

He acted as though he were going on. And they urged him, saying, 'Stay with us, for it is getting towards evening, and the day is now far spent.' And he went in with them. And it came to pass when he reclined at table with them, that he took the bread and blessed and broke and began handing it to them. And their eyes were opened, and they recognized him; and he vanished from their sight. And they said to each other, 'Was not our heart burning within us while he was speaking on the road and explaining to us the Scriptures?' (Luke 24.13–33)

Who were these two disciples? We're told one was called Cleophas, a not uncommon man's name in that century. Because it's spelled κλέοπας in the manuscripts, he was presumably not the same Cleophas (or Clopas) who was the older brother of St Joseph and father of James the Less, 'brother of the Lord'. This Cleophas spelled his name differently – κλῶπας – but English can be rather insensitive to the niceties of Greek vowels. The Cleophas who was walking to Emmaus was also a follower of Christ, but this is the only certain mention of him in Scripture.

Who was the other disciple? Some commentators have advanced the opinion that he was St Luke, but Scripture says merely that 'two of them' (in Greek, δύο ἐξ αὐτῶν) were going to Emmaus. Naturally, the αὐτῶν is masculine plural. If one had been a woman, the Greek text would read the same and leave the reader none the wiser. 'They were talking to each other' is rendered αὐτοὶ ὥμιλον πρὸς ἀλλήλους, and so on through the remainder of the story, all pronouns being set quite properly in the discreet masculine plural. Cleophas' companion is never quoted as a person, but always speaks as one half of 'they', and our Lord address only 'them'.

Could this other disciple have been a woman?

Solange Hertz

Solange Hertz, *Searcher of Majesty* (Westminster, MD, The Newman Press, 1963), p. 139.

But because one thing alone is necessary (Luke 10.42), I bear witness to that one thing and encourage you, for love of him to whom you have offered yourself as a holy and pleasing sacrifice (Rom. 12.1), that, like another Rachel (cf. Gen. 29.16), you always remember your resolution and be conscious of how you began.

What you hold, may you always hold.
What you do, may you always do and never abandon.
But with swift pace, light step,
    and unswerving feet,
    so that even your steps stir up no dust,
go forward
    securely, joyfully, and swiftly,
on the path of prudent happiness,
    believing nothing,
    agreeing with nothing
    which would dissuade you from this resolution
    or which would place a stumbling block for you on the way,
so that you may offer your vows to the Most High
in the pursuit of that perfection
to which the Spirit of the Lord has called you.

Clare of Assisi

Francis and Clare: the Complete Works. Classics of Western Spirituality. Tr. and introd. Regis J. Armstrong OFM Cap and Ignatius Brady OFM (London, SPCK; Mahwah, NJ, Paulist Press, 1982), p. 196.

Then she took her husband home with her and looked after him for as long as he lived. And she worked very hard for in his last days he turned childish again and lost touch. So he could not control his bowels and use a seat, or else he would not, but like a child he voided in his linen at the fire or at the table, wherever he was sitting; he spared no place. And therefore she had much more work washing and wringing and much more expense in drying, and she was kept to a great extent from contemplation. Many times she would have resented her work, except she remembered the many delectable thoughts, fleshly lust and inordinate love she had for him in her youth. And therefore she was glad to be punished with the same person and she took it more easily and served him and helped him, she thought, as she might have done Christ himself.

Margery Kempe

The Book of Margery Kempe. Tr. Susan Dickman. Quoted in *Medieval Women's Visionary Literature*, ed. Elizabeth Alvilda Petroff (Oxford University Press, 1986), p. 327.

To confess our sins is to accuse ourselves of them; quite a different thing from merely telling them. We may tell our sins by way of boast, we may tell them to intimate friends for the sake of sympathy; but to confess them is to acknowledge their guilt; to recognize them as an injury to another; to own to our action in the matter and yet be willing to repudiate it. For it is not more contrary to the essence of true confession to deny our deed than to defend it; in the former case we try, fruitlessly, to obliterate the past; in the latter we endeavour to carry over the past into the future and to crystallize the attitude in which we find ourselves. True confession consists in telling our deed in such a way that our soul is changed in the telling of it. What is done in the external and material order can never be undone or altered; but the spiritual act, which is in the soul itself, is never really past, and can be qualified, and transformed, like all living things, by the infusion of new elements. Thus do we modify our sin in the telling of it, and become again pleasing instead of displeasing to the one against whom we have sinned. And this is done, not by making out an act to be other than it was, but, on the contrary, by taking towards it the attitude prescribed by truth and justice.

Maude Petre

Maude D. Petre, 'Devotional Essays' in *The Method of Theology* (London, Catholic Truth Society, 1902), pp. 40–1.

After living for a year with her father, Mme Martin was called to the help of her sister and brother-in-law. This man, whom Brémond described as a 'travelling nabob' was an agent for the transport of merchandise and goods all over France. He was said to keep the largest establishment in the whole province – men, horses, coaches, carriages, the whole equipment of a great livery-stable and clearing-house. Life there was an incessant turmoil, a whirl of arrivals and departures, shouting, cracking of whips, neighing of horses, lumbering of wheels, everyone was overworked and overwhelmed.

This was the atmosphere in which little Claude Martin grew up and which his solitude-loving mother had to endure. For some years she helped in the kitchen, then she was promoted to the office:

'I found myself among the noise of merchants and yet my spirit was sunk in the Divine Majesty. I spent whole days in a stable which served as an office; sometimes it was midnight and I was still at the gate seeing to the loading and unloading of merchandise. My usual companions were ostlers and coachmen and even the fifty or sixty horses for which I was responsible. I had also all the affairs of my brother-in-law and sister on my shoulders when they were in the country as often happened.'

Marie de l'Incarnation

Marie de l'Incarnation in Lucy Menzies, ed., *Mirror of the Holy* (Oxford, Mowbray, 1928), p. 263.

Madeleine came in the evening and there was no one there who knew her, and I was on the farm on Staten Island. She was unostentatious in her dress, a tall thin woman, nervous in manner. She was referred by whoever it was in charge of the office, then to the Salvation Army, where she could get a bed for the night for thirty-five cents, sharing a huge dormitory with the derelict women from the Bowery. I was not too much surprised at this, since on several occasions I myself had been taken for a Bowery woman, both at the Municipal lodging house and at a Catholic nursery where I was abruptly dismissed by a busy young nun at a day nursery. I had gone there trying to get the child of a young unwed mother taken care of, but before I could even make my wants known I had the door shut in my face with the curt remark, 'Go away, I can do nothing for you!' I could well understand a young nun in the midst of some crisis with a score of tiny children being hasty and thought nothing of it – was even glad to be so closely identified with the poor as to share the insults and contempt they encountered.

But Madeleine – sick as she always was! And our benefactor! But she went where she was told, and shared the lodging of the poor, overwhelmed with compassion for them. As though this encounter with our hospitality was not enough, when she came to Spring Street for a cup of tea the next morning she was met with more rudeness. She asked for a cup of hot water and was brought coffee instead, which she gave to an old woman sitting next to her. When she went over to the sink to get some of the boiling hot water from the faucet, the dish washer snarled at her, 'Don't you like the way we wash dishes around here?' But she finally got the cup of hot water to make her tea from the tea bag she carried in her purse, and she got the direction to Staten Island and visited us there and when she told me the story, she felt only sadness at the way poor, old and unattractive women are treated. As for herself, 'This then was perfect joy,' bringing her a bit nearer to the sufferings of Christ and by her very sharing, lightening to some degree the burden of others.

Dorothy Day

Dorothy Day, *On Pilgrimage: The Sixties* (New York, Curtis Books, 1972), pp. 198–9.

You have heard how wonderfully silk is made – in a way such as God alone could plan – how it all comes from an egg resembling a tiny pepper-corn. Not having seen it myself, I only know of it by hearsay, so if the facts are inaccurate the fault will not be mine. When, in the warm weather, the mulberry trees come into leaf, the little egg which was lifeless before its food was ready, begins to live. The caterpillar nourishes itself upon the mulberry leaves until , when it has grown large, people place near it small twigs upon which, of its own accord, it spins silk from its tiny mouth until it has made a narrow little cocoon in which it buries itself. Then this large and ugly worm leaves the cocoon as a lovely little white butterfly.

If we had not seen this, but had only heard of it as an old legend, who could believe it? Could we persuade ourselves that insects so utterly without the use of reason as a silkworm or a bee would work with such industry and skill in our service that the poor little silk-worm loses its life over the task? This would suffice for a short meditation, sisters, without my adding more, for you may learn from it the wonders and the wisdom of God. How if we knew the properties of all things? It is most profitable to ponder over the grandeurs of creation and to exult in being the brides of such a wise and mighty King.

Teresa of Avila

Teresa of Avila in *An Anthology of Mysticism*. Ed. Paul de Jaegher sj (London, Burns, Oates and Washbourne, 1935), p. 138.

For the change that has come to women is a change, not in environment merely, not in wealth and habits merely, not in occupation merely, but in the very mind, the very being of the race itself.

As a woman, standing in the front lines of service to humanity, it is with an unbounded enthusiasm of gratitude that I hail the dawn of this long-awaited day of opportunity. The forces of prejudice, of selfishness, of ignorance, which have arrested the progress and curtailed the influence of womankind for centuries, are receding from the foreground of the future, and with astonished vision we look upon the limitless fields of progress. Across all oceans, however tempestuous, over all frontiers, however mountainous, into all countries, however remote and inhospitable, the women's movement is spreading, the exhilaration and invigoration of its spirit is in the very air we breathe, bracing the nerves, stimulating the will, and reinforcing the faculties.

Evangeline Booth

Evangeline Booth, *Woman* (New York, Fleming H. Revell, 1930), p. 7.

Ten women got together, pooling their savings, and bought the house in an old run down neighbourhood, with the intention of helping the pastor work among the Negroes, catechizing and performing the corporal works of mercy. One of the girls died of leukemia and there were grave rumours around the section that the girls led too rigorous a life, denied themselves too much and so on. They were scornfully called the 'detachers' because they tried to detach themselves from the world to follow Christ. But certainly they were women of good solid sense, with a background of hard work and a readiness for sacrifice. Two of the women left to work on their own, one went to the South to a group in Greenwood, Mississippi, to work with the poorest of the Negroes (Alma was a good musician and gave music lessons and tutored anyone who asked). Seven remained, of whom Dorothy McMahon teaches, Jane Judge, Lucille Lynch and Rose McDonnell nurse, Marion Judge is a receptionist and Mary Hlebain is a housekeeper. They pool all their resources, take simple promises of Poverty, Chastity and Obedience from year to year and now live in this delightful rural spot of Maryhouse, little Canada, living the contemplative life in the world, the beginnings of a secular institute.

Dorothy Day

Dorothy Day, *On Pilgrimage: The Sixties* (New York, Curtis Books, 1972), p. 27.

I had been left guardian of a child whose parents had not been married, and I had taken a cottage in a small village as a weekend retreat for myself and as a home for his mother and himself.

In due course the story of his birth was discovered by someone in the small community, and the mother and boy found themselves shunned and boycotted. I myself was about to leave England on a tour abroad when a message from my friend in great distress about her position in the village reached me. I hurried down to see what I could do, and although not at that time even personally interested in the Church, I went in desperation to the vicar as spiritual head of the parish. I put the case to him (I hardly knew him, and had never been to his church) and asked his help.

Without one question or any sign of curiosity about the facts, he asked first had the child been baptised, and might he undertake this next day, and stand godfather. He then offered to look after the mother and the boy in every way, and indeed put this into immediate practice one evening shortly afterwards at a village concert, when he had the mother to sit beside him with the boy on his knee, so showing everyone that they were under his care and his affection.

This, in a small place, to a little family under the stigma of illegitimacy, seemed to me the real practice of Christianity. It gave me a great sense of the availability of the Church as an institution, of its reliability, and above all of its quick, practical response to a request for help, without any prying into circumstances, or with any conditions imposed.

Athene Seyler

Athene Seyler in *They became Anglicans*. Ed. Dewi Morgan (London, Mowbray, 1959), pp. 146–7.

Never be astonished at the faults of the community or of any individual Sister, for to be shocked at our Sisters' faults, to pick them apart, examine them, to get all upset about them is the sign of a narrow-mindedness which has no insight into human frailty, and very little charity or forbearance. That is why those who are inclined to be so righteous should close their eyes to what is going on around them and remind themselves constantly that charity does not go looking for evil, and when she does come upon it, she looks the other way and excuses those who commit it. This should be our attitude toward our Sisters who are our companions.

Jane de Chantal

Jane de Chantal in *Francis de Sales, Jane de Chantal: Letters of Spiritual Direction*. Classics of Western Spirituality. Sel. and introd. Wendy M. Wright and Joseph F. Power OSFS (Mahwah, NJ, Paulist Press, 1986), p. 261.

We acquired two rooms in a working class area, found a woman doctor bold enough to officiate, and two nurse-midwives bold enough to assist her, and in 1925 opened what I think was the first provincial birth-control clinic.

Our premises were in one respect fortunately situated; for they were on an upper floor, approached through a shop which sold meat pies. This meant that shy clients were not readily identifiable from the street as visitors to the clinic – they might equally well be regarded as pie purchasers. In another respect we were less fortunately placed, because our clinic was in the near neighbourhood of a large Roman Catholic church, and officially the Roman Catholics did not like us at all. Indeed, they did all they could to frustrate our venture; even to the extent of organizing a huge protest meeting at which one speaker accused us of practising abortion. The result of this meeting was not, however, all that its promoters could have wished; because for some time after its occurrence our routine question: 'How did you hear of the clinic?' might provoke the answer: 'At the Protest'.

On one occasion Charis Frankenburg and I found ourselves described in a Roman Catholic publication as 'the kind of idle women who visit matinées and sit with cigarettes between their painted lips'. This image of ourselves afforded us some pleasure because we were apt to envisage ourselves as rather dowdy social workers. On another occasion the access to our clinic was described as 'through a stinking entry'. This was a half-truth, because though a potent aroma certainly followed one up its staircase, it was a pleasant and comforting aroma of freshly cooked meat pies.

In view of authoritative Catholic doctrine, the attitude of our local Roman Catholic clergy was easy to understand. Less easy to understand was the non-committal but on the whole, hostile aloofness of the Anglican Church. Its attitude was well portrayed in a contemporary play by St John Ervine entitled *Robert's Wife*. In many clerical minds, and indeed many other minds, birth-control was associated with irregular sex relations, as indeed it well may be. It was also, in those far-off days, associated with strange myths which we often encountered and, as time went on, were able to dispel; for instance that it caused cancer, or that once practised, it produced subsequent sterility.

Mary Stocks

Mary Stocks, *My Commonplace Book* (London, Peter Davies, 1970), pp. 160–1.

1 Lord, for to-morrow and its needs
   I do not pray;
   Keep me, my God, from stain of sin,
   Just for to-day.

2 Let me both diligently work,
 And duly pray;
 Let me be kind in word and deed,
 Just for to-day.

3 Let me be slow to do my will,
 Prompt to obey;
 Help me to mortify my flesh,
 Just for to-day.

4 Let me no wrong or idle word
 Unthinking say;
 Set thou a seal upon my lips,
 Just for to-day.

5 Let me in season, Lord, be grave,
 In season, gay;
 Let me be faithful to thy grace,
 Just for to-day.

6 And if to-day my tide of life
 Should ebb away,
 Give me thy sacraments divine,
 Sweet Lord, to-day.

7 In Purgatory's cleansing fires
 Brief be my stay;
 Oh, bid me, if to-day I die,
 Go home to-day.

8 So, for to-morrow and its needs,
 I do not pray;
 But keep me, guide me, love me, Lord,
 Just for to-day.

Sister M. Xavier

Sister M. Xavier in *The Westminster Hymnal* (London, Burns, Oates and Washbourne, 1953), no. 191.

Before I forget, I must tell you about some mortifications which I have heard are being practised at Malagón. The Prioress says that one of the nuns is to be given a sudden blow, and tells another nun to strike her; this, it is said, is a device which she learned here. It looks as if the devil is teaching them to do these things, under the guise of perfection, and thus imperilling souls by making them offend God. On no account must you ever order, or allow, any nun to strike another – and that applies to pinching too – or bring up your nuns with the severity which you saw practised at Malagón; for they are not slaves, and the only point in their practising mortifications is that they should profit by them. I tell you, my daughter, you need to look very carefully at these things which inexperienced prioresses take it into their heads to do: they cause me immense distress. What things have been disclosed to me quite recently! May God make you holy for me. Amen.

Teresa of Avila

Teresa of Jesus, *The Letters of Saint Teresa*, vol. 1. Tr. E. Allison Peers (London, Sheed and Ward, 1980), p. 340.

And I beseech that Sister who shall be entrusted with the care of the Sisters to govern others more by her virtues and holy life than by her office, so that, encouraged by her example, they may obey her not only out of duty but rather out of love. Let her be prudent and watchful toward her Sisters as a good Mother toward her daughters; and from the alms which the Lord shall give let her take care to provide for them according to the needs of each one. Let her also be so kind and approachable that they may reveal their necessities without fear and have recourse to her at any hour with all confidence as may seem good to them for themselves or for their Sisters.

But the Sisters who are under her should remember that they have renounced their own wills for God's sake. Therefore I will that they obey their Mother as they have of their own free will promised the Lord; and thus the Mother, seeing their charity and humility and the unity that exists among them, will carry more lightly the burdens of her office, and what is painful and bitter will, by their holy living, be turned to sweetness for her.

Clare of Assisi

Clare of Assisi in *Medieval Women's Visionary Literature*. Ed. Elizabeth Alvilda Petroff (Oxford University Press 1986), p. 279.

Because she loved all the kings, she prayed for the life of each, and instructed us to pray without interruption for the stability of their kingdoms. Whenever she heard that they had turned against each other with hatred, she was greatly shaken and sent letters to the one and the other imploring them not to wage war and take up arms against each other but to conclude peace so that the country should not perish. In the same way, she sent great men to give salutary advice to the illustrious kings so that the country should be made more salubrious both for the king and the people. She imposed letters and continuous vigils upon the congregation, and instructed us with tears in her eyes to pray for the kings without interruption.

Baudonivia

Baudonivia, *De Vita s. Radegundis*, 10 MGH Script. rer.mer. 2:384. Quoted in *Medieval Religious Women* vol. 2: *Peace Weavers*, ed. by John A. Nichols and Lillian Thomas Shanks (Kalamazoo, MI, Cistercian Publications, 1987), p. 44.

Thus speaks a beggar woman in her prayer to God:

Lord, I thank you that since with your love you have taken from me all earthly riches, you now clothe and feed me out of the goodness of others, for all that clothes my heart in the desire of possession has become foreign to me.

Lord, I thank you that since you have taken from me the power of my eyes, you now serve me through the eyes of others.

Lord, I thank you that since you have taken from me the power of my hands . . . Lord, I thank you that since you have taken from me the power of my heart, you now serve me with the hands and hearts of others.

Lord, I ask you to reward them here on earth with your divine love so that they might beseech and serve you with all virtues until they come to a holy end.

Mechthild of Magdeburg

Mechthild of Magdeburg, *The Flowing Light of the Godhead* 7, 64. Tr. Joan Howard. Quoted in *Medieval Women Writers*, ed. Katharina M. Wilson (Manchester University Press 1984), pp. 26–7.

She continually consoled the sick, visiting them frequently and sustaining them with holy exhortation. In the spirit of charity, she suffered with the sufferers, rejoiced with the joyful, and often suggested to the abbess that those in need of healing be comforted. The abbess, as a mother, responded amicably to all her requests because, in keeping with the apostolic tradition, they were one in heart and soul, loving each other tenderly and fully in Christ.

Balthilda

Vita s. Balthildis, 11 MGH Script. rer.mer. 6:497. Quoted in *Medieval Religious Women* vol. 2: *Peace Weavers*, ed. John A. Nichols and Lillian Thomas Shanks (Kalamazoo, MI, Cistercian Publications, 1987), p. 45.

When the flame is lit

Regarding the sisters who are ill, the Abbess is strictly bound to inquire with all solicitude by herself and through other sisters what these sick sisters may need both by way of counsel and of food and other necessities and, according to the resources of the place, she is to provide for them charitably and kindly. This is to be done because all are obliged to serve and provide for their sisters who are ill just as they would wish to be served themselves if they were suffering from any infirmity. Each should make known her needs to the other with confidence. For if a mother loves and nourishes her daughter according to the flesh, how much more lovingly must a sister love and nourish her sister according to the Spirit.

Those who are ill may lie on sackcloth filled with straw and may use feather pillows for their head; and those who need woollen stockings and quilts may use them.

Clare of Assisi

Francis and Clare: the Complete Works. Classics of Western Spirituality. Tr. and introd. Regis J. Armstrong OFM Cap and Ignatius Brady OFM (London, SPCK; Mahwah, NJ, Paulist Press, 1982), p. 220.

To wear your tunic in summer is ridiculous. And, if you want to please me, you will take it off as soon as you get this letter, however much it mortifies you to do so. As all the nuns realize why you need to do this, they will suffer no loss of edification. You will be doing your duty to our Lord because you will be following my wishes. Do not act otherwise, for I have experienced the heat at Seville, and it is much better to be fit to do your work in the community than to have all the nuns ill. I also mean this injunction to apply to anyone else where you may think it necessary.

Teresa of Avila

Teresa of Jesus, *The Letters of Saint Teresa*, vol. 2. Tr. E. Allison Peers (London, Sheed and Ward, 1980), p. 718.

The abbess is true love who has much sanctified sense with which she rules the community in the body and soul to the letters and honour of God. She gives her sisters much holy teaching of the will of God whereby her own soul is set free.

The chaplain-of-love is divine humility so utterly subject to love that pride has to stand aside.

The prioress is the holy peace of God; patience is added to her good-will that she may teach the community with divine wisdom.

The sub-prioress is loving-kindness . . .

Hope is the chantress filled with holy, humble devotion, so that even temerity of heart in singing before God, sounds so sweetly that he loves the melody sung from the heart . . .

Gentleness is the steward always happily doing good . . .

Watchfulness is the portress filled with holy desire to do whatever she is bidden. Thus nothing she does is ever lost and she comes quickly to God when she would pray; there he is with her in holy stillness . . .

Thus the convent abides in God . . . Blessed are they who dwell therein!

Mechthild of Magdeburg

Lucy Menzies, *The Revelations of Mechthild of Magdeburg* (London 1953). Quoted in *Medieval Religious Women* vol. 2: *Peace Weavers*, ed. John A. Nichols and Lillian Thomas Shanks (Cistercian Publications 1987), p. 235.

How I like things to be done quietly and without fuss. It is the fuss and bustle principle, which must proclaim itself until it is hoarse, that wars against truth and heroism. Let truth be done in silence 'till it is forced to speak,' and then should it only whisper, all those whom it may concern will hear.

Caroline Fox

The Journals of Caroline Fox 1835–1871. Ed. Wendy Monk (London, Elek, 1972), p. 145. Entry for 14 June 1843.

O blessed poverty
who bestows riches on those who love
and embrace her!

O holy poverty
to those who possess and desire you
God promises the kingdom of heaven
and offers indeed eternal glory and blessed life!

O God-centred poverty
    whom the Lord Jesus Christ,
    who ruled and now rules heaven and earth,
    who spoke and things were made
    condescended to embrace before all else.

Clare of Assisi

Francis and Clare: the Complete Works. Classics of Western Spirituality. Ed. Regis J. Armstrong o F M Cap and Ignatius Brady o F M (London, S P C K; Mahwah, NJ, Paulist Press, 1982), p. 193. Quoted in *Medieval Religious Women* vol. 2: *Peace Weavers*, ed. John A. Nichols and Lillian Thomas Shanks (Kalamazoo, MI, Cistercian Publications, 1987), p. 172.

History shows no war averted by the influence of women; none against which women, as women, have worked, or organized, or offered more than here and there a sporadic protest. Queens have been no more reluctant than kings to look on the dead bodies of men and say, 'It is nothing'. The fact that war brings to women personally no glory, but only suffering, is empty of significance; they are well accustomed to vicarious glory and well accustomed to suffering. The appeal to their loyalty comes with irresistible force. 'We cannot fight', they say; 'let us at least be willing to suffer.'

Not what is noble only, but what is ignoble in women, is enlisted easily in the service of war. The importance of fear as a factor in war-making cannot be overlooked, and can hardly be over-estimated. Any politician can play on panic when he wishes to stampede a people into war. The fear of being attacked enables him to blind them, and makes them an easy tool for a war which is really one of aggression. And in the creation of panic a sex trained to timidity is hardly likely to play a restraining part. Personal courage is the one quality held indispensable in a man: it has not been extraordinarily admired in women, and since fear is the mother of cruelty, it should not surprise any of us if those who have never been expected to be brave should sometimes outdo the men in vindictiveness. That so many women remain untainted by fear should rather give us hope. Nevertheless, it is reasonable to remember that so long as fear plays a part in the making of wars, women are hardly likely as a sex to be more uncompromising in their desire for peace than men.

It should, therefore, have surprised no one (though, in fact, it surprised many of us) that women throughout Europe have accepted war as an inevitable evil, or even, in the earnestness of their loyalty, as a spiritual good. Nor does their attitude towards war in general, or this war in particular, prove those wrong who have believed that the Woman's Movement is one of the great influences making for peace. It is true that its effect will not be so direct or so obvious as had been supposed. The mistake has been rather about the nature of its influence than about its ultimate effect.

Maude Royden

Maude Royden, 'War and the Woman's Movement' in *Towards a Lasting Settlement*. Ed. Charles Roden Buxton (London, George Allen and Unwin, 1915), pp. 136–7.

There is a woman,
An old woman, who shuffles along,
With a jug for a pint of beer.
Almost oblivious,
Seeking oblivion.

Her hair is in metal curlers,
Under an old tweed cap.
Her face is the poor face
Of someone drowned in the sea.

She has never been young,
And her mind is dumb:
And she does not see,
She only floats to the surface,
A terrible accusation to me.
A poor, drowned, bloated face,
floating up from the sea
Of accepted misery.

And I,
Who lower my eyes for shame
As I go by,
Am more ashamed,
Because I wonder why,
Despair,
Troubles to curl her hair.

Caryll Houselander

Caryll Houselander, 'Woman with a Jug' in *The Flowering Tree* (London, Sheed and Ward, 1945), p. 25.

Chastened by rightful rebukes of meaningless talk can we talk about God? What do we really want to talk about? The word or a meaning?

When the flame is lit

Suppose we become acquainted with two girls. One is called Grace, but unfortunately we do not catch the name of the other. Each meeting with the two of them makes it more certain that the one whom we are eager to know better is not Grace, who has the meaningful and self-giving name but the other one, who is in being gracious and friendly. What, we will ask, is in a name? It is the reality we are looking for: so we swallow our pride and address the gracious one. It could be like this in the matter of God: that the visual images of childhood, the pictures we drew and hymns we sang have the name attached to them, but that if we looked around our experience we would find that in it which we deem more worthy of a commitment than the child's old man in the sky or the angry authoritarian, or the indifferent world mechanic.

There are those who say 'our image of God must go': the old man in the sky must be burnt like Guy Fawkes and we must set out to find a new way of thinking of God. I do not see it quite that way. I have had experience of waiting on the platform for a train: it comes in, but from the opposite direction: I get in and it moves off. Nothing corrects the overmastering impression that I am headed away from my desti-nation. Thinking back to the place I was in and the journey to the station only confirms my worst forebodings of lost connections and broken engagements. I try to read, I look out of the window. Suddenly without being able to say why or how I feel I am travelling the opposite way: the train, the rails, the scenery have all done a volte-face. I can in my mind now repeat my journey to the station mirror-wise. I believe this happens in relation to the experience of God. What one thinks one ought to believe contradicts or does not connect with a lot of what one experiences and most values in life: you do what is the practical right next thing (get on the train in spite of the nagging 'ought I not to have faith and go the other way?') and lived experience asserts itself as reality and reorganizes past experience into continuity with it.

This may well be a form of conversion experience in the modern world: that from searching the heavens to find God and attempting to be very spiritually-minded one slowly or suddenly becomes aware that what one needed but could not express was discernible by clues or flashes of insight or unexpected awareness as one's life was opened up to receive whatever would come largely unsought through events, sights, sounds, encounters, delights and afflictions.

Kathleen Bliss

Kathleen Bliss, *The Future of Religion* (London, Pelican Books, 1972), pp. 162–3.

I would climb the dark stairs of No. 10 and pass through the heavy door to No. 12 and the *Nineteenth Century* office. It was a small room with no windows, and in the middle, Helen would be sitting at a huge desk, a horrible angular desk-lamp shining like a spotlight on her white head and the books and papers scattered over the desk. Dim piles of books and papers rose out of the fringes of the shadows beyond the light, and merged into the darkness. Helen would glance up at the sound of the opening door, her abstracted expression turning to one of welcome. 'Mollie, I think I've at last got it to my liking. Listen to this –

O Father, give the spirit power to climb
To the fountain of all light, and be purified.
Break through the mists of earth, the weight of the clod,
Shine forth in splendour, Thou that art calm weather,
And quiet resting place for faithful souls.
To see Thee is the end and the beginning.
Thou carriest us, and Thou dost go before

A pause as she finished reading, and then – 'isn't it a lovely last line' –

'Thou art the journey, and the journey's end.'

Helen Waddell *(as related by Felicitas Corrigan)*
Dame Felicitas Corrigan o s b, *Helen Waddell* (London, Gollancz, 1986), p. 338.

If language is a creative faculty, then we have to use it boldly to describe for ourselves and others whatever has the ring of truth and genuineness for us. By disciplining this use, bringing to bear on it a necessary economy and sincerity, we examine our lives, finding what frustrates and what enhances our knowledge and practice of truth and love. If we are open to the possibilities of language we will be sensitive to the use of it by others and recognize that others may be speaking of profoundly religious matters without using traditional language.

Kathleen Bliss
Kathleen Bliss, *The Future of Religion* (London, Pelican Books, 1972), p. 164.

There has never been any question but that women of the poor should toil alongside their men. No angry, and no compassionate, voice has been raised to say that women should not break their backs with harvest work, or soil their hands with blacking grates and peeling potatoes. The objection is only to work that is pleasant, exciting or profitable – the work that any human being might think it worth while to do. The boast, 'My wife doesn't need to soil her hands with work', first became general when the commercial middle classes acquired the plutocratic and aristocratic notion that the keeping of an idle woman was a badge of superior social status. Man must work, and woman must exploit his labour. What else are they there for? And if the woman submits, she can be cursed for her exploitation; and if she rebels, she can be cursed for competing with the male: whatever she does will be wrong, and that is a great satisfaction.

Dorothy L. Sayers

Dorothy L. Sayers, *Are Women Human?* (Grand Rapids, MI, Eerdmans, 1971), p. 43.

1 Blessed Lamb of Calvary,
   Let thy Spirit fall on me;
   Let the cleansing, healing flow
   Wash and keep me white as snow,
   That henceforth my life may be
   Bright and beautiful for thee.

2 Burn out every selfish thought,
   Let thy will in me be wrought,
   Fan my love into a flame,
   Send a pentecostal rain,
   That henceforth my life may be
   Spent in winning souls for thee.

3 Teach me how to fight and win
   Perfect victory over sin;
   Give me a compassion deep,
   That will for lost sinners weep,
   That henceforth my life may prove
   That I serve thee out of love.

Barbara Stoddart

Barbara Stoddart in *The Song Book of the Salvation Army* (London, 1986 edn).

In my ninth year . . . my dear mother took me to London Yearly Meeting . . . and there for the first time, I had the privilege of listening to that eminent servant of the Lord, Elizabeth Fry. I shall never forget the impression she made upon my young mind by her sweet voice, beautiful face, and her earnest pleading, as she spoke of the prisoners, the suffering and the outcast. I was too young to understand one half of what she said, yet good seed was sown then and there which led to active labour in after years. In the solemn silence that followed, after she took her seat, my childish heart was lift in the prayer that I might grow as good as she was, and work in the same way . . . I expressed to my mother a fear that God would not care for a little child like me. She replied by lifting me up to see a bird's nest in the hedgerow, and explaining to me that God taught the little bird to build its nest, and to rear its young; and then bade me pluck a little flower at my feet, and pointed out how nothing was so small to escape his notice . . .

Elizabeth L. Comstock

Life and Letters of Elizabeth L. Comstock (London, Headley, 1895), pp. 2–3. Quoted in *Daily Readings from Quaker Writings Ancient and Modern* ed. Linda Hill Renfer (Oregon, Serenity Press, 1988), p. 271.

No person will deny the importance attached to the character and conduct of a woman, in all her domestic and social relations, when she is filling the station of a daughter, a wife, a mother, or a mistress of a family. But it is a dangerous error to suppose that the duties of females end here. Their gentleness, their natural sympathy with the afflicted, their quickness of discernment, their openness to religious impressions, are points of character (not unusually to be found in our sex) which evidently qualify them, within their own peculiar province, for a far more extensive field of usefulness.

In endeavouring to direct the attention of the female part of society to such objects of Christian charity as they are most calculated to benefit, I may now observe that no persons appear to me to possess so strong a claim on their compassion, and on their pious exertion, as the helpless, the ignorant, the afflicted, or the depraved, of their own sex. It is almost needless to remark, that a multitude of such persons may be found in many of our public institutions.

I rejoice to see the day in which so many women of every rank, instead of spending their time in trifling and unprofitable pursuits, are engaged in works of usefulness and charity. Earnestly is it to be desired that the number of these valuable labourers in the cause of virtue and humanity may be increased, and that all of us may be made sensible of the infinite importance of redeeming the time, of turning our talents to account, and of becoming the faithful, humble, devoted, followers of a crucified Lord, who went about DOING GOOD.

Elizabeth Fry

Elizabeth Fry, *Observations on the Visiting, Superintending and Government of Female Prisoners* (London 1827), pp. 2, 3.

It was in prison that I first saw drug addiction close at hand. Addicts are known there even by the special robe they wear. I would not have known this if I had not picked out one of these wrappers as being my size, and having it taken away from me as 'only for addicts'. It is made of seersucker, a coverall with big pockets and it is a more adequate garment, more all-embracing than the other sleazy affairs they hand out for our wear in jail. But I suppose they are given it because all other clothes are taken away from them. The last time Dean Mowrer and I served a brief sentence of ten days, we were put in a dormitory and the young woman next to me, usually very taciturn, spoke one day.

'When I wake up you are reading that prayer book and when I go to sleep you are reading it.' (It was a little Fr Frey psalm book.) 'As for me, the first thing I think of in the morning is how I'll get me a fix as soon as I get out, and it is the last thing I think of at night.'

'And me too,' another woman, an older white woman, called out from across the aisle.

There was a young Negro in the end bed, who had made a shrine by her bedside. She was reading Keyes' life of the Little Flower, and she came over to me. She frankly admitted to being an addict. One had to, in the Woman's House of Detention, because the method of treating it there is the cold turkey cure. In other words nothing is given to enable the women to endure the breaking off pains, and their suffering is most obvious to all. A mild tranquillizer is the extent of their medication.

She was not talking of a 'fix', but of the book she was reading. 'If I had had a home like this,' she cried, showing her book. She had become a Catholic the year before, and though she might fall again seventy times seven – still, there was something to go on, and who can tell how the grace of God would work in that soul.

Dorothy Day

Dorothy Day, *On Pilgrimage: The Sixties* (New York, Curtis Books, 1972), pp. 45–6.

Nor are we the lazy ones, the thriftless ones. Jesus defended us, in the person of Magdalen. He was at table, Martha was waiting upon him, Lazarus eating with him and his disciples. Mary never gave a thought to her food, but only how she might give pleasure to one she loved; so she took a vessel filled with perfume of great price and breaking the vessel poured it upon Jesus' head, and all the house was filled with the odour of the ointment, but the apostles murmured against Magdalen.

It is very much the same with us, the most fervent Christians, the priests consider that we are too extreme, that we ought to serve with Martha instead of consecrating to Jesus the vessels of our lives with the

perfumes contained in them . . . but after all, what matter that our
vessels are broken, since Jesus is consoled, and since, in spite of itself,
the world is forced to awareness of the perfumes they breathe forth,
perfumes which serve to purify the poisoned air the world is ever
breathing.

The infirmarian would be glad if you could find in Caen a half bottle
of Tissérand water – 2 francs 50 – if there are only whole bottles don't
get one, they can be had here in Lisieux.

Sister Marie of the Sacred Heart would like seven or eight nutcrackers.

Thérèse of Lisieux

Thérèse of Lisieux, *Collected Letters* (London, Sheed and Ward, 1949),
pp. 210–11.

Saint Martha was holy, but we are not told that she was a contemplative. What more do you want than to be able to grow to be like that
blessed woman, who was worthy to receive Christ our Lord so often in
her house, and to prepare meals for him, and to serve him and perhaps
to eat at table with him? If she had been absorbed in devotion all the
time, as the Magdalen was, there would have been no one to prepare a
meal for this Divine Guest. Now remember that this little community
is Saint Martha's house and that there must be people of all kinds here.
Nuns who are called to the active life must not murmur at others who
are very much absorbed in contemplation, for contemplatives know
that, though they themselves may be silent, the Lord will speak for
them, and this, as a rule, makes them forget themselves and everything
else.

Remember that there must be someone to cook the meals and count
yourselves happy in being able to serve like Martha. Reflect that true
humility consists to a great extent in being ready for what the Lord
desires to do with you and happy that he should do it, and in always
considering yourselves unworthy to be called his servants. If contemplation and mental and vocal prayer and tending the sick and
serving in the house and working at even the lowliest tasks are of
service to the Guest who comes to stay with us and to eat and take his
recreation with us, what should it matter to us if we do one of these
things rather than another?

Teresa of Avila

Teresa of Jesus, *The Complete Works*, vol. 2. Tr. and ed. E. Allison Peers (London
and New York, Sheed and Ward, 1946), pp. 70–1.

. . . The whole house with its manifold and graded activities must be a house of prayer. It does not mean keeping a Quiet Room to which we can retreat, with mystical pictures on the walls, and curtains over the windows to temper the disconcerting intensity of the light; a room where we can forget the fact that there are black beetles in the kitchen, and that the range is not working very well. Once we admit any violent contrast between the upper and lower floor, the 'instinctive' and 'spiritual' life, or feel a reluctance to investigate the humbling realities of the basement, our life becomes less, not more, than human; and our position is unsafe. Are we capable of the adventure of courage which inspires the great prayer of St Augustine: 'The house of my soul is narrow; do thou enter in and enlarge it! It is ruinous; do thou repair it'? Can we risk the visitation of the mysterious Power that will go through all our untidy rooms, showing up their short-comings and their possibilities; reproving by the tranquillity of order the waste and muddle of our inner life? The mere hoarded rubbish that ought to go into the dustbin; the things that want mending and washing; the possessions we have never taken the trouble to use?

Evelyn Underhill

Evelyn Underhill, *Concerning the Inner Life with the House of the Soul* (London, Methuen, 1947), p. 70.

Of the Woman and the Hen

A woman was sitting
before her gate, watching
as her hen scratched
and gathered her food.
The hen worked hard all day with great steps.
The woman spoke to her with great love:
'Beauty', she said, 'let it be,
you don't have to scratch so much.
Each day I'll give you
a full measure of grain to your desire.'
The hen replied:
'Why do you say this, lady?
Do you think I like your wheat better
than what I have always had?
Not at all, not at all,' said the hen.
'If there were half a bushel before me,
every day, full, I would not stop
nor would I delay
to seek more every day

according to my nature and my custom.'
By this example, it is shown
that many people can find
goods and whatever they need,
but they cannot change
their nature or their habits;
every day their courage revives.

Marie de France

The *Fables of Marie de France*. Tr. Joan M. Ferrante in *Medieval Women Writers*, ed. Katharina M. Wilson (Manchester University Press 1984), pp. 26–7.

I am convinced it is a great art to know how to grow old gracefully, and I am determined to practise it . . . I always thought I should love to grow old, and I find it is even more delightful than I thought. It is so delicious to be done with things, and to feel no need any longer to concern myself much about earthly affairs . . . I am tremendously content to let one activity after another go, and to await quietly and happily the opening of the door at the end of the passage way, that will let me in to my real abiding place.

Hannah Whitall Smith

Hannah Whitall Smith, *A Religious Rebel, the Letters of H. W. Smith* (1949), pp. 156–7. Quoted in *Christian Faith and Practice in the Experience of the Society of Friends* (London Yearly Meeting of the Religious Society of Friends 1960), no. 519.

Read, Reader, the Little Verses of this Epitaph
Dhuoda's body, formed of earth,
Lies buried in this tomb.
Immense king, receive her!
Here the earth has received in its bowels
The all too fragile clay which belonged to it.
   Benign King, grant her pardon!
Under and over her are the opaque depths
Of the grave, bathed in her wounds.
   O King, forgive her sins!
O you of all ages and sexes who come
And go here, I beg you, say this,
   Great Hagios, unlock her chains!

Detained by dire death in the depths
Of the tomb, she has ended her earthly life.
  O King, pardon her sins!
As that dark serpent wishes to capture
Her soul, pray against him this prayer:
  Clement God, come to her aid!
No one should leave her without having read.
I urge all that they may pray, saying this:
  Almus, give her rest!
And command, Benign One, that she be given
Eternal light with the saints in the end.
  And may she receive Amen after her death!

Dhuoda

Dhuoda's *Manual*, ed. Jean Mabillon, *Patrologia Latina 106, 109–18*. Quoted in *Medieval Women Writers*, ed. Katharina M. Wilson (Manchester University Press 1984), pp. 26–7.

We all know that there is a tendency to skip or skim through those passages in the Gospel which disconcert us, and to form a conception, not only of Christ, but of his special relationship to ourselves, by the passages which are as we say most 'consoling' to us.

When I hear Christians discussing economics, I remember a figure who often loomed in my childhood; a very large figure, too, seated squarely and heavily in an armchair on one of the several famous green lawns in her grounds. At her side is a box of sodamint, and a little way behind her back, her acquaintances, whispering – between yawns and within hearing of the child among them taking notes – that her prodigious wealth was derived from the rents of slums. Now this old lady was exacting in piety and a devoted reader of the Bible; whether she ever read any other passages, I do not know, but the passage that she always read to me was the one in which 'The Lord is my Shepherd: I shall not want' occurs.

We all tend to that sort of scripture reading. And though we do not depend only on reading, yet it is really necessary, in our search for Christ, to read the Gospel, and to read it all without flinching; or if we must flinch, at least without giving up the attempt.

But we are still faced with the fact that Christ lives with us, in the same room, and we do not know him.

Caryll Houselander

Caryll Houselander, *The Reed of God* (London, Sheed and Ward, 1955), p. 80.

The Church's approach to an intelligent carpenter is usually confined to exhorting him not to be drunk and disorderly in his leisure hours, and to come to church on Sundays. What the Church should be telling him is this: that the very first demand that his religion makes upon him is that he should make good tables. Church by all means, and decent forms of amusement, certainly – but what use is all that if in the very centre of his life and occupation he is insulting God with bad carpentry? No crooked table-legs or ill-fitting drawers ever, I dare swear, came out of the carpenter's shop at Nazareth. Nor, if they did, could anyone believe that they were made by the same hand that made heaven and earth. No piety in the worker will compensate for work that is not true to itself; for any work that is untrue to its own technique is a living lie. Yet in her own buildings, in her own ecclesiastical art and music, in her hymns and prayers, in her sermons and in her little books of devotion, the Church will tolerate, or permit a pious intention to excuse, work so ugly, so pretentious, so tawdry and waddling, so insincere and insipid, so bad as to shock and horrify any decent craftsman. And why? Simply because she has lost all sense of the fact that the living and eternal truth is expressed in work only so far as that work is true in itself, to itself, to the standards of its own technique. She has forgotten that the secular vocation is sacred. Forgotten that a building must be good architecture before it can be a good church; that a painting must be well painted before it can be a good sacred picture; that work must be good work before it can call itself God's work.

Dorothy L. Sayers

Dorothy L. Sayers, *Creed or Chaos* (New York, Harcourt, Brace, 1949), pp. 55–6. Quoted in Rosamond Kent Sprague, *A Matter of Eternity: Selections from the Writings of Dorothy L. Sayers* (London and Oxford, Mowbray, 1973), pp. 16–17.

I would to God that all men understood this verity, that women, if they will, may be perfect, and if they would not make us believe we can do nothing and that we are 'but women', we might do great matters.

There was a Father that came recently to England, whom I heard say that he would not for a thousand worlds be a woman, because he thought that a woman could not apprehend God! I answered nothing but only smiled, although I could have answered him by the experience I have of the contrary. I could have been sorry for his want of judgment. I mean not his want of judgment, for he is a man of very good judgment – his want is in experience.

So we may say of men: if we look upon them as prophets, we shall see their imperfections; but if we look upon them as men, we shall see them as far otherwise. That you may not be deceived, you may know them by the fruits of their counsels.

Mary Ward

Till God Will: Mary Ward through her Writings. Ed. M. Emmanuel Orchard I B V M (London, Darton, Longman and Todd, 1985), p. 58.

It is nonsense to say that women have never had any power in the Churches: they have had immense power, but power in the form of influence, which is irresponsible power. Nobody can call to account the wife or mother who gets her way with husband or son and is known to be the real director of his opinion and vote. This is the form of power to which women, especially very able women, have been confined by their exclusion from responsible power. Wherever democratic ideals prevail in society, influence of all kinds is discredited. Open attempts are made to prevent pressure on political leaders and on those who make appointments, issue honours and privileges and make executive decisions in every walk of life. That influence is discredited is not to say that it is abolished. Women have wielded influence with very great skill over the centuries and many still prefer it to any form of responsibility which brings them out into the open. But the choice between influence and responsibility is one that women have to make, and Churches have to make in relation to women.

Kathleen Bliss

Kathleen Bliss, *The Service and Status of Women in the Churches* (London, SCM, 1952), p. 183.

5
As silence gathers into stillness

'Prayer is naught else but a yearning of the soul.' The encounter with God has its own integrity. Sometimes it is accompanied by a call. Sometimes it is experienced in the midst of life or in the whole direction of an individual's life. In this chapter women like Mechthild of Magdeburg reflect upon the 'wonderous place' where God and the soul 'speak much of love'.

With Olive Wyon 'we turn to prayer quietly'. With Maude Petre, the Roman Catholic, there are times when we experience doubt more than faith – and this hurts: 'The best prayer will be that which makes the soul realize most fully the tragedy and pathos of its actual existence.' Like Caryll Houselander's cat there are moments when we too will be 'raddled with fear'. It is this note of realism which serves to remind the reader time and again that the women whose testimonies are recorded here were writing about the experience of prayer from the inside. Hence their authority. They do not pretend that prayer is easy, nor that it will always be hard. What they do say is that it is important.

So Thérèse of Lisieux can claim that the 'apostolate of prayer' is 'lifted higher, so to speak, than the apostolate of preaching' and add: 'What have priests that we need envy!'

Evelyn Underhill, whose writings on mysticism were accompanied by a rich life of prayer of her own, can remind us about the 'mysterious beauty of our human vocation; so utterly a part of the fugitive and creaturely life of this planet and yet so deeply coloured by eternity'. And the Anglican contemplative sister Mother Maribel can reflect in a more prosaic way that 'dog-tiredness is such a lovely prayer'.

No one tradition has a monopoly on prayer: Elizabeth of the Trinity, a Carmelite nun, writes movingly and with complete simplicity, 'I am never alone. My Christ is always present, always praying in me and I pray in him.' But equally the Quaker child, Mary Proude, who can barely form her letters, composes 'a pretty large prayer concerning. . . an assurance of pardon for my sins'. Access to God is open to all, in spite of the historian Hilda Graef's comment that: 'In Christian antiquity nothing at all is heard of women mystics.' We must not assume that women were not enjoying the same kind of access to God as the women whose writings appear in this chapter just because we have no record of it. The philosophical justification for this silence given by Hilda Graef is in fact contradicted by Evelyn Underhill's *sharp piece on the two seals Slushy and Sophy. Here it is the clarity of the female mind which saves from the welter of feelings represented by Slushy.*

A further insight which cannot go unmentioned as it is such a good example of this kind of clarity: Kathleen Bliss notes that, 'If we are open to the possibilities of language we will be sensitive to the use of it by others and recognize that others may be speaking of profoundly religious matters without using traditional language.' This kind of sensitivity is not gender-specific; the women whose experience and understanding of God is recorded in this chapter nevertheless show it to an extraordinary degree. Not only the uncomplicated 'lay' language they use but also their imagery demonstrates that they know their way round the 'quiet homely ways' in which God blesses and consecrates the material of our ordinary life. Then in turn, like Clare of Assisi, they can bless each other: 'Always be lovers of God and your souls and the souls of your sisters.' Familiarity with the ordinary gives us access to the divine and we too are gathered into stillness.

In heaven prayer will be synonymous with joy and peace, because our life will have been made one, disruption and division will no longer be possible; the beatitude of the soul will be also its deepest reality. But on earth this deepest life consists rather in continuous pain and struggle, hence, in disclosing the one, prayer must also disclose the other, and the truest and best prayer will be that which makes the soul realize most fully the tragedy and pathos of its actual existence.

We understand then what spiritual writers mean when they tell us to make our prayer practical, and to aim at some definite resolution. We are not to understand this as though prayer were chiefly practical in so far as its result is merely external. What is meant is that it is not to be a matter of superficial sentiment, of feeling, in the more trivial sense of the word. Prayer is practical when it affects our outer conduct, but still more when it affects our inward activity, and the best of resolutions is that which contains in itself its own fulfilment, being not merely a promise for the future, but a performance in the present, a subjection of the soul to her Maker, and an advance of the kingdom of God within her.

Maude Petre

Maude D. Petre, 'Devotional Essays' in *The Method of Theology* (London, Catholic Truth Society, 1902), pp. 18–19.

There is one thing which happens in a deep rapture and of which I want to give warning here: when the period has passed during which the soul is in union and its faculties are wholly absorbed – and this period, as I have said, is short – the soul will still be recollected, and be unable, even in outward things, to return to itself; two of the faculties – memory and understanding – will be quite bewildered, and almost in a state of frenzy. This, as I say, sometimes happens, especially at the beginning. It may, I imagine, be a result of the inability of our natural weakness to endure such spiritual vehemence, and of the weakening of the imagination. I know this happens to some people. I should think it is a good idea for them to force themselves to give up prayer and to take it up again later, at some time when they have leisure, for if they try to pray while in that state they may come to great harm. And I have experience of this and of the wisdom of considering what our health can bear.

In all this we need experience and a director; for, when the soul has reached this stage, many things will occur which it will need to discuss with someone. Yet, if it seeks such a person unsuccessfully, the Lord will not fail it, for, even though I am what I am, he has not failed me. I believe there are few who have acquired experience of all these things, and without experience it is useless to attempt to bring a soul relief – one will bring it only disquiet and distress. This the Lord will also take into account, for which reason it is better, as I have said on other occasions, to discuss the matter with one's confessor. All that I am saying now I have said already, but I do not remember it very well, and I am sure the relations of penitent and confessor, and the type of confessor to be chosen, are very important matters, especially to women. The Lord gives these favours far more to women than to men: I have heard the saintly Fray Peter of Alcántara say that, and I have also observed it myself. He would say that women made much more progress on this road than men, and gave excellent reasons for this, which there is no point in my repeating here, all in favour of women.

Teresa of Avila

Teresa of Jesus, *The Complete Works*, vol. 1. Tr. and ed. E. Allison Peers (London and New York, Sheed and Ward, 1946), p. 293.

I am never alone. My Christ is always present, always praying in me and I pray in him. If only I could teach you the secret of happiness, as God has taught it to me. You say I have no worries nor sufferings. It is true that I am very happy, but if you only knew how one can still be completely happy even when one is crossed. One has only to keep one's gaze continually on God. At first one has to make efforts when one feels boiling inside, but gradually, by dint of patience and with

God's help, one succeeds. You must build for yourself as I have done, a little cell in the depths of your soul. Remember that God is there and enter his presence from time to time. When your nerves are on edge, or you are unhappy, hasten into this cell and tell the Master all about it. If only you knew him a little better, prayer would not bore you. To me it seems a relaxation, a rest. With complete simplicity one has recourse to him whom one loves. One remains very close to him, as close as a little child in its mother's arms, and one allows one's heart to go out to him.

Elizabeth of the Trinity

Elizabeth of the Trinity, *Spiritual Writings*. Ed. M. M. Philipon O P (London, Geoffrey Chapman, 1962), p. 59.

My way is all of trust and love, I don't understand souls who are afraid of so loving a Friend. Sometimes, when I read spiritual treatises, in which perfection is shown with a thousand obstacles in the way and a host of illusions round about it, my poor little mind grows very soon weary, I close the learned book, which leaves my head muddled and my heart parched, and I take the holy scripture. Then all seems luminous, a single word opens up infinite horizons to my soul, perfection seems easy; I see that it is enough to realize one's nothing-ness, and give ourself wholly, like a child, into the arms of the good God.

Leaving to great souls, great minds, the fine books I can't under-stand, I rejoice to be little, because 'only children, and those who are like them, will be admitted to the heavenly banquet.' I am so happy that 'in the kingdom of God there are many mansions', for if there were but the one, the description of which and the way to which seem to me incomprehensible, I could not get in.

Thérèse of Lisieux

Thérèse of Lisieux, *Collected Letters* (London, Sheed and Ward, 1949), p. 292.

My relations made this cross very heavy; but as at length I happily gave up, divested of reasonings, not consulting how to provide for the flesh, I received strength to attend the meetings of these despised people which I never intended to meddle with, but found truly of the Lord, and my heart owned them. I longed to be one of them, and minded not the cost or pain; but judged it would be well worth my utmost cost and pain to witness such a change as I saw in them – such power over their corruptions. I had heard objected against them, that they wrought not miracles; but I said that they did great miracles, in that they turned them that were in the world and the fellowship of it, from all such things. Thus, by taking up the cross, I received strength against many things which I had thought impossible to deny; but many tears did I shed, and bitterness of soul did I experience, before I came thither; and often cried out: 'I shall one day fall by the over-powering of the enemy'. But Oh! the joy that filled my soul in the first meeting ever held in our house at Chalfont. To this day I have a fresh remembrance of it. It was then the Lord enabled me to worship him in that which was undoubtedly his own, and give up my whole strength, yea, to swim in the life which overcame me that day. Oh! long had I desired to worship him with acceptation, and lift up my hands without doubting, which I witnessed that day in that assembly. I acknowledged his great mercy and wonderful kindness; for I could say, 'This is it which I have longed and waited for, and feared I never should have experienced.'

Mary Penington

Mary Penington, *Experiences in the Life of Mary Penington* (1911), pp. 44–5. Quoted in *Christian Faith and Practice in the Experience of the Society of Friends* (London Yearly Meeting of the Religious Society of Friends 1960), no. 29.

The worship is prayer and praise to God, as the almighty Creator of heaven and earth, Fountain of eternal light, love and goodness, One in essence, Dual in manifestation, Father and Mother, manifested and expressed in humanity and in all the beauties and sublimities of the natural world.

Shakers regard all life and activity animated by Christian love as worship. They invoke the Divine Father-Mother in silent prayer together before each meal, partake of their food in a worshipful spirit and go about their duties in a cheerful, happy, helpful temper, feeling that 'Labour is worship and prayer'.

No form of worship, however sacred, is regarded as established, only so far as it expresses the gift and leading of the Spirit; no form but may be changed or dispensed with. The life of the spirit, not the form of expression, is regarded as essential.

Anna White

Anna White(?) in *Testimonies*. Ed. Seth Wells, pp. 30–2. Quoted in *The Shakers: Two Centuries of Spiritual Reflection*, ed. Robert Edward Whitson (Mahwah, NJ, Paulist Press, 1984), pp. 268–9.

Prayer is an exercise of the spirit, as thought is of the mind. To pray about anything is to use the powers of our spirit on it, just as to think clearly is to use our mental powers. For the best solution of every problem, the best carrying out of every action, both thought and prayer are necessary . . . To pray about any day's work does not mean to ask for success in it. It means, first, to realize my own inability to do even a familiar job, as it truly should be done, unless I am in touch with eternity, unless I do it 'unto God', unless I have the Father with me. It means to see 'my' work as part of a whole, to see 'myself' as not mattering much, but my faith, the energy, will and striving, which I put into the work, as mattering a great deal. My faith is the point in me at which God comes into my work; through faith the work is given dignity and value. And if, through some weakness of mine, or fault of others, or just 'unavoidable circumstances', the work seems a failure, yet prayer is not wasted when it is unanswered, any more than love is wasted when it is unreturned.

Mary F. Smith

Mary F. Smith, 'The Place of Prayer in Life' in Gerald K. Hibbert, ed., *Studies in Quaker Thought and Practice* (2nd edn 1936), pp. 25–6.

Here let me give what I understand to be the spiritual
    sense of the Lord's Prayer:

Our Father which art in heaven,
    Our Father-Mother God, all-harmonious,

Hallowed by thy name.
    Adorable One.
Thy kingdom come.
    Thy kingdom come; thou art ever-present.

Thy will be done in earth, as it is in heaven.
    Enable us to know – as in heaven, so on earth, – God is
        omnipotent, supreme.

Give us this day our daily bread;
    Give us grace for to-day; feed the famished affections;

And forgive us our debts, as we forgive our debtors.
    And Love is reflected in love;

And lead us not into temptation, but deliver us from evil;
    And God leadeth us not into temptation, but delivereth us from
    sin, disease, and death.

For thine is the kingdom, and the power and the glory,
                                                    forever.
    For God is infinite, all-power, all Life, Truth, Love,
                                            over all, and All.

Mary Baker Eddy

Mary Baker Eddy, *Science and Health with Key to the Scriptures* (Boston, MA,
Christian Science Publishing, 1890), pp. 16–17. Quoted in Rosemary Radford
Ruether, *Womenguides* (Boston, Beacon Press, 1985), pp. 16–17.

Queer things one gets involved in. I now have an invitation to a wine-
tasting party in the cellars of the London branch of a Port Wine
shipping firm of Oporto. This, and my having been asked to write a
foreword to their brochure, is what comes of writing so eruditely about
port wine in that book: a fascinating subject of which actually I know
less than nothing. But I did like those Oporto wine shippers; I stayed
with one of them, and every hour [or] so when I was indoors port was
brought in on a tray; it wouldn't do for long. Their Factory House (18th
century) is a magnificent affair. It seems to me the most romantic of the
English colonies abroad. I am going to ring up Fr Wilkins after
Whitsunday and go and call, as he said I could. How much difference
is there between communicating and not communicating, when one
goes to the service? Of course I know one sometimes does and
sometimes not: but how nearly is it the same thing? This seems an
ignorant and confused question; but then I *am* ignorant and confused
still. I *feel* a difference between them; but could one communicate
mystically? Then I suppose it wouldn't be a sacrament. I am probably
talking nonsense. Anyhow I must stop. Did I tell you I copy out some
of those short Latin prayers and put them in my prayer book and say
them in church, which I like to do. It seems to link one with tradition
and the whole Catholic church. Tho' for sheer *beauty*, I think our own
liturgy and prayers beat any, owing to the fortunate language-period of
our P[rayer] B[ook].

Rose Macaulay

Rose Macaulay, *Letters to a Friend* 1950–2 (London, Fontana Books, 1961),
p. 126.

Each Friend who feels called upon to rise and deliver a lengthy discourse might question himself – and herself – most searchingly, as to whether the message could not be more lastingly given in the fewest possible words, or even through his or her personality alone, in entire and trustful silence. 'Cream always must rise to the surface.' True. But other substances rise to the surface besides cream; substances that may have to be skimmed off and thrown away before bodies and souls can be duly nourished. 'Is my message cream or scum?' may be an unusual and is certainly a very homely query. Still it is one that every speaker, in a crowded gathering especially, should honestly face. Some of the dangers of silent worship can best be guarded against by its courtesies.

L. Violet Holdsworth

L. Violet Holdsworth, *Silent Worship, the Way of Wonder* (Swarthmore Lecture 1919), pp. 77–8. Quoted in *Christian Faith and Practice in the Experience of the Society of Friends* (London Yearly Meeting of the Religious Society of Friends 1960), no. 290.

Perhaps some of you have read Dr Doolittle's Circus, a book which is nearly as full of spiritual wisdom as Alice in Wonderland. There is, you remember, one admirable member of the circus; a most steady and responsible creature called Sophy the Wise Seal. But unfortunately Sophy had a husband, whose name was Slushy. Now in the spiritual life Sophy is one of the best and most reliable of companions; but we have to keep a very sharp look-out for Slushy. He has his pious moments, when he tries to push his quiet wife on one side and suggest to us what a helpful animal he is – such a good appearance, so fervent, and so full of feeling. But Slushy, like all sentimentalists, is really a very self-indulgent creature. What he calls zest is mostly feverishness; and what he calls worship is mostly basking. There are some devotional books in which one seems to hear nothing but Slushy flapping his tail; just as in others the quiet wise Sophy finds a few humble words, which yet convey her utter submission to God. Slushy, though at first sight very attractive, with his warm devotional colour and soft fur, is really wrapped up in nothing better than his own feelings. Sophy may not have such a good coat; but she keeps in much better condition, because she looks at herself and her own feelings very little, and at God and the mighty purposes of God and the needs of the children of God a very great deal. It is by keeping company with

Sophy, sharing her point of view and sense of proportion, that we shall achieve a deep, healthy, self-forgetful inner life.

Evelyn Underhill

Collected Papers of Evelyn Underhill. Ed. Lucy Menzies, (London, Longmans, 1946), pp. 179–80.

It is with this latter kind of doubt that we are here concerned. It arises in the soul where untroubled faith had hitherto existed, and brings with it an inevitable sense of suffering or loss. It is the sudden disappearance beneath the horizon of something which had been fully visible; it is the melting into shadow of something we had held as substance – we tighten our grasp to find that our hands have closed on nothing; it is the violent withdrawal of the basis on which we thought ourselves securely settled, a withdrawal which seems to precipitate us into a chaos wherein all is shifting and uncertain; it is a meta-morphosis in which things seem to change their relative size and position – what was great becomes small, what was near grows far, and we stagger amidst the shifting confusion, asking ourselves, Do we dream? or were we dreaming and are we now awake? or is it that all we look upon is a dream?

This state is no more like that of mere questioning and investigation than the doubt which might seize us as to the sincerity of an old friend is like the dispassionate manner with which we might study the character of a new one, or than the visionary's doubt as to the solidity of the earth on which he walks is like the critical spirit in which we might receive the reported discovery of a new island. The doubt which precedes belief is not necessarily painful; the doubt which follows is like the freezing of a warm limb, the blinding of a sound eye.

Maude Petre

Maude D. Petre, 'The Temperament of Doubt' in *The Method of Theology* (London, Catholic Truth Society, 1902), pp. 7–8.

One day I was pondering over what I could do to save souls; a phrase from the gospel showed me a clear light; Jesus said to his disciples, pointing to the fields of ripe corn: 'Lift up your eyes and see the countries. For they are white already to harvest', and a little later, 'The harvest indeed is great, but the labourers are few. Pray ye therefore the Lord of the harvest that he send forth labourers'.

How mysterious it is! Is not Jesus all powerful? Do not creatures belong to him who made them? Why then does Jesus say: 'Pray ye the Lord of the harvest that he send forth labourers . . .'? Why? . . . Surely because Jesus has so incomprehensible a love for us, that he wants us to have a share with him in the salvation of souls. He wants to do nothing without us. The creator of the universe waits for the prayer of a poor little soul to save other souls redeemed like itself at the price of all his blood.

Our vocation, yours and mine, is not to go harvesting in the fields of ripe corn; Jesus does not say to us, 'Lower your eyes, look at the fields, and go and reap them'; our mission is still loftier. Here are Jesus' words: 'Lift up your eyes and see . . .' See how in my heaven there are places empty; it is for you to fill them . . . each one of you is my Moses praying on the mountain; ask me for labourers and I shall send them, I await only a prayer, a sigh from your heart!

Is not the apostolate of prayer lifted higher, so to speak, than the apostolate of preaching? Our mission, as Carmelites, is to form those gospel labourers, they will save millions of souls, whose mothers we shall be . . . Celine, if these were not the very words of our Jesus, who would dare to believe them? . . . I find our lot most beautiful! . . . What have priests that we need envy!

Thérèse of Lisieux

Thérèse of Lisieux, *Collected Letters* (London, Sheed and Ward, 1949), pp. 152–3.

Dog-tiredness is such a lovely prayer, really, if only we would recognize it as such. Sometimes I hear, 'I'm so dog-tired when I get to chapel, I can't pray'. But what does it matter? We don't matter. Our Lord can pray just as well through a dog-tired body and mind as through a well-rested one, better perhaps. It is the same with pain and suffering of all kinds. Our advance guard on the Infirmary Wing would tell us that.

Mother Maribel of Wantage

Sister Janet csmv, *Mother Maribel of Wantage* (London, SPCK, 1972), p. 65.

As for prayer, don't burden yourself with making considerations; neither your mind nor mine is good at that. Follow your own way of speaking to our Lord sincerely, lovingly, confidently, and simply, as your heart dictates.

When you have committed some fault, go to God humbly, saying to him, 'I have sinned, my God, and I am sorry.' Then, with loving confidence, add: 'Father, pour the oil of your bountiful mercy on my wounds, for you are my only hope; heal me.' A little later: 'By the help of your grace, I shall be more on my guard and will bless you eternally,' and speak like this according to the different movements and feelings of your soul. Sometimes put yourself very simply before God, certain of his presence everywhere, and without any effort, whisper very softly to his sacred heart whatever your own heart prompts you to say.

When you are experiencing some physical pain or a sorrowful heart, try to endure it before God, recalling as much as you can that he is watching you at this time of affliction, especially in physical illness when very often the heart is weary and unable to pray. Don't force yourself to pray, for a simple adherence to God's will, expressed from time to time, is enough. Morever, suffering borne in the will quietly and patiently is a continual, very powerful prayer before God.

Jane de Chantal

Jane de Chantal in *Francis de Sales, Jane de Chantal: Letters of Spiritual Direction*. Classics of Western Spirituality. Sel. and introd. Wendy M. Wright and Joseph F. Power o s f s (Mahwah, NJ, Paulist Press, 1986), pp. 202–3.

Jesus be with you. I said in the letter that went by the Alba courier that the sardines had arrived in good condition and that the sweets had duly arrived too, though I would rather you had kept the best ones. May God reward you.

It is well with us both just now. What great things our Lord is doing! He seems to be pleased to show forth his greatness in raising up wretched creatures and doing us all these favours – and I know of none more wretched than you and I. I must tell you that, for over a week, I have been in such a condition that, if I were to go on, I should hardly be able to attend to all my business. Since before I wrote to you I have had raptures again, and they have been most distressing. Several times I have had them in public – during Matins, for example. It is useless to resist them and they are impossible to conceal. I get so dreadfully ashamed that I feel I want to hide away somewhere. I pray God earnestly not to let them happen to me in public: will you make this prayer for me too, for it is an extremely awkward thing and I don't believe my prayer is any the better for it? Latterly I have been going about almost as if I were drunk; but at least it is clear that the soul is well employed, for, as the faculties are not free, it is a grievous thing for the soul to have to occupy itself with anything save the object of its desire.

Previously, for nearly a week, I had been in such a state that I could hardly think a single good thought, so severely was I suffering from aridity.

Teresa of Avila

Teresa of Jesus, *The Letters of Saint Teresa*, vol. 1. Tr. E. Allison Peers (London, Sheed and Ward, 1980), pp. 408–9.

It came into my mind to write a prayer of my own composing, to use in the mornings. So I wrote a prayer, though I then could scarcely join my letters, I had so little a time learned to write. It was something of this nature: that as the Lord commanded the Israelites to offer up a morning sacrifice, so I offered up the sacrifice of prayer, and desired to be preserved during that day. The use of this for a time gave me some ease, and I soon left off using my books, and as the feelings arose in me, I wrote prayers according to my several occasions. The time when this circumstance took place, was when the spirit of Puritanism began to be manifested in the churches. The reading of the common prayers of the Church of England Prayer-book, both in public and private worship, was one of the practices to which these Puritans – as they were in ridicule called – objected.

The next prayer I wrote was for an assurance of pardon for my sins. I had heard one preach, how God pardoned David his sins of his free grace; and as I came from our place of worship, I felt how desirable a thing to be assured of the pardon of one's sins; so I wrote a pretty large prayer concerning it.

I felt a fear of being puffed up with praise, as several persons had praised me for the greatness of my memory; so I wrote a prayer of thanks for the gift of memory and expressed my desires to use it to the Lord.

Mary Proude

Mary Proude in 1635. Quoted in *Daily Readings from Quaker Writings Ancient and Modern*, ed. Linda Hill Renfer (Oregon, Serenity Press, 1988), p. 188.

So we turn to prayer quietly, confidently, as God's beloved, forgiven children, and we use the tender word that Jesus gave us, saying 'Abba, Father'. Our prayer will be transformed if we always take time for a moment or two of preparation – if we reflect on the greatness and the mercy and the nearness of the God to whom we are coming. Instead of plunging immediately into distracted petitions about our own affairs (which only increases our confusion of mind), we shall begin by waiting upon God in quiet faith. Our prayer will be more real, and far more effective, if we remember to make a brief pause for preparation, if for a few moments we stop talking, and try to hold ourselves still before God. As we wait we can make brief acts of faith such as 'God is here, and God is love . . . Christ is here with me at this moment . . . he will never let me go . . . He says Fear not!' Simple affirmations of this kind enable us to put ourselves and our needs into God's hands, and to seek first of all that he may be glorified. Once we have entered into this rest, which may coincide with a normal active life, our hearts will be strangely lightened, we shall find that we are less self-centred, less troubled by the sight of our sins and miseries, for we are now more willing to face the truth about ourselves. Then we can rejoice in God, in his love and beauty, his power and his grace, knowing that his love is constantly being poured out upon us, and upon all the world.

Olive Wyon

Olive Wyon, *Prayer* (London, Fontana Books, 1962), p. 43.

It is important to understand that God doesn't lead all by one path, and perhaps the one who thinks she is walking along a very lowly path is in fact higher in the eyes of the Lord.

So, not because all in this house practise prayer must all be contemplatives; that's impossible. And it would be very distressing for the one who isn't a contemplative if she didn't understand the truth that to be a contemplative is a gift from God; and since being one isn't necessary for salvation, nor does God demand this, she shouldn't think anyone will demand it of her.

Teresa of Avila

The Collected Works of St Teresa of Avila. Tr. Kieran Kavanaugh and Otilio Rodriguez. Vol. 1: *The Book of Her Life; Spiritual Testimonies; Soliloquies* (Washington DC, I C S Publications, 1976). Quoted in *Medieval Religious Women* vol. 2: *Peace Weavers,* ed. John A. Nichols and Lillian Thomas Shanks (Kalamazoo, MI, Cistercian Publications, 1987), p. 349.

In Christian antiquity nothing at all is heard of women mystics. This may seem strange at first glance; but there is probably an historic reason for it. In the second-century Montanist heresy discussed in the chapter on St Augustine, the pseudo-ecstasies of two so-called prophetesses played an essential part. Very likely this is why, in the Patristic age, women were not encouraged to divulge any ecstatic experiences they may have had. Moreover, the austere mystic theology of antiquity, with its 'negative' way on the one hand and its Platonism on the other, did not lend itself to the feminine temperament, which is by nature so much more attracted to the sensible and the personal. But the new medieval devotion to the humanity of Christ appealed to it most powerfully, and so women now began to take their full share in the mystic life of the Church.

The feminine mystic movement began in Germany, where women had always been held in far higher esteem than in the Latin countries, and where even in pagan times they were believed to be endowed with some numinous quality that made them particularly susceptible to divine influences. Thus, at the time when Bernard preached the humanity of Christ, Hildegard of Bingen and Elisabeth of Schönau began to write down their mystic visions. Then came the great movement of the Mendicant Orders who exercised a profound influence also on women through their Second (contemplative nuns) and Third Orders (men and women living 'in the world'), so that women mystics began to flourish all over Europe.

Hilda Graef

Hilda Graef, *The Light and the Rainbow* (London, Longmans, 1959), p. 242.

Lying long in my bed of sickness, in the 1170th year of the Lord's incarnation, I saw – awake in body and spirit – a most beautiful image of womanly form, most peerless in gentleness, most dear in her delights. Her beauty was so great that the human mind could not fathom it, and her height reached from earth as far as heaven. Her face shone with the greatest radiance, and her eye gazed heavenward. She was dressed in the purest white silk, and enfolded by a cloak studded with precious gems – emerald, sapphire and pearls; her sandals were of onyx. Yet her face was covered in dust, her dress was torn on the right side, her cloak had lost its elegant beauty and her sandals were muddied. And she cried out . . . 'The foxes have their lairs, and the birds of the sky their nests, but I have no helper or consoler, no staff on which to lean or be supported by'.

Hildegard of Bingen

Hildegard of Bingen in Peter Dronke, *Women Writers of the Middle Ages: a critical study of texts from Perpetua to Marguerite Porete* (Cambridge University Press 1984), p. 170.

My cat (I can't neglect him for long, as to-day he is my spiritual director!) is a tabby. Just now he was in the garden when a black cat came loping along the garden wall, a very unpleasant fellow, I must admit, definitely marked by the underworld; my tabby became very anxious. He rushed to the window, his pink mouth wide open, his face raddled with fear. I let him in, and no sooner had he jumped on my lap than he relaxed, he went limp, not with fear, but happily, deliciously limp, and indicated by various signs known to me that he wanted his ears scratched – that done, he went to sleep.

This is a lesson in prayer. There are many ways of prayer: to 'lift up the heart and mind to God' covers a huge range. There is prayer like that of Moses, when he lifted his arms and held them up, straining and agonizing, before God; there is the prayer which Christ describes in one of his parables, which could be called 'the prayer of importunity', a continual hammering and beating on the door of heaven until we get what we want; and many others. But now, with such great anxiety pressing upon us, the prayer in which we can relax is surely among the most creative.

We certainly should pray all the time, praying with our hands, our bodies, our will, our acts, but in order to delight God and to build up the peace of our souls, besides the prayer in which we offer ourselves to God should be the prayer in which we let God give himself to us. We should learn to receive the love of God in silence and joy – that is what is meant by relaxing.

There should be, even in the busiest day, a few moments when we can close our eyes and let God possess us. He is always present, always giving us life, always round us and in us, like the air we breathe; there should be moments at least when we become more conscious of his presence: when we become conscious of it as the only reality, the only thing that will last for ever.

Caryll Houselander

Caryll Houselander, *The Comforting of Christ* (London, Sheed and Ward, 1947), pp. 14–15.

We all know the woman who is exaggeratedly house-proud, who concentrates on the neatness, cleanliness, beauty of her house, to the exclusion of its comfort. Her house is not a home, nothing must ever be left about, out of place. To come in with muddy shoes is a crime, it is a crime to disarrange the cushions! In such a house one can neither work nor rest, one is never at home, because it is not a home.

There are many women who are 'soul-proud' in the same way. They spend their whole time cleaning up their soul, turning out the rubbish, dusting and polishing. Like the house-proud woman they become nervous, tired, there is nothing left in them to give, they have wasted themselves on the silver, the curtains, the ornaments.

Christ wants to be at home in your soul. He will not go away and leave you if the house is chilly and uncomfortable; he loves you too much to leave you, but how often, how tragically often, he must say nowadays: 'The Son of Man has nowhere to lay his head.'

Christ asks for a home in your soul, where he can be at rest with you, where he can talk easily to you, where you and he, alone and together, can laugh and be silent and be delighted with one another.

All this may seem daring, but it is true, it is the meaning of the Incarnation; we should all realize that it is true were it not that often Christ has been treated as if he were not real at all.

Caryll Houselander

Caryll Houselander, *The Comforting of Christ* (London, Sheed and Ward, 1947), pp. 68–9.

Prayer is naught else but a yearning of soul . . . when it is practised with the whole heart, it has great power. It makes a sour heart sweet, a sad heart merry, a poor heart rich, a foolish heart wise, a timid heart courageous, a sick heart well, a blind heart full of vision, a cold heart ardent. For it draws down the great God into the little heart; it drives the hungry soul up to the plenitude of God; it brings together these two lovers, God and the soul, in a wondrous place where they speak much of love.

Mechthild of Magdeburg

Mechthild of Magdeburg in Lucy Menzies, ed., *Mirror of the Holy* (Oxford, Mowbray, 1928), p. 50.

Love God from the depths of your heart and Jesus, his Son, who was crucified for us sinners. Never let the thought of him leave your mind but meditate constantly on the mysteries of the cross and the anguish of his mother as she stood beneath the cross.

Pray and watch at all times! Carry out steadfastly the work you have begun and fulfill the ministry you have undertaken in true humility and holy poverty. Fear not, daughter! God, who is faithful in all his words and holy in all his deeds, will pour his blessings upon you and your daughters. He will be your help and best comforter for he is our Redeemer and our eternal reward.

Let us pray to God together for each other for, by sharing each other's burden of charity in this way, we shall easily fulfill the law of Christ.

Clare of Assisi

Francis and Clare: the Complete Works. Classics of Western Spirituality. Tr. and introd. Regis J. Armstrong OFM Cap and Ignatius Brady OFM (London, SPCK; Mahwah, NJ, Paulist Press, 1982), p. 220.

There is a woman who prays
as grey as the stone,
without a name or a face,
she assumes a unique majesty,
only by being still,
in a world that is ever moving,
moving and ever moving
on the surge of its own unrest.

She is the still water
in the hollow of the rock,
beside the driven sea,
she is the still water
receiving the light.
She is alone,
but in her strong hands
she folds the feeble hands
of the marionette.
And in her limited life
the whole world is gathered
to its neglected God.
She gathers the whole world
like a contemplative
who, alone in his cell
gathers the whole world
under the wide wings
of the crucifix.
Yet she remains,
with her unique majesty
and her shadowless peace,
in the complete solitude
of adoration.

Caryll Houselander

Caryll Houselander, 'Afternoon in Westminster Cathedral' in *The Flowering Tree* (London, Sheed and Ward, 1945), pp. 87–8.

How did I know, he asked me, that the Lord was not desirous of using me in order to help a great number of people and perhaps to do other things (it seems now that he was prophesying what the Lord afterwards did with me)?

By resisting the consolations and favours of God I gained this – that His Majesty himself taught me. For previously I had thought that, if I was to receive favours in prayer, I must go apart by myself a great deal, and so I had hardly dared to stir. Then I began to see how little this had to do with it; the more I tried to think of other things, the more completely the Lord enveloped me in that sweetness and glory until I felt so completely surrounded by it that I could not flee from it in any direction; and thus matters continued. I was so much concerned about this that it caused me distress. The Lord, however, was much more concerned, during those two months, to grant me favours and to reveal himself to me more than he had been wont to do, so that I might the better understand that resistance was no longer in my power. I began to conceive a new love for the most sacred Humanity. My prayers now began to take shape like an edifice with solid foundations.

Teresa of Avila

Teresa of Jesus, *The Complete Works* vol. 1. Tr. and ed. E. Allison Peers (London and New York, Sheed and Ward, 1946), p. 153.

Next, what type of house does the soul live in? It is a two-storey house. The psychologist too often assumes that it is a one-roomed cottage with a mud floor; and never even attempts to go upstairs. The extreme transcendentalist sometimes talks as though it were perched in the air, like the lake dwellings of our primitive ancestors, and had no ground floor at all. A more humble attention to facts suggests that neither of these simplifications is true. We know that we have a ground floor, a natural life biologically conditioned, with animal instincts and affinities; and that this life is very important, for it is the product of the divine creativity – its builder and maker is God. But we know too that we have an upper floor, a supernatural life, with supernatural possibilities, a capacity for God; and that this, man's peculiar prerogative, is more important still. If we try to live on one floor alone we destroy the mysterious beauty of our human vocation; so utterly a part of the fugitive and creaturely life of this planet and yet so deeply coloured by eternity; so entirely one with the world of nature, and yet, 'in the Spirit', a habitation of God.

Evelyn Underhill

Evelyn Underhill, *Concerning the Inner Life with the House of the Soul* (London, Methuen, 1947), p. 67.

A Friends' meeting, however silent, is at the very lowest a witness that worship is something other and deeper than words, and that it is to the unseen and eternal things that we desire to give the first place in our lives. And when the meeting, whether silent or not, is awake, and looking upwards, there is much more in it than this. In the united stillness of a truly 'gathered' meeting there is a power known only by experience, and mysterious even when most familiar. There are perhaps few things which more readily flow 'from vessel to vessel' than quietness. The presence of fellow-worshippers in some gently penetrating manner reveals to the spirit something of the nearness of the Divine Presence. 'Where two or three are gathered together in his name' have we not again and again felt that the promise was fulfilled and that the Master himself was indeed 'in the midst of us'? And it is out of the depths of this stillness that there do arise at times spoken words which, springing from the very source of prayer, have something of the power of prayer – something of its quickening and melting and purifying effect. Such words as these have at least as much power as silence to gather into stillness.

Caroline E. Stephen

Caroline E. Stephen, *Light Arising* (1908). Quoted in *Christian Faith and Practice in the Experience of the Society of Friends* (London Yearly Meeting of the Religious Society of Friends 1960), no. 246.

Silence is not a thing we make; it is something into which we enter. It is always there. We talk about keeping silence. We keep only that which is precious. Silence is precious, for it is of God. In silence all God's acts are done; in silence alone can his voice be heard and his word spoken.

All we can make is noise, and that we do thoroughly these days! We desecrate the silence which is of God. While 'night is in the midst of her swift course', man makes the most hideous noise he can, and out of the noise he pours down on his fellow men death and destruction.

I see vividly two pictures. In one I see what man does, and in the other I see what God does, 'when all things are in quiet silence and night is in the midst of her swift course, and his almighty Word leaps down from heaven out of his royal throne.'

Mother Maribel of Wantage

Sister Janet c s m v, *Mother Maribel of Wantage* (London, SPCK, 1972), pp. 63–4.

As silence gathers into stillness

Lord! going out from this silence, teach me to be more alert, humble, expectant, than I have been in the past: ever ready to encounter you in quiet, homely ways: in every appeal to my compassion, every act of unselfish love which shows up and humbles my imperfect love, may I recognize you: still walking through the world. Give me that grace of simplicity which alone can receive your mystery.

> Come and abide with me!
> Meet me, walk with me!
> Enlighten my mind!

And then, Come in! Enter my humble life with its poverty and its limitations as you entered the stable of Bethlehem, the workshop of Nazareth, the cottage of Emmaus.
Bless and consecrate the material of that small and ordinary life.

> Feed and possess my soul.

Evelyn Underhill

Evelyn Underhill on Prayer. Ed. Tony Castle (London, Marshall Pickering, 1989), p. 42.

When in this state of quiet, I, who understand hardly anything that I recite in Latin, particularly in the psalter, have not only been able to understand the text as though it were in Spanish but have even found to my delight that I can penetrate the meaning of the Spanish. Let us leave out of account occasions when these learned men have to preach or teach, for then it will be well for them to make use of their learning, so as to help poor ignorant creatures like myself, for charity is a great thing, and so is a constant care for souls, when undertaken simply and purely for the sake of God. In these periods of quiet, then, let the soul repose in its rest; let them put their learning aside; the time will come when they will use it in the Lord's service and will esteem it so much that they would not have failed to acquire it for all the treasures imaginable, simply because they can serve His Majesty with it and for this purpose find it a great help. But in the sight of Infinite Wisdom, believe me, there is more value in a little study of humility and in a single act of it than in all the knowledge in the world. So in this state there is no room for argument but only for a plain recognition of what we are, a presenting of ourselves in our simplicity before God, whose will is that the soul should become a fool, as in truth it is in his sight, for it is due to His Majesty's great humility, we being what we are, that he suffers it to be near him.

Teresa of Avila

Teresa of Jesus, *The Complete Works* vol. 1. Tr. and ed. E. Allison Peers (London and New York, Sheed and Ward, 1946), p. 92.

In the name of the Father and of the Son and of the Holy Spirit. Amen.

May the Lord bless you and keep you. May he show his face to you and be merciful to you. May he turn his countenance to you and give you peace.

I, Clare, a handmaid of Christ, a little plant of our holy Father Francis, a sister and mother of you and the other Poor Sisters, although unworthy, ask our Lord Jesus Christ, through his mercy and through the intercession of his most holy Mother Mary, of Blessed Michael the Archangel and all the holy angels of God, and of all his men and women saints, that the heavenly Father give you and confirm for you this most holy blessing in heaven and on earth. On earth, may he increase his grace and virtues among his servants and handmaids of his Church Militant. In heaven, may he exalt and glorify you in his Church Triumphant among all his men and women saints.

I bless you in my life and after my death as much as I can and more than I can with all the blessings with which the Father of mercies has and will have blessed his sons and daughters in heaven and on earth. Amen.

Always be lovers of God and your souls and the souls of your Sisters, and always be eager to observe what you have promised the Lord.

May the Lord be with you always and, wherever you are, may you be with him always. Amen.

Clare of Assisi

Francis and Clare: the Complete Works. Classics of Western Spirituality. Tr. and introd. Regis J. Armstrong OFM Cap and Ignatius Brady OFM (London, SPCK; Mahwah, NJ, Paulist Press, 1982), pp. 233–4.

6

The steady eyes of women

According to Catherine Booth, God sanctions the ministry of women. The Salvation Army, from its earliest days, has enabled women to use their skills in the divine service. Other Christian groups have been less than enthusiastic about the ministry of women or have seen it in very narrow terms. This is because ministry has been understood exclusively as the work of the ordained.

The selection of writings in this chapter shows us that God has been calling women to active service in the Church since its earliest origins. Primitive records suggest that this ministry was eucharistic. The story of Pope Joan reminds us that it could also lead women into positions of considerable authority. But equally the preaching of a Maude Royden demonstrates that God calls women to a variety of roles within the active life of the Church. Sometimes this ministry can lead women to build churches, like Lady Anne Clifford, or to compensate for the inadequacies of Roman Catholic nuns by providing nice English Church Sisters on the mission fields! Let it also be said that God can call a man to be the convent cook.

With the passing of the centuries, the liberating vision preached by Jesus has faded. Paul understood this vision to mean that there would be no more insiders or outsiders, no more Greek or Jew, no more male or female, no more 'them' and 'us'. Instead the Church has introduced a strong clerical/lay divide and restricted the sphere and authority of women by refusing them access to the clerical side. Certain activities, such as giving out doughnuts to boys in the trenches or sumptuous teas to clerics are valued, while others are not. Whatever the call of God might be, the co-operation of men is uncertain.

This is why the testimony of women from the free Churches is so fascinating. Admission to ordination does not guarantee instant happiness. The root question is about the acceptance of women whatever they do in the divine service. So what can women bring to ministry – whether it is ordained ministry or not? The eminent Quaker, Elizabeth Fry, suggests that it is the spirit 'not of judgement, but of mercy'. The Anglican deaconess Isabella Gilmore suggested that it was the ability to 'help without doing harm'. The broadcaster Kathleen Bliss singles out their 'scholarship, piety and Christian witness in martyrdom'. And Catherine Booth verges on a sexist stance when she claims that 'God has given to woman a graceful form and attitude, winning manners, persuasive speech and, above all, a finely-toned emotional nature'. More simply, Clare of Assisi relied on the witness of a 'holy manner of life'.

What is painful is that these human gifts, which are the basis of what women bring to ministry simply because they are human beings, are so easily ignored. And the irony, as Hatty Baker saw, is that other women can do this ignoring as easily as men. As Mary Ward realized, there is nothing so dismissive as the attitude which 'expects to see women fail'. Each of us can sympathize with the German convert, Gertrude Le Fort, and beg the Church to 'protect me from yourself'. Few of us would find the courage to say with the mystic Mechthild of Magdeburg, that 'God calls the cathedral clergy goats'. But it is comforting to know that women have met with the same kind of rigidity and lack of recognition (even to the extent of confusing their names) before us.

On a more hopeful note the Anglican Edith Picton-Turberville reminds us that 'the coming order will be potent in bringing a more complete and fuller type of Christianity to the world'. In this type of Christianity we must believe that it will be safe for every woman to give the Church what Florence Nightingale so longed to give, 'my head, my hand, my heart'.

God having once spoken directly by woman, and man having once recognized her divine commission and obeyed it, on what ground is omnipotence to be restricted, or woman's spiritual labours ignored? Who shall dare say unto the Lord, 'What dost thou?' when he 'pours out his Spirit upon his handmaidens', or when it is poured out shall I render it null with impunity? If, indeed, there is 'in Christ Jesus neither male nor female', but in all touching his kingdom 'they are one', who shall dare thrust woman out of the Church's operations, or presume to put my candle which God has lighted under a bushel?

If God has given her ability, why should not woman persuade the vacillating, instruct the penitent, and pour out her soul in prayer for sinners?

Catherine Booth

Catherine Booth, 'The Call and Ministry of Woman', in Bramwell Booth, *Echoes and Memories* (London, Hodder and Stoughton, 1925), pp. 45–6.

You are spectacles to God, angels and men. It is certain God has looked on you as he never looked upon any. I say not 'better', nor 'in a greater or more excellent manner', nor 'with more love', for I intend not to make any comparisons. But I say 'as he never looked upon any', and that is certain. The angels, we may believe, look upon you and upon all other creatures according to the will of God. Men, you know, look diversely upon you: all look upon you as new beginners of a course never thought of before, marvelling at what you intend, and what will be the end of you. Some thinking we are women and aiming at greater matters than was ever thought women capable of, they expect perhaps to see us fail, or fall short, in many things. Others esteem us 'but women' and, with a kind of emulation that we should compass and bring about things beyond the limit of such weak creatures as they have ever esteemed women to be, expect to see our fervour decay, and all come to nothing, ourselves to shame and confusion.

Mary Ward

Till God Will: Mary Ward through her Writings. Ed. M. Emmanuel Orchard I B V M (London, Darton, Longman and Todd, 1985), p. 59.

No life has less glamour, less chance of a career, poorer financial reward or more hard work. Yet women write of their work with great affection, saying that there is no other reason for doing it than the inner irrepressible conviction that they are being called by God and cannot do anything else. Women who have been compelled by changes in church law to give up the pastoral work they did during the war speak of the loss of it with grief.

The ministry of women directly affects only a very tiny minority of women in the Church, whether one looks at the number who are actually ordained or at those who might want to be if the situation in their Church were different. It is no slight upon the service of these women to their own Churches to say that the most important part about the discussion of the ministry of women has been its indirect influence. The raising of the question 'should women be ministers?' has compelled those charged with answering it to re-examine the nature of the ministry, and without exception all Churches which have seriously discussed the question of women in the ministry have also had to look to the broader aspect of the place of all women in the Church.

Kathleen Bliss

Kathleen Bliss, *The Service and Status of Women in the Churches* (London, SCM, 1952), pp. 160–1.

Greatest of all claims made for women in the Church, is the assertion that there has been a woman pope. Here indeed is debatable ground, and bitter has been the controversy in the Romish Church over this affirmation. A woman in the line of apostolic succession from St Peter! Should we elect to take sides in the discussion, it must be acknowledged that records are confusing, often mythical, with regard to the earliest years of the papacy. There is much obscurity, evidence is ambiguous and conflicting and of such doubtful genuineness that conclusions can be but conjectural. For instance, various lists of the popes are found, but the later Latin ones in no wise agree with the earlier Greek. The first Latin list was the Catalogus Liberianus; there are two other Latin lists also of some authority, but earlier still Irenaeus drew up a Greek list; while it is generally understood that in still earlier days Hegesippus compiled a Greek table which is, however, not extant. But as in all these records there are considerable discrepancies, a correct list, seriatim, of every name in the line of successors, is problematical. A woman may possibly have figured therein, although the Romish Church, naturally, denies the authenticity of the report.

Hatty Baker

Hatty Baker, *Women in the Ministry* (London, C. W. Daniel, 1911), pp. 28–9.

You do know now . . . what a home the Catholic Church is. And yet what is she to you compared with what she would be to me? No one can tell, no man can tell, what she is to women, their training, their discipline, their hopes, their home . . . For what training is there compared to that of the Catholic nun? . . . I have seen something of different kinds of nun, am no longer young, and do not speak from enthusiasm but from experience. There is nothing like the training (in these days) which the Sacred Heart or the Order of St Vincent gives to women.

Florence Nightingale

The Dublin Review, vol. CLXI, October, 1917, p. 181. Quoted in *Women of Spirit*, ed. Rosemary Radford Ruether and Eleanor McLaughlin (New York, Simon Schuster, 1979), pp. 190–1.

Many people think that the women of the Salvation Army are lassies who, in the main, spend their time and energies on waving the tambourine and shouting their 'Hallelujahs'. During the war, our girls achieved a reputation scarcely less embarrassing. It was supposed that their whole energies were devoted to serving out the doughnuts to the boys in the trenches and gaily welcoming bombardment as a short cut to glory.

Of the courage of our women officers, I would be the last person in the whole world to utter a word of depreciation. 'Tis conscience that makes cowards of us all, and if shell fire no longer alarms, it is because hell fire has lost its terrors.

But death and danger had not been the only trial of these women's faith. They had faced dirt, they had handled disease, they had not flinched before uttermost degradation, they had not been dismayed by the most awful defacements of God's image, imprinted on our race; there is no depth of misery, of despair, of iniquity that is concealed from the steady eyes of the women of the Salvation Army.

Evangeline Booth

Evangeline Booth, *Woman* (New York, Fleming H. Revell, 1930), pp. 28–9.

Much depends on the spirit in which the visitor enters upon her work. It must be the spirit, not of judgment, but of mercy. She must not say in her heart, I am more holy than thou; but must rather keep in perpetual remembrance, that 'all have sinned, and come short of the glory of God' – that, therefore, great pity is due from us even to the greatest transgressors among our fellow-creatures – and that, in meekness and love, we ought to labor for their restoration. The good principle in the hearts of many abandoned persons may be compared to the few remaining sparks of a nearly extinguished fire. By means of the utmost care and attention, united with the most gentle treatment, these may yet be fanned into a flame, but, under the operation of a rough and violent hand, they will presently disappear, and may be lost for ever.

Elizabeth Fry

Elizabeth Fry, *Observations on the Visiting, Superintending and Government of Female Prisoners* (London 1827), pp. 21–2.

In the morning I open school with one of the Sunday school prayers . . . I have a Bible class – Testament class – Psalter class . . . Instructing the Bible or Testament class I always begin with the parables, which we explain to them in the most familiar manner. ('I chiefly recollect,' wrote Marianne Thornton later, 'Mrs Hannah's or Mrs Patty's eloquent exhortation to the whole school in the most familiar homely language, full of anecdotes of the people round them, as well as of the good people that lived in old times.')

I also encourage them, by little bribes of a penny a chapter to get by heart certain fundamental parts of scripture . . . It is my grand endeavour to make everything as entertaining as I can, and to try to engage their affections; to excite in them the love of God, and particularly to awaken their gratitude to their Redeemer. Once in six weeks I give a little gingerbread.

Hannah More *(editorial commentary in brackets)*

Hannah More, Letter to William Wilberforce. Quoted in Margaret Cropper, *Sparks among the Stubble* (London, Longmans, 1955), p. 163.

People who are untrained themselves cannot realize how much there is to teach in parochial work. There was once an idea that any old woman could visit the poor, or worse still, some utterly inexperienced girl; this is fast dying out, and the good district visitor, who really loves and cares for her people, is thankful to turn her really serious cases over to the skilled hands and thought of the woman who has been taught to help without doing harm.

Isabella Gilmore

Janet Grierson, *Isabella Gilmore* (London, SPCK, 1962), pp. 74–5.

So long as there was a service into which they could put their strength and affection, the women were willing to ignore the disabilities that faced them in general church work . . . But when the church, by action taken by the men of the church with but the slightest consultation with the women . . . decided to absorb these agencies which had been built up by the women, the by-product of such a decision was to open the whole question of the status of women in the church.

Among thinking women there arose a serious question as to whether their place of service could longer be found in the church when a great organization which they had built could be autocratically destroyed by vote of male members of the church without there seeming to arise in the mind of the latter any question as to the justice, wisdom and fairness of their actions.

Katherine Bennett and Margaret Hodge

Katherine Bennett and Margaret Hodge, 'Causes for Unrest among the Women of the Church' (Report of the Special Committee to the General Council of the Presbyterian Church in the USA 1927), pp. 10, 11. Quoted in *Women of Spirit* ed. Rosemary Ruether and Eleanor McLaughlin (New York, Simon Schuster, 1979), pp. 314–15.

And we find from Church history that the primitive Christians thus understood it; for that women did actually speak and preach amongst them we have indisputable proof. God had promised in the last days to pour out his Spirit upon all flesh, and that the daughters as well as the sons of mankind should prophesy.

And Peter says most emphatically, respecting the outpouring of the Spirit on the day of Pentecost, 'This is that which is spoken of by the prophet Joel', etc. (Acts 2.16–18). Words more explicit, and an application of prophecy more direct than this, does not occur within the range of the New Testament.

Commentators say: 'If women have the gift of prophecy, they must not use that gift in public'. But God says, by his prophet Joel, they shall use it, just in the same sense as the sons use it. When the dictation of men so flatly opposes the express declaration of the 'sure word of prophecy', we make no apology for its utter and indignant rejection.

Catherine Booth

Catherine Booth, *Female Ministry: an Address by Mrs General Booth* (London, Salvation Army Book Department, 1909), p. 12.

Let me illustrate this opportunity for service by outlining the career of one of our women-Officers.

Some years ago a well-educated lady, a governess, offered herself for service in The Army, and passed through our Training Home at Clapton. She was appointed, partly because of her knowledge of languages, to work abroad. At first she took charge of a Corps, or local branch of work; then of a small Training Home for Women; and, subsequently, of a Division. That is, she had the oversight of several local branches, and of the Officers in charge of them. Later she received an appointment to India, and served on the Staff of the Headquarters there, acquainting herself with two or three of the languages of that great country. This lady is, at present, in command of a Territory – a portion of country comprising several Divisions, in which she has under her direction two hundred and fifty school-teachers, all men, and four hundred Officers; two Training Homes – one for men and one for women; two Industrial Schools for Orphans; three hundred Corps or Societies, and one Peasant Settlement. Her devotion and piety are held in high esteem by all who know her.

In thus going forward until she reached this place of large opportunity she has but followed in the steps of many other noble Salvationist women. I wish, for the inspiration of all here, that I could give you an idea of this woman's capacity for leadership; of her trained powers in handling difficult undertakings; of her resourceful promptitude in meeting emergencies. She possesses, in short, all that pertains to true Christian statesmanship, and is an example of what a woman can become, and of what a woman can do for others. Thousands look up to her and call her blessed.

Sitting in this congregation, I verily believe, are women of equal force and mental capacity. What you need to lead you into wide spheres of usefulness is a realization that Christ requires your service; an entire consecration of yourself to that service; a ready obedience to dare to go forward in the face of criticism and opposition; and a simple faith in God.

Florence Booth

Florence Booth, *Mothers and the Empire* (London, Salvation Army Book Department, 1914), pp. 45–6.

Deacons, choristers, churchwardens, acolytes, servers and thurifers, even the takers-up of the collection, are almost exclusively men. If at any time not one male person can be found to collect, the priest does it himself, or, after a long and anxious pause, some woman, more unsexed than the rest, steps forward to perform this office. In one church, I am told, it was the custom for collectors to take the collection up to the sanctuary rails, till the war compelled women to take the place of men, when they were directed to wait at the chancel steps. In another it was proposed to elect a woman churchwarden, when the vicar vehemently protested on the ground that this would be a 'slur on the parish'. In another, the impossibility of getting any male youth to ring the sanctus-bell induced a lady to offer her services. After anxious thought the priest accepted her offer 'because the rope hung down behind a curtain, so no one would see her'.

Maude Royden

Maude Royden, *Women and the Church of England* (1916), pp. 8–9. Quoted in Sheila Fletcher, *Maude Royden: A Life* (Oxford, Basil Blackwell, 1989), p. 150.

A meeting at which Miss Maude Royden was to speak on Women in the Church was vetoed, though on what grounds I do not know. Meeting the Rev. Dr Selbie, Principal of Mansfield College, in the street one day, I raised the problem. He said he could only suppose that the Vice-Chancellor had confused Maude Royden with Maud Allan, a dancer who was at the time in some trouble over a nude show in London.

Mary Stocks

Mary Stocks, *My Commonplace Book* (London, Peter Davies, 1970), pp. 136–7.

But when the Restoration came, she refused to go to Court for the quaint reason that she would require blinkers – as do ill-sighted and unruly horses – lest 'she should see and censure what she could not competently judge of'.

The churches she built were those of Appleby, Skipton, Bongate, Brougham, Ninekirks, Mallerstang, and Barden. She founded the almshouses at Appleby, and restored the one built by her mother there. She erected the monument to Spenser in Westminster Abbey, and that to Daniel in Beckington Church, Somersetshire. She raised a tomb for her father at Skipton, and a monument to her mother (by whose side she herself was subsequently buried) at Appleby. And she erected the 'Pillar in the Road', about a quarter of a mile from Brougham, on the way to London, where she last parted with her mother on earth. She had 'an eye to charity in all her buildings, by which she did set the poor on work, thus curing idleness, as well as supplying their indigency'.

Lady Anne Clifford *(as related by Mrs Aubrey Richardson)*

Lady Anne Clifford, Countess of Pembroke, Dorset and Montgomery in Mrs Aubrey Richardson, *Women of the Church of England* (Chapman and Hall 1908), pp. 68–9.

Therefore, beloved sisters, we must consider the immense gifts which God has bestowed on us, especially those which he has seen fit to work in us through his beloved servant, our blessed Father Francis, not only after our conversion but also while we were still living among the vanities of the world.

For, almost immediately after his conversion, while he had neither brothers nor companions, when he was building the Church of San

Damiano in which he was totally filled with divine consolation, he was led to abandon the world completely. This holy man, in the great joy and enlightenment of the Holy Spirit, made a prophecy about us which the Lord fulfilled later. Climbing the wall of that church he shouted in French to some poor people who were standing nearby: 'Come and help me build the monastery of San Damiano, because ladies will dwell here who will glorify our heavenly Father throughout his holy Church by their celebrated and holy manner of life.'

In this, then, we can consider the abundant kindness of God toward us. Because of his mercy and love, he saw fit to speak these words about our vocation and selection through his saint. And our most blessed Father prophesied not only for us, but also for those who were to come to this same holy vocation to which the Lord has called us.

Clare of Assisi

Francis and Clare: the Complete Works. Classics of Western Spirituality. Tr. and introd. Regis J. Armstrong OFM Cap and Ignatius Brady OFM (London, SPCK; Mahwah, NJ, Paulist Press, 1982), p. 227.

The next service was at 8 p.m.; the church was then quite full, mostly of women. The light was furnished by small benzoline lamps. We had evensong led by the catechist, and I again gave an address which was interpreted to the women. This went on till 9.45 and I then thought we should have finished; but no, the women begged that they might go on longer. So I said, 'Very well, you can go on, and I will stay'. We sang another hymn and then Magdalena Mathiba (the catechist's wife, and quite naturally a leader among them) read out a passage. I think it was about Mary and Martha and Lazarus, and she then harangued the women for forty minutes. I remember she spoke to them of the work women might do, not only in their own homes but outside; it was a revelation of what even some native women are thinking and feeling about their lives. At 10.45, tired out after my journey, and three services, I quietly retired to rest, and shortly after the others followed my example. In the morning before dispersing we had mattins, and I gave another short address. They all crowded round to say 'Sala Nantle' 'Good-bye'. Two or three heathen women, whom the others had induced to come, came running across the veldt determined not to be left out. One last thing was a request: 'Deaconess, So-and-so has just got a baby born, will you name it?'

Isabella Gilmore

Janet Grierson, *Isabella Gilmore* (London, SPCK, 1962), p. 196.

But although much might be written concerning these things, that which has struck me as most astonishing is the reception according to me by those of my own sex. 'You will be very successful in speaking to men', was said to me once by a well-known Scotch divine. This has proved true, but what has most profoundly moved me is the large-hearted response which I have ever received from those whom I venture to call the highest class of our intellectual women. No two women are like, and the men-preachers and writers who classify them as all of one mould, err, and err greatly. That is a notable instance in Prof. George Adam Smith's Commentary on Isaiah, when he writes, without differentiation, of 'the besetting sins of women', as if every woman possessed the same categorical list of sins! But while there are women who still prefer to listen to a man-preacher of whatever quality so long as he be of the male genus, this but serves to accentuate the fact of the response on the part of the more advanced and the intellectual women.

It is sadly true that women of this type are dropping out of the Churches – at least out of the orthodox, conventionally organized Church of whatever denomination. I have been amazed at the letters received from, and the interviews held with, such women, to discern their gradual awakening.

Hatty Baker

Hatty Baker, *Women in the Ministry* (London, C. W. Daniel, 1911), pp. 38–9.

The Church will never believe that women have a religious message until some of them get, and take, the opportunity to prove that they have. My taking it in a Nonconformist church will ultimately lead, I believe, to other women being given it in the Church of England.

Maude Royden

Maude Royden to Miss A. M. Procter (20 March 1917). Quoted In Sheila Fletcher, *Maude Royden: A Life* (Oxford, Basil Blackwell, 1989), p. 162.

I was asked, not long since, by an enterprising newspaper in search of 'copy', what had struck me during the years I have been a woman preacher. I did not answer, as I might well have done, 'the unanimity with which all classes of people of somewhat narrow doctrines and antiquated views bombard me with St Paul' (they place a big emphasis on the 'St'!). Nor yet the manner in which it has lost me the friendship (so-called friendship) of men-ministers. In earlier years, seeing the celerity with which ministers use women for Sunday School teachers, leaders of bible classes, choir singing, organizing bazaars, etc., I thought, in all innocence, that did a woman offer herself for the ministry she would be received with the open hands of a kindly brotherhood, as a valuable ally in the fight against the world, the flesh and the devil. For so long they had preached to us that we should live for the highest, should use every talent given by God, should consecrate all to the Divine service, that it came as a distinct shock to find that they meant this with the reservation 'in a woman's own sphere'.

Did a man offer himself for the ministry he was received at least with kindness, his wish was considered. Had he been in business and not received a college training, if young enough, some rich Church might be responsible for his 'Course'; if not, let him be 'called' to a Church – a country one by preference – where, while he undertook the full offices of pastor, he could at the same time go through the 'Three Years' Theological Course'. This, by the way, is a venture which, I have heard, does not always turn out satisfactorily. But if a woman happens to offer herself, if she too feels 'called of God' and ready to consecrate her all to the service: she may be a 'born preacher', but let her do so, and note the result!

Hatty Baker

Hatty Baker, *Women in the Ministry* (London, C. W. Daniel, 1911), pp. 37–8.

But perhaps you think women are not to preach, therefore their words are not to be regarded. It is certain that the words of everyone whosoever, man or woman, that by their place are to speak, are to be regarded, and every word, though never so little esteemed, let it not pass as if spoken by chance. It is good to take every word and action that cometh from anyone soever, who hath cause to speak, as from God.

Mary Ward

Till God Will: Mary Ward through her Writings. Ed. M. Emmanuel Orchard IBVM (London, Darton, Longman and Todd, 1985), p. 58.

Mabillon records the evangelisation of Europe to be in great part the work of Benedictine nuns, many of whom 'publicly preached and taught'.

That women held the office of ministers, that they preached, presided, taught, visited the sick, and fulfilled the duties of pastor in the early Christian Church, we find abundant record. One more reference, and this is noteworthy.

In the early days of the Church, that somewhat curious and, as we term it, apocryphal book, 'The Shepherd of Hermas', was valued by Catholics and received as part of the New Testament scriptures in the Romish Church, as authenticated to them as are any of the more exclusively Protestant books to us. Zahn thinks it was written as early as the year 97 AD. The prophet Hermas herein clearly alludes to women being pre-eminent as religious teachers; he represents that he is himself taught by a woman 'seated on a chair white like snow, on which she sat down alone, unfolding the book in her hand, and bidding him give ear to the glories of God'. While in the next vision 'an ivory seat is prepared for her'.

Were women regularly ordained in the early Christian Church, or did they merely fall, as it were, into office, or as some Free Churchmen of to-day exclaim contemptuously, 'creep by the back-door into the ministry'? It seems to me that if the inflow of the Spirit of the great God has filled them; if the Holy Ghost has set his seal on their work, then being possessed of God they are indeed independent of men; little does ordination – the mere laying on of a man's hands – matter; less still, as long as work is faithfully performed when once therein, whether they have entered by the front door or by the back. 'The Holy Spirit has in the past, and does in our day, very remarkably set his seal upon the preaching of women', one testified not long since.

Women were regularly ordained, with the consent of people and clergy, by the Bishop. The first Ecumenical Council provided for such ordination, and in the Ordo Romanus, the rite is found. 'The ordination of men and women is identical, both by the imposition of hands.' 'The Bishop placed the Stole on her neck after Consecration, saying: *'Stola jucunditatis induit te Dominus'*, after which she took the veil from the altar and clothed herself with it. She also received a maniple, ring and crown.

Hatty Baker

Hatty Baker, *Women in the Ministry* (London, C. W. Daniel, 1911), pp. 26–7.

I shall never forget his face when he came at the appointed time and found the church half full of women and children, some of them quite big. 'What are we going to do?' he said breathless. I said, 'You will baptize them'. I told him we had planned it all out. Every woman had a slip with all particulars about the child, in fact a copy of the register, and she would hand it to me, and as the child was baptized I should hand it on to my dear Helen who would do nothing else but take charge of them. Everything went quite evenly but the vestry meeting which waited for an hour. Ninety-three children were made members of Christ, and I don't think any baptisms have ever seemed so real to me. There was a family of three children, a little girl of ten who carried a baby quite young and held on to a fat little brother of four. As she came up to me she said, 'Deaconess dear, Mother was too drunk to come so I brought them myself'. I held the baby and the boy while she was baptized, and then she gave the other two to the vicar. I can see her proud and happy face now; shall I meet her in that life to come? It was indeed blessed to give those poor neglected ones into Christ's holy keeping. After that we could have a week-night for baptisms when we wanted it. The people in the poor degraded streets always called it a 'public baptism'.

Isabella Gilmore

Janet Grierson, *Isabella Gilmore* (London, SPCK, 1962), pp. 89–90.

A nun of Campsey, an Austin house consisting at the time of a prioress and eighteen nuns, complained at the visitation of the house in 1532 of the unpunctuality of the meals, which she ascribed to the fault of the cook (*culpa coci*), – using a term which suggests that the cook in this case was a man.

An appointment in the nunnery which has led to some controversy is that of chaplain, it being alleged by some writers that the chaplain of the convent was necessarily a man. Certainly in most houses, especially in the wealthier ones, there were men chaplains; for example at the nunnery of Shaftesbury, where men chaplains are mentioned by the side of the abbess in various early chapters and played an important part. Again at St Mary's, Winchester, at the time of the dissolution, men chaplains were among those who are described as resident in the monastery; at Kilburn nunnery the fact that the chaplain who dwelt on the premises was a man is evident from the arrangement of the dwellings, – three chambers which lie together being designated as set apart for the chaplain and the hinds or herdsmen. But the fact that the chaplain's office could be and was held by a woman is established beyond a doubt by the following information. In consequence of an episcopal visitation (1478) of the Benedictine convent of Eastbourne, injunctions were sent to the prioress, one of which directs that 'every week, beginning with the eldest, excepting the sub-prioress, she shall select for herself in due course and in turns one of her nuns as chaplain (*capellanissam*) for divine service and to wait upon herself'.

Lina Eckenstein

Lina Eckenstein, *Women under Monasticism* (Cambridge University Press 1896), p. 282.

The steady eyes of women

The Encyclopaedia Britannica records that the story of the pontificate of Joan was received as fact from the 13th to the 15th century, but was discredited by later authorities. It thus tells her history. Pope Joan was supposed to be of English descent, though born in Ingelheim, or Mainz. Falling in love with a Benedictine monk, she assumed male monastic dress and lived in the Monastery of Fulda. Her lover died while studying with her in Athens, whereupon she went to Rome, became a great professor of learning, and was finally elected by the cardinals to be Pope after Leo IV. The catastrophe of her giving birth to a male child during a procession to the Vatican blasted her reputation. She is reported to have been stoned.

Tuker and Malleson record 'One of the pontiffs in the 8th or 9th century is said to have been a woman, and as such her bust appeared in the series of reliefs of the Popes in the Cathedral of Siena. It was inscribed *"Johannes VIII, femina de Anglia"*. In 1600, this bust was altered at the suggestion of Pope Clement 8th, into that of Pope Zacharias.'

Hatty Baker

Hatty Baker, *Women in the Ministry* (London, C. W. Daniel, 1911), pp. 30–1.

The first and most common objection urged against the public exercises of women, is, that they are unnatural and unfeminine. Many labour under a very great but common mistake, viz. that of confounding nature with custom. Use, or custom, makes things appear to us natural, which, in reality, are very unnatural; while, on the other hand, novelty and rarity make very natural things appear strange and contrary to nature. So universally has this power of custom been felt and admitted, that it has given birth to the proverb, 'Use is second nature'. Making allowance for the novelty of the thing, we cannot discover anything either unnatural or immodest in a Christian woman, becomingly attired, appearing on a platform or in a pulpit. By nature she seems fitted to grace either, God has given to woman a graceful form and attitude, winning manners, persuasive speech, and above all, a finely-toned emotional nature; all of which appear to us eminent natural qualifications for public speaking.

Catherine Booth

Catherine Booth, *Female Ministry: an Address by Mrs. General Booth* (London, Salvation Army Book Department, 1909), p. 1.

I know of a truth that Christ was manifested in her; because I know that I received the spirit of Christ through her ministration. I have obeyed her testimony and I have ever found the same spirit in all her successors, down to the present day.

Prudence Hammond

We have taught thru the years that the manifesting spirit of God – the Christ of the Ages – incarnates wherever man or woman with sincere purpose, honest effort and faithful obedience lives a pure life, and in self-denial and devotion to others becomes by self-effort and spiritual baptism at one with God.

Anna White

The Shakers: Two Centuries of Spiritual Reflection. Ed. Robert Edward Whitson (Mahwah, NJ, Paulist Press, 1984), p. 85.

I can say, for one, that I have not been led blindfold by a vain imagination these forty-five years past. I know by the revelation of God in my soul, that Mother was the Lord's anointed, and that Christ really began his second appearance in her, and dwelt in her, and that her body was a temple for the Holy Spirit. (See 1 Cor. 6.19.) However incredible this may appear to an unbelieving world, we know that we are not left in darkness and doubt concerning these things; they are as clear and as certain to us as the light of the sun in a clear day. Here we find the promise of Christ verified: 'He that followeth me shall not walk in darkness.' (John 8.12.)

I know of a certainty, that Mother Ann had the gift of prophecy and the revelation of God, by which she was able to search the hearts of those who came to see her; for I have myself been an eye and ear witness of it. I have known some to come to her under a cloak of deception, thinking to conceal their sins in her presence; and I have seen her expose them by the searching power of truth, and set their sins before them, so that they have been constrained to confess, with guilt and shame, that she had told them the truth, and to acknowledge that the light and revelation of God was in her. I am not insensible of the spirit of unbelief which prevails in the world against the spirit of truth, and especially against testimonies of this kind; but I can say with the apostle Paul, 'I speak forth the words of truth and soberness;' my eyes have seen and my ears have heard what I have stated; it is no vain imagination.

By obedience to the testimony of the gospel, which I received from Mother Ann and the Elders who stood with her, I have found salvation from sin; and this, I can truly say, feels more precious to me than all created things. Why then should I hold my peace? I regard not the sneers of an unbelieving world. I am not ashamed to acknowledge Mother Ann as my mother in Christ.

I know she lived a pure and sinless life; and I know that she was not guilty of any of those shameful crimes which the wicked have laid to her charge. I know that she loved righteousness and hated iniquity; and I can bear witness that her soul abounded in goodness and love; and that she was able to administer the same to others; I have seen and felt it in numberless instances. I know that the spirit of Christ was formed in her; and I have ever found the same spirit in all her faithful followers. I have been well acquainted with all her successors in the Ministry, and I have always found in them the same godly example, and the same Christ-like spirit; and I feel a firm and unshaken confidence that, in obedience to her precepts, they follow her as she followed Christ. Under their ministration, and in obedience to this gospel, I feel my faith established and my soul resting on a sure foundation, against which the tongue of slander and the gates of hell can never prevail.

Hannah Cogswell

Hannah Cogswell in *Testimonies*. Ed. Seth Wells, pp. 30–2. Quoted in *The Shakers: Two Centuries of Spiritual Reflection*, ed. Robert Edward Whitson (Mahwah, NJ, Paulist Press, 1984), pp. 48–9.

When Marie de l'Incarnation looked round her after more than thirty year's work in Canada, she saw churches and houses where before had been broken-down huts. And she had not merely established a material convent but had laid the foundations of a community which would outlast the centuries, spreading over New France the blessings of civilization as well as of religion. She had lived through all the perils which had beset the young colony; fire, famine, siege, pestilence, not to mention the awful cold from which she and her Sisters suffered bitterly if uncomplainingly, their habits being inadequate for that climate. All danger from the Iroquois was now a thing of the past; they welcomed gladly the brothers of the priests they had so cruelly put to death. New churches were springing up; the Jesuits had opened a college where five hundred students were being trained.

Of the great men she met out there it is interesting to remember the Abbé Bernières, nephew of the early benefactor of the mission; the Abbé Fénelon, brother of the great Archbishop of Cambrai; the Mgr de Laval, the first Bishop of New France. Bossuet was only echoing their estimate of her when he described her as the French Teresa; 'French,' Bremond adds, 'to her finger-tips'.

She also earned for herself the title of the Teresa of the New World. She had to deal with secular and ecclesiastical rulers in the interests of the young colony, she had to bargain with merchants, and she had to lead her nuns and her scholars in the way of perfection. None of all that drew her away from the presence of God in which she lived. 'The closer one lives to God,' she said, 'the more clearly one sees one's way in temporal things.'

Marie de l'Incarnation *(as related by Lucy Menzies)*

Lucy Menzies, ed., *Mirror of the Holy* (Oxford, Mowbray, 1928), pp. 292–3.

The so-called 'surplus' women in this country are surplus only to those who have no other ideal for woman at all, no other conception of her value to the State, apart from her relation to man as wife and partner in the physical creation of the race. We venture – but quite unhesitatingly – to stigmatize this as non-Christian if not distinctly anti-Christian thought; it harmonizes with Mohammedan and Hindu conception – though not with Hinduism at its purest period. The coming order in the Church of God will be potent in bringing a completer and fuller type of Christianity to the world, simple, strong, shorn, we believe, of much hampering tradition and pagan thought.

It is impossible sometimes not to find oneself in the somewhat wearying position of the small child who is perpetually asking the question why? Why, if a women is able and capable, and above all else spiritually fitted for certain service, may she not find a recognized and complete outlet within the ministry of the Church? Can the reply be simply because she is a woman? Then again we ask, is that answer worthy of one professing the Christian faith, and does any one really believe that such a reply will satisfy the present generation?

Edith Picton-Turberville

Edith Picton-Turberville, *Women and the Church* (London, T. Fisher Unwin, 1917), pp. 36–7.

Often a woman's zeal has been damped down and discouraged by the Church, her gifts of mind and spirit refused, her devotion and labour frittered away on trifles. In 1852 Florence Nightingale wrote to Dean Stanley, an intimate friend, her own inner thoughts about the Church of England of which she was a member. She said: 'I would have given her my head, my hand, my heart. She told me to go back and to crochet in my mother's drawing-room. "You may go to the Sunday School if you like," she said. But she gave me no training even for that. She gave me neither work to do for her, nor education for it.' Other women have felt the same about their churches.

Yet the purposes of God in Florence Nightingale were not thwarted by the blindness of the Church of England to the service which women might have rendered. Clinging to her faith in her own inner call to relieve human suffering, she met nothing but failure in attempting in England to equip herself as a nurse. But when she was almost overwhelmed by despair the way opened for her to go to Kaiserwerth to the new and almost unknown mother-house of the deaconesses whom Pastor Fliedner was training, and in their hospital she learned. And this is only one of many examples of the essentially ecumenical character of any study of women in the Church, for when one Church loses all consciousness, apparently, of the very existence of women able and willing to serve, another Church or another branch of the same Church, is beginning to take action.

There have been periods in the life of almost all branches of the Christian Church in which women are honoured, when many are able to use their gifts in a variety of ways, and a few attain to great eminence in the Church. Such times are to be found in the Eastern Orthodox Church between the fourth and ninth century when numbers of women ordained by bishops to be deaconesses taught in schools and in congregations and when a small but significant number attained wide reputations for their scholarship, piety and Christian witness in martyrdom. Palladius describes the deaconess Sylvia who 'loved the divine Scripture and turned nights into days in order to read the writings of the exegetists.' Deaconess Makrina, sister of St Basil of Cappadocia, was a philosopher and theologian of no mean distinction. Phebronia had such a gift for explaining Scripture that 'the whole town of Nisibia gathered together to listen to her; everybody praised her scholarship'. Two deaconesses, Dominica and Mavra, opened the first school for Christian girls. Many suffered martyrdom and some, like Tatiana, Nonna, Olympiada, Xenia, Nina, Susanna and Irina were canonized by the Eastern Church. So great was the influence of women that Lucenius, in the last persecution, issued an edict forbidding men and women to worship together – not in the interests of morality but because of the great influence of women in the Christian movement. Nor did these women whose names are here mentioned (and there were very many others) work unofficially, with the Church authorities half disapproving and half tolerating their efforts. More than one Ecumenical Council discussed and regulated the work of women, and demanded a high standard of theological attainment, and State laws of successive Emperors applied legal sanctions to breaches of discipline among deaconesses.

Women also had a high status in Anglo-Saxon Britain. Women, especially women of noble birth, were the first converts to the Christian faith and took up from the missionaries, from whom they learned the task of evangelizing their tribes. It was Queen Bertha who made to St Augustine and his followers the grant of land on which to build the cathedral of Canterbury: and many are the stories of tribal queens and princesses suffering martyrdom for the new faith. Soon religious houses for women were established in Anglo-Saxon England, and even mixed houses (separate departments of a single religious community). At the close of the seventh century there were five such mixed houses in Kent alone, all governed by women. In the councils of the Church the position of honour given to abbesses was next to that of bishops. St Hilda presided at the great Synod of Whitby in 664, and five abbesses put their names to the Acts of the Great Council of Beckenham in 694.

Kathleen Bliss

Kathleen Bliss, *The Service and Status of Women in the Churches* (London, SCM, 1952), pp. 14–15.

To that parish came some few years ago, for the week-end, a woman of peculiar holiness and beauty of character. She is living still, and her name would probably be known to many of my readers. She has done a great work in the city in which she lives, and is popularly known as the Guardian Angel of that city. Her presence is a benediction, and when she speaks on spiritual things seems to lift her hearers into the very arms of God. The ardent desire for her to be allowed to speak in the church at the Morning Service was openly expressed. It could not be. True she could speak in a parish room, a barn, a stable, but why no room for her in the church? No room in what should be the spiritual home of the people, no room within the walls of the Mother Church.

Edith Picton-Turberville

Edith Picton-Turberville, *Women and the Church* (London, T. Fisher Unwin, 1917), p. 70.

When the mother of one of the children first approached me, explaining that she wished her child baptized at the City Temple, that she was obliged to leave London almost immediately, and that she wished

me to conduct the service, it literally never entered my head to refuse
. . . Baptism by the laity is as old as the Church.

Maude Royden

Maude Royden, Letter to the *Challenge*, 1917. Quoted in Sheila Fletcher, *Maude Royden: A Life* (Oxford, Basil Blackwell, 1989), p. 171.

To be betrothed to you, Jesus, to be a Carmelite, to become, through
my union with you, a mother of souls – surely that ought to be enough
for anybody? But, somehow, not for me; those privileges I've mentioned are the stuff of my vocation, but I seem to have so many other
vocations as well! I feel as if I were called to be a fighter, a priest, an
apostle, a doctor, a martyr; as if I could never satisfy the needs of my
nature without performing, for your sake, every kind of heroic action
at once. I feel as if I'd got the courage to be a Crusader, a Pontifical
Zouave, dying on the battle-field in defence of the Church. And at the
same time I want to be a priest; how lovingly I'd carry you in my hands
when you came down from heaven at my call; how lovingly I'd bestow
you upon men's souls! And yet, with all this desire to be a priest, I've
nothing but admiration and envy for the humility of St Francis; I'd
willingly imitate him in refusing the honour of the priesthood. Dear
Jesus, how am I to reconcile these conflicting ambitions, how am I to
give substance to the dreams of one insignificant soul? Insignificant as
I am, I long to enlighten men's minds as the prophets and doctors did; I
feel the call of an Apostle. I'd like to travel all over the world, making
your name known and planting your cross on heathen soil; only I
shouldn't be content with one particular mission, I should want to be
preaching the gospel on all five continents and in the most distant
islands, all at once. And even then it wouldn't do, carrying on my
mission for a limited number of years; I should want to have been a
missionary ever since the creation, and go on being a missionary till
the world came to an end.

Thérèse of Lisieux

Thérèse of Lisieux, Autobiography of a Saint. Tr. Ronald Knox (London, Fontana Books, 1960), pp. 183–4.

It is essential to the work of Church Extension, for which this Order
has made itself responsible, that our Sisters should be able and willing
to found Centres of Church life and labour, not only among the
teeming population of the great towns of England, but also in her most
distant colonies and dependencies. Consequently, our Mother House
must now be regarded more and more as the Training quarters of the
Society, the place where its members will be instructed and exercised

in that unity of thought, aim and action, which is so indispensable to success.

There has been no hanging back on the part of the Sisters from this arduous and honourable sphere of labour. More than enough have been found ready and desirous to go forth and do battle *Pro Ecclesia Dei.* Their calling is not without its crosses and trials, but let us not doubt, it has also its compensations. Almighty God knows how to reward any sacrifices made for him; and in this case the recompense will probably be in proportion to the distance, difficulty and isolation of the position so cheerfully accepted.

Emily Ayckbowm

A Valiant Victorian: the Life and Times of Mother Emily Ayckbowm 1836–1900 (London, Mowbray, 1964), p. 135.

Let us as Christians face the attitude of the Founder of our faith to women and their ministry, and then compare it with the attitude of the Church today. Is there not indeed a wide gulf fixed between the two? Women are prohibited from conducting the simplest of services within the walls of our Church. The reason why a woman could not lead an intercession service in church, as given by a clergyman of the Church of England (who was by no means indisposed to permit it in his church, but genuinely regretted his inability to do so) was because the church was consecrated.

Mary was by Christ permitted to break the vase of precious ointment over his head. Abelard, writing of this matchless scene, says: 'Judge thereby of the dignity of woman, by her the living Christ was anointed twice, ointment being poured on feet and on head; from her he received the unction of King and of Priest.' It is true that many a churchman will speak with much tenderness of the sacredness and dignity of womanhood; yet it appears that fundamentally their attitude of mind belies their words, else they could not be so disturbed at the thought of a woman leading an intercession service in a consecrated building. We cannot compare the attitude of our Lord and the attitude of the Church towards women fully here, suffice it to say that in Christ's attitude no trace can be found of relegating woman to the place she now holds in the Church of today, nor is there a single note in all his teaching of either class or sex distinction. There is no suggestion in any words uttered by Christ that women were to be excluded from the highest ministry. To women was given the first great Easter message of new life and power, given, let it be noted, that they might pass it on.

Edith Picton-Turberville

Edith Picton-Turberville, *Women and the Church* (London, T. Fisher Unwin, 1917), pp. 30–1.

The steady eyes of women

There is no such difference between men and women; yet women, may they not do great matters, as we have seen by example of many saints who have done great things? And I hope in God it will be seen that women in time will do much.

This is verity: to do what we have to do well. Many think it nothing to do ordinary things. But for us it is. To do ordinary things well, to keep our Constitutions, and all other things that be ordinary in every office or employment whatsoever it be. To do it well: this is for us, and this by God's grace will maintain fervour.

Heretofore we have been told by men we must believe. It is true, we must, but let us be wise and know what we are to believe and what not, and not to be made think we can do nothing. If women are so inferior to men in all things, why are they not exempted in all things as they are in some?

I confess, wives are to be subject to their husbands, men are head of the Church, women may not administer sacraments nor preach in public churches, but in all other things, wherein are we so inferior to other creatures that they should term us 'but women'? As if we were in all things inferior to some other creation, which I supose to be men! Which, I dare be bold to say, is a lie and, with respect to the good Father, may say it is an error.

Mary Ward

Till God Will: Mary Ward through her Writings. Ed. M. Emmanuel Orchard I B V M (London, Darton, Longman and Todd, 1985),p. 57.

Not even a beginning has been made in breaking down the peculiarly loathsome superstitions which bar the sanctuary to women. It is true that many people neither understand this prohibition nor are aware of its existence. It remains a fact that it crystallizes a prejudice indescribably insulting to womanhood, and one which, when a young woman first hears of it, fills her with a very deep (and honourable) sense of resentment.

Maude Royden

Maude Royden, *The Lambeth Conference on 'The Position of Women'* in *The Manchester Guardian* (20 August 1920). Quoted in Sheila Fletcher, *Maude Royden: A Life* (Oxford, Basil Blackwell, 1989), p. 198.

Twenty years nearly since God sent me to you, it seems such a long time, and yet how short for the work I had to do. I often wonder how

God looks at it all. I know many of its faults and sins, but God saw them all. One thing, dear friends, he did know, that my desire however I failed in its accomplishment, was to bring you closer to him and help you by love and sympathy, to show you something of his love who died for you.

You see I had always had this great joy, that he did send me, and that my place was with you and my work for you, and so it came about that I could go on so long and not be greatly troubled when things seemed to go wrong, for I knew that God saw it all and cared, though I did not always understand why things should be so difficult here on earth.

Thank you so much for your dear gift, and thank you still more for all your love. In that after life may we meet and praise him, not with weak and faithless hearts, such as we often have here, but filled then with his fulness, who will then fill us and all things.

Believe me always,
Your affectionate servant and friend,
Isabella Gilmore,
Deaconess

Isabella Gilmore

Janet Grierson, *Isabella Gilmore* (London, SPCK, 1962), p. 188.

SERVICE OF ORDINATION

The deaconess is set apart by the bishop at a special service, generally associated with a celebration of Holy Communion. The ordination takes place preferably at a public service in the cathedral or a parish church of the diocese; this is fitting, as the deaconess is the servant of the Church. It is a matter of great regret that bishops who ordain deaconesses have not agreed upon a uniform service. At the present time the use varies, though often only slightly, in different dioceses. Since the revival of the order about 400 deaconesses have been set apart. There are at present seven deaconess houses in the province of Canterbury (two of which do not provide training for the diaconate), two in the province of York, and one in Scotland, three in India, one in China, one in New Zealand, and one in Australia.

The Ministry of Women. A Report by a Committee appointed by His Grace the Lord Archbishop of Canterbury (London, SPCK, 1919), p. 209.

Here I trust the clergy will forgive me if I remind them that their deaconess is, from her position, far more lonely than their curate, and also that from her being a woman she is in far greater need of this sympathy and help. They will find that they will be the gainers in the end, by their deaconesses being kept fresh and bright, and most certainly that approaching failures in health will be detected more quickly by one who knows them well.

Isabella Gilmore

Janet Grierson, *Isabella Gilmore* (London, SPCK, 1962), pp. 162–3.

Early in the year (1892) we had a beautifully expressed letter from the Bishop of Adelaide (Bp. Kennion), urging us to send Sisters to Australia especially to his own diocese. He put it so forcibly we could hardly hold back. His request was backed up by a visit from a friend of his, Miss Lang, who came to see me at St Mary's, Broadstairs, as I could not get to Kilburn, and urged the matter with much eloquence, offering to pay the passages of four Sisters to Adelaide, and provide a house there. Simultaneously with the good Bishop's appeal came one to the same effect from Hobart, and these are by no means the first we have had. All tell the same tale – in all that vast continent, there is not a single English Church Sister, while every town is over-run with Roman Catholic nuns. The letters were made public in the Community, and it ended by a number of Sisters volunteering, out of whom five were chosen to go out with Sister May as organizer, to sail at the end of July.

Emily Ayckbowm

A Valiant Victorian: the Life and Times of Mother Emily Ayckbowm 1836–1900 (London, Mowbray, 1964), p. 126

God calls the cathedral clergy goats because their flesh stinks of impurity with regard to eternal truth, before his holy Trinity . . .

Alas! Crown of holy Church, how tarnished you have become. Your precious stones have fallen from you because you are weak and you disgrace the holy Christian faith. Your gold is sullied in the filth of unchastity, for you have become destitute and do not have true love. Your purity is burned up in the ravenous fire of gluttony; your humility has sunk to the swamp of your flesh; your truth has been destroyed in the lie of this world; the flowers of all your virtues have fallen from you. Alas, crown of holy priesthood, you have disappeared, and you have nothing left but your external shape – namely, priestly power – with this you do battle against God and his chosen friends. Therefore God will humble you before you know what has happened. For our Lord speaks thus: I will touch the heart of the pope in Rome with great sadness and in this sadness I will speak to him and lament to him that my shepherds from Jerusalem have become murderers and wolves, for they slaughter the white lambs before my eyes. And the old sheep are all sickly, for they cannot eat of the healthful pasture which grows on the high mountains, that is, love and holy doctrine. Whoever does not know the way to hell, let him behold the depraved priesthood, how its path goes straight to hell with women and children and other public sins . . .

Mechthild of Magdeburg

Mechthild of Magdeburg, *The Flowing Light of the Godhead* 5, 34. Tr. Joan Howard. Quoted in *Medieval Women Writers*, ed. Katharina M. Wilson (Manchester University Press 1984), p. 170.

Mother, I lay my head between your hands: protect me from
    yourself.
For the law of faith that you impose is terrible.
It is strange to me on every level of my sight.
The valleys of my hours and the spaces of the stars know nothing
    of it.
My feet stumble and slip on it as on an icy floe,
And my spirit is splintered as against rocks of glass.
Are you so certain, mother, that the messenger from the abyss did
    not deceive you?
Or that wildings from the hall of angels did not mock you?
You bid me quench my only light and bid me rekindle it at the
    darkness of night –
You order me blindess that I may see and deafness that I may
    hear!
Do you know what you do? – Mother, I lay my head between
    your hands. Protect me from yourself.

Gertrude von le Fort

Gertrude von le Fort, *Hymns to the Church* (New York, Sheed and Ward, 1953), p. 39.

When women grow tired of organizations and meetings they go back to their homes and begin again in the way that is a second nature to them, talking in the queue and over the garden fence and bringing in a couple of friends to drink a cup of tea, meeting the children from school and getting to know the teacher and the health visitor and the tradesmen. They, in other words, have in their hands most of the slender threads which can re-unite the Church to the local community. Where the woman is at work, there also the Church can be at work through her. Many young Christian women have their husband's full support: the modern Christian home is a shared responsibility, and the husband rejoices to see his wife use her gifts outside the home and thereby enriching her own contribution to the life of the family.

'The questions you have asked are certainly very interesting,' writes a woman from Berlin in answer to the World Council's questionnaire, 'but please do not be angry if I say that the most important question has not been asked at all. The life of the Church is no longer carried on chiefly through its organisations, but in the houses and families, the factories and offices where Christians meet with others. So the first question should be, What does the Church mean in the lives of women? What chance does the Church give to women to be its representatives at home and in their work?' Women are beginning to answer these questions by experiment in living encounter between the Gospel, their families, friends and work.

Kathleen Bliss

Kathleen Bliss, *The Service and Status of Women in the Churches* (London, SCM, 1952), p. 201.

7
Driven to desire

The themes of desire and abandonment feature strongly in the spiritual writing of women. Catherine of Siena is not the only woman who can say: 'I am driven to desire . . . for by the light of understanding within your light I have tasted and seen your depth, eternal Trinity, and the beauty of your creation.' God kindles desire and God satisfies desire. More than that, creation, created reality, the people and places one loves all serve to satisfy desire because with the self-disclosure of God comes a new understanding of reality. Desire is not about withdrawal; rather it leads to a new and passionate kind of engagement. It drives us out of ourselves and sends us towards others in passion, tenderness and love.

Catherine Booth's description of her courtship makes a telling point. She knew she wanted to marry a minister; she fancied that he should be tall and dark and had a special liking for the name William. 'Singularly enough, in adhering to my essentials, my fancies were also gratified.' The point being that it helps a great deal if you actually know what it is that you want.

Christian spirituality has been cautious about desires and has viewed them with suspicion. Women in particular have not been encouraged to know what they want. Edith Stein puts it bluntly: 'Man uses her as a means to achieve his own ends in the exercise of his work and in pacifying his lust.' This is all such a long way away from the regime envisaged by the French nun, Jane de Chantal: 'Govern your community with great expansiveness of heart: give the sisters a holy liberty of spirit and banish from your mind and theirs a servile spirit of constraint.'

Generations of Anglo-Saxons have prayed to be freed from following too much the 'devices and desires' of their own hearts. All our desires are known only to God and God is expected to cleanse them. Within such a framework it is hard to feel good about wanting anything, let alone greeting one's own desires as a place of disclosure of the divine purpose.

Hence the value of the material in this chapter. 'If we are to obey this Supreme Light, we must of course learn to recognize it; and in order to do so we must be quiet.' The testimony of the Quaker tradition is especially valuable in enabling us to attend to our own desires and learn to discern them and Caroline Stephen makes an important connection. The discernment we make when in a state of quiet is about the 'search after truth and the God of Truth'. With Hadewijch, we are able to 'to follow your being in which God has created you'.

This truth and integrity give new authority to women who are able to listen to their desires.

And it leads them to offer themselves in love. The theme of abandonment to God is probably best handled in the hymns, the fourth verse of Christina Rossetti's 'In the bleak midwinter' being a marvellous example of this: 'Yet what I can I give him – Give my heart.' Mother Maribel reminds us why this self-offering is safe: 'He waits for our Fiat *before taking possession.'*

But there are other kinds of abandonment too and some of them are far less safe. The American lay woman, Solange Hertz, speaks for many when she writes that 'the business world, the marriage bed and the nursery yield problems for which theology must indeed be developed', stipulating that this theology must come from lay people. Those who experience the demands of conflicting desires are best able to deal with them. Admittedly most of us will lack the temerity of the young Thérèse of Lisieux whose attitude to discernment was formed by a childhood experience in which she found herself saying: 'I choose the lot'. But choices there are, and we will be better able to face them when empowered by desire.

O eternal Trinity, fire and abyss of charity, dissolve this very day the cloud of my body! I am driven to desire, in the knowledge of yourself that you have given me in your truth, to leave behind the weight of this body of mine and give my life for the glory and praise of your name. For by the light of understanding within your light I have tasted and seen your depth, eternal Trinity, and the beauty of your creation. Then, when I considered myself in you, I saw that I am your image. You have gifted me with power from yourself, eternal Father, and my understanding with your wisdom – such wisdom as is proper to your only-begotten Son; and the Holy Spirit, who proceeds from you and from your Son, has given me a will and so I am able to love.

You, eternal Trinity, are the craftsman; and I your handiwork have come to know that you are in love with the beauty of what you have made, since you made me a new creation in the blood of your Son.

O abyss! O eternal Godhead! O deep sea! What more could you have given me than the gift of your very self?

Catherine of Siena

Catherine of Siena, *The Dialogue*. Classics of Western Spirituality. Tr. Suzanne Noffke (London, SPCK; Mahwah, NJ, Paulist Press, 1980). Quoted in *Medieval Religious Women* vol. 2: *Peace Weavers*, ed. John A. Nichols and Lillian Thomas Shanks (Kalamazoo, MI, Cistercian Publications, 1987), p. 287

Christ said to us 'Be ye perfect.' He spoke not only to the apostles, nor only to a nation, nor only to a sex. He said to every man and woman in the world, 'Be ye perfect.' In what sense did he say it? Did he say, 'In those virtues which become your class,' or 'your sex'? He said 'Be ye perfect, even as your Father which is in heaven is perfect.'

Maude Royden

Maude Royden, 'The Religious Aspects of the Women's Movement' (1912). Quoted in Sheila Fletcher, *Maude Royden: A Life* (Oxford, Basil Blackwell, 1989), p. 101.

While Mr Sackville was commending us and our course and telling how much it was esteemed by men of judgment among the cardinals at Rome, Father Minister, who was present, answered: 'It is true – while they are in their first fervour, but fervour will decay and when all is done, they are but women.'

I would know what you all think he meant by this speech of his 'but women', and what fervour is. Fervour is a will to do well, that is, a preventing grace of God and a gift given freely by God, which we could not merit. It is true that fervour doth many times grow cold, but what is the cause? Is it because we are women? No, but because we are imperfect women. There is no such difference between men and women.

Therefore, it is not because we are women but, as I said before, because we are imperfect women and love not verity but seek after lies. '*Veritas Domini manet in aeternum*': the verity of the Lord remains for ever. It is not *veritas hominum*, the verity of men, nor the verity of women, but *veritas Domini*, and this verity women may have as well as men. If we fail, it is for want of this verity, and not because we are women.

Mary Ward

Till God Will: Mary Ward through her Writings. Ed. M. Emmanuel Orchard IBVM (London, Darton, Longman and Todd, 1985), pp. 56–7.

If we are to obey this Supreme Light, we must of course learn to recognize it; and in order to do so we must be quiet. True inward quietness is not that which may be produced by shutting out all outward causes of distraction – a process which, when carried out too severely, may intensify the inward ferment of the mind, especially in the young. It is rather a state of stable equilibrium; it is not vacancy, but stability – the steadfastness of a single purpose.

Inwardness and true quietness indeed appear to be but two aspects of the same thing – of a 'truly centered' life. In the innermost religion of life there is perpetual calm; perturbations and excitements belong to the comparatively superficial part of our natures. In cleaving to the Centre we cannot but be still; to be inwardly still is to be aware of the Centre. This may be mystical language, unfamiliar to those to whom it has not occurred that all parts of our nature are not on one level, and do not respond to the same plane in our environment; but it is also the language of hard common sense. The Centre means whatever is most unchangeable, most real, most truly important. Not withstanding all possible dangers from perversion or exaggeration in the teaching of quietness, the need for it lies too deep in human nature to be forgotten while the search for truth and the God of truth holds its place among us.

Caroline Stephen

Caroline Stephen, *Light Arising* (London, Headley, 1908). Quoted in *Daily Readings from Quaker Writings Ancient and Modern*, ed. Linda Hill Renfer (Oregon, Serenity Press, 1988), p. 9.

I beg you, my dear Sister, govern your community with great expansiveness of heart: give the Sisters a holy liberty of spirit, and banish from your mind and from theirs a servile spirit of constraint. If a Sister seems to lack confidence in you, don't for that reason show her the least coldness, but gain her trust through love and kindness. Don't entertain thoughts against any one of the Sisters, but treat them all equally. Lead them, not with a bustling, anxious kind of concern, but with a care that is genuine, loving and gentle. I know there is no better way to succeed in leading souls. The more solicitous, open and supportive you are with them, the more you will win their hearts. This is the best way of helping them advance toward the perfection of their vocation. So be present at the community exercises as often as you can, and let the Sisters know how much you enjoy being with them.

Jane de Chantal

Jane de Chantal in *Francis de Sales, Jane de Chantal: Letters of Spiritual Direction*, Classics of Western Spirituality. Sel. and introd. by Wendy M. Wright and Joseph F. Power OSFS (Mahwah, NJ, Paulist Press, 1986), p. 265.

I sometimes remember the complaint of that holy woman, Martha; her complaint was not merely of her sister – I feel sure that the chief cause of her sorrow was the thought that thou, Lord, hadst no compassion on her for the labour that she was enduring nor caredst whether or no she was with thee. Perhaps she thought that thou hadst less love for her than for her sister, and this would have troubled her more than serving one whom she loved so dearly, for love turns labour into rest. And so she said nothing to her sister, but made her complaint to thee, Lord, alone, for love made her bold enough to ask why thou hadst no care for her. Thine answer, which seems to imply that the source of her complaint was as I have been saying, was that it is love alone which gives value to all things and that the most needful thing is that it should be so great that nothing can hinder its operation. But how can we have this love, my God, in the degree merited by the Beloved, if the love which thou hast for us is not united with it? Shall I complain with this holy woman? Ah, I have no reason to do so, for I have ever found in my God far greater and stronger proofs of love than I have known how to ask or to desire. I have nothing to complain of save that thy loving-kindness has borne with me too long. What, then, can one ask of thee so wretched as I? That thou wilt give to me, my God (as Saint Augustine said), so that I may give to thee, to repay thee some part of all that I owe thee; that thou wilt remember that I am thy handiwork; and that I may know who my creator is, and so may love him.

Teresa of Avila

Teresa of Jesus, *The Complete Works* vol. 2. Tr. and ed. E. Allison Peers (London and New York, Sheed and Ward, 1946), p. 406.

There is a story told of an old woman who went into a shop and asked for a quarter of a pound of 2/- tea. The grocer asked her what sort of tea she expected to get. She replied that she hoped for the best, but was prepared for the worst. This, of course, was not the virtue of hope.

Hope, the second of those spiritual powers in man which tend towards God, is a completely confident expectation; that sureness and certitude with which the awakened soul aims at God and rests in God. It is the source of that living peace, that zest and alertness, that power of carrying on, which gives its special colour to the genuine Christian life. Hope brings the exalted vision of faith into the wear and tear of our daily life. When we descend from the watch-tower, where we feel that we can do all things – or rather that in us all things can be done – and try to do the things, the first result is usually disillusion. Unless hope has come downstairs with us to sweeten fortitude, permeate the content of our minds, the last result may be apathy and despair.

The old moralists said that hope was the virtue which purified memory and made it fit for God; and by memory they meant all our funded experience, that hoarded past which we drag along with us, and which conditions our whole outlook on life. In respect of all this, hope teaches us the art of wise forgetting; of dropping the superfluous, the outgrown, the trivial. It cleanses the mind from all those half realities which impede the total concentration of our love and will on God; and lifts up all the rest of our experience into the eternal light, saying: 'Even though I do not see the meaning, yet I know all this is conditioning my growth, purifying my spirit, taking me towards you; and nothing matters but that.'

Hope finds all life penetrated by a significance that points beyond itself, and has a trustful expectation that the ceaseless stream of events, thoughts, joys, trials – the whole stuff of experience – means something, contributes to something; and only has value because it points beyond itself to God, is an earnest of rich fields of experience awaiting the soul. Such hope is the bright side of self-abandonment. Much so-called self-abandonment is conceived in the spirit of the 2/- tea but the real self-abandonment to God which is the supreme expression of our human freedom, should be a delighted act of hope. 'O God, my hope is in thee,' does not mean, 'I have tried everything else first.' It means that the final achievement of his hidden purpose is what we really care about, and that we entirely depend on him for the power of achieving our little bit of his plan.

Thus the pain and disappointment, the tragedy and frustration of existence, are transfigured when hope purifies the mind. If faith enlarges and illuminates the understanding, shows it the fields of experience that lie beyond its span, hope integrates faith's vision with the very texture of our common thoughts, our mental life as a whole; merging the interests of that little life in the vast interests of the divine love and will.

Evelyn Underhill

Evelyn Underhill, *Concerning the Inner Life with the House of the Soul* (London, Methuen, 1947), pp. 124–5.

During the time I was in hospital I had frequent opportunity of witnessing the utterly friendless condition of many poor outcasts who sought admission to its charity, the filthy plight of their persons and clothing proving their need of a female hand to rectify disorder . . . how I would wish to dedicate the time I have to spare (it might be two or three hours a day), not so much to the decent poor . . . but to the lost and degraded of my own sex, whom from their vicious lives, no tenderly reared female would be likely to approach; but to me, who, by God's mercy, was preserved in my youth from a like fate, such scenes will have no terror . . . It will be enough for her to require my aid – such as cleansing and washing and repairing her garments.

Marian B.

Marian B. in L. N. R[anyard], *The Missing Link: or Bible-Women in the Homes of the London Poor* (London 1859). Quoted in Brian Heeny, *The Women's Movement in the Church of England* (Oxford, Clarendon Press, 1988), pp. 46–7.

My mother, too, was a very virtuous woman, who endured a life of great infirmity: she was also particularly chaste. Though extremely beautiful, she was never known to give any reason for supposing that she made the slightest account of her beauty; and, though she died at thirty-three, her dress was already that of a person advanced in years. She was a very tranquil woman, of great intelligence. Throughout her life she endured great trials and her death was most Christian.

We were three sisters and nine brothers: all of them, by goodness of God, resembled their parents in virtue, except myself, though I was my father's favourite. And, before I began to offend God, I think there was some reason for this, for it grieves me whenever I remember what good inclinations the Lord had given me and how little I profited by them. My brothers and sisters never hindered me from serving God in any way.

I had one brother almost of my own age. It was he whom I most loved, though I had a great affection for them all, as had they for me. We used to read the lives of saints together; and, when I read of the martyrdoms suffered by saintly women for God's sake, I used to think they had purchased the fruition of God very cheaply; and I had a keen desire to die as they had done, not out of any love for God of which I was conscious, but in order to attain as quickly as possible the fruition of the great blessings which, as I read, were laid up in heaven. I used to discuss with this brother of mine how we could become martyrs. We agreed to go off to the country of the Moors, begging our bread for the love of God, so that they might behead us there; and, even at so tender an age, I believe the Lord had given us sufficient courage for this, if we could have found a way to do it; but our greatest hindrance seemed to be that we had a father and a mother. It used to cause us great astonishment when we were told that both pain and glory would last for ever. We would spend long periods talking about this and we liked to repeat again and again 'For ever – ever – ever!' Through our frequent repetition of these words, it pleased the Lord that in my earliest years I should receive a lasting impression of the way of truth.

Teresa of Avila

Teresa of Jesus, *The Complete Works* vol. 1. Tr. and ed. E. Allison Peers (London and New York, Sheed and Ward, 1946), p. 11.

Driven to desire

A day came when Léonie, thinking she was too old now to play with dolls, came along to us with a basket full of dresses and pretty little bits of stuff for making others, with her own doll lying on the top. 'Here you are, darlings,' she said, 'choose which of these you'd like; they're all for you.' Céline put her hand in and brought out a little ball of silken braid which had taken her fancy. I thought for a moment, and then said, as I held out my hand: 'I choose the whole lot!' Then, without further ceremony, I took over the basket. Everybody said I was quite within my rights, and Céline never dreamt of making any protest. (As a matter of fact she was never hard up for toys; her godmother was always giving her presents, and Louise could always manage to get her anything she wanted.)

Only a childish trait, perhaps, but in a sense it's been the key to my whole life. Later on, when the idea of religious perfection came within my horizon, I realized at once that there was no reaching sanctity unless you were prepared to suffer a great deal, to be always on the look-out for something higher still, and to forget yourself. There were plenty of degrees in spiritual advancement, and every soul was free to answer our Lord's invitation by doing a little for him, or by doing a lot for him; in fact, he gave it a choice between various kinds of self-sacrifice he wanted it to offer. And then, as in babyhood, I found myself crying out: 'My God, I choose the whole lot. No point in becoming a saint by halves. I'm not afraid of suffering for your sake; the only thing I'm afraid of is clinging to my own will. Take it, I want the whole lot, everything whatsoever that is your will for me.'

Thérèse of Lisieux

Thérèse of Lisieux, *Autobiography of a Saint*. Tr. Ronald Knox (London, Fontana, 1960), pp. 38–9.

Not long ago in a diocesan newspaper I ran across a column in which a Reverend Monsignor attempted to advise a mother writing in to him concerning an acute child-feeding problem! That he heroically tried to answer her thorny question has led me to recognize that the American hierarchy is being driven to sacrifice itself way above and beyond the call of duty, being all things to all men, and women too. There are all kinds of child-feeding problems, some of them spiritual, which are the special province of an enlightened laity equipped to cope with them at ground level. Let's not expect the impossible of our busy clergy, whose special contribution must always be theological and liturgical. The business world, the marriage bed, and the nursery yield problems for which theology must indeed be developed by them, but these are specifically lay terrain, to be worked by the layman himself if he is to leaven society as he should.

Solange Hertz

Solange Hertz, *Searcher of Majesty* (Westminster, MD, The Newman Press, 1963), p. 129.

My views on birth control are very tentative 'half-way' ones, first because I am not married and feel that the question of the nervous strain imposed on married people by long-continued abstinence from intercourse is one which it is practically impossible for an unmarried person to gauge; and, secondly, because I believe that we have no adequate scientific knowledge to guide us yet. I believe that the average man and woman are not quite normal about sex; I think most of us are rather unnaturally over-sexed, and over-preoccupied with sex, and that this greatly complicates the question of birth control.

Subject to these very serious limitations my views are roughly:-

1. That some form of birth control is necessary; because very few people can afford to marry young if they are to look forward to having a child born every year; because such frequent child-bearing is too great a strain both physically and in other ways on the mother; and because the children do not get a sufficiently prolonged babyhood or sufficiently individual care if they come every year.

2. I believe the ideal method of birth control to be abstinence except when a child is desired.

3. Nevertheless I am in favour of the use of contraceptives where the alternative is (a) unfaithfulness or alienation on the part of the partner who refuses to use self-control or remains unconvinced that it is either necessary or right. (b) Undue nervous strain where self-control is exercised or attempted. (c) The birth of an unwanted child. (d) The exhaustion by child-bearing of the mother. (f) Indefinite postponement of marriage, unless the number of children to be born can be limited.

4. Considering that these dangers are exceedingly serious, I advocate the dissemination of knowledge on the subject of contraceptives, and of birth control generally, by properly qualified medical men and women. I believe that this knowledge should be given not only to the rich but to the poor, and that doctors at clinics should be not only allowed but definitely instructed to give it where it is asked for.

Maude Royden

Maude Royden, *The Ethics of Birth Control* (London, Macmillan, 1926), pp. 92–3.

Driven to desire

Nothing dwells or can dwell in Love, nor can anything touch her except desire. And 'touch' is Love's most secret name, which springs forth from Love herself. For Love is always desiring and touching and consuming within herself. And yet she is complete within herself. Love can dwell in all things. She can dwell in charity, while charity cannot dwell in Love, any more than mercy can, or graciousness, or humility, or reason, or fear, or thrift, or moderation, or anything at all. And yet she can dwell in all these things, which are all sustained by Love. And yet nothing sustains Love herself but her own wholeness.

Hadewijch of Brabant

Hadewijch of Brabant in *Beguine Spirituality*. Ed. Fiona Bowie (London, SPCK; New York, Crossroad, 1989), p. 112.

1 In the bleak midwinter
　　Frosty wind made moan,
Earth stood hard as iron,
　　Water like a stone;
Snow had fallen, snow on snow,
　　Snow on snow,
In the bleak midwinter,
　　Long ago.

2 Our God, heaven cannot hold him,
　　Nor earth sustain;
Heaven and earth shall flee away
　　When he comes to reign:
In the bleak midwinter
　　A stable-place sufficed
The Lord God almighty,
　　Jesus Christ.

3 Angels and archangels
　　May have gathered there,
Cherubim and seraphim
　　Thronged the air –
But his mother only,
　　In her maiden bliss,
Worshipped the beloved
　　With a kiss.

4 What can I give him,
　　Poor as I am!
If I were a shepherd

I would bring a lamb;
If I were a wise man,
I would do my part;
Yet what I can I give him –
Give my heart.

Christina Rossetti

Christina Rossetti in *The Baptist Hymn Book* (London, Psalms and Hymns Trust, 1962), no. 99.

Since I was ten years old I have been so overwhelmed by intense love that I should have died, during the first two years when I began this, if God had not given me other forms of strength than people ordinarily receive, and if he had not renewed my nature with his own Being. For in this way he soon gave me reason, which was enlightened to some extent by many a beautiful disclosure; and I had from him many beautiful gifts, through which he let me feel his presence and revealed himself. And through all these tokens with which I met in the intimate exchange of love between him and me – for as it is the custom of friends between themselves to hide little and reveal much, what is most experienced is the close feeling of one another, when they relish, devour, drink, and swallow up each other – by these tokens that God, my Love, imparted to me in so many ways at the beginning of my life, he gave me such confidence in him that ever since that time it has usually been in my mind that no one loved him so intensely as I. But reason in the meantime made me understand that I was not the closest to him; nevertheless the chains of love that I felt never allowed me to feel or believe this. So that is how it is with me: I do not, finally, believe that he can be loved the most intensely by me, but I also do not believe there is any man living by whom God is loved so much. Sometimes Love so enlightens me that I know what is wanting in me – that I do not content my Beloved according to his sublimity; and sometimes the sweet nature of Love blinds me to such a degree that when I can taste and feel her it is enough for me; and sometimes I feel so rich in her presence that I myself acknowledge she contents me.

Hadewijch of Brabant

Hadewijch, *The Complete Works*. Classics of Western Spirituality. Tr. and introd. Mother Columba Hart o s b (London, S P C K; Mahwah, NJ, Paulist Press, 1980), p. 60.

Driven to desire

1 In full and glad surrender,
   I give myself to thee,
   Thine utterly and only
   And evermore to be.

2 O Son of God, who lov'st me,
   I will be thine alone;
   And all I have, and am, Lord,
   Shall henceforth be thine own.

3 Reign over me, Lord Jesus,
   O make my heart thy throne;
   It shall be thine, dear Saviour,
   It shall be thine alone.

4 O come and reign, Lord Jesus,
   Rule over everything;
   And keep me always loyal,
   And true to thee, my king.

Frances Ridley Havergal

Frances Ridley Havergal in *The Baptist Hymn Book* (London, Psalms and Hymns Trust, 1962), no. 439.

But God forbid that you should say or assume that I am a teacher, for that is not and never was my intention; for I am a woman, ignorant, weak and frail. But I know very well that what I am saying I have received by the revelation of him who is the sovereign teacher. But it is truly love which moves me to tell it to you, for I want God to be known and my fellow Christians to prosper, as I hope to prosper myself, by hating sin more and loving God more. But because I am a woman, ought I therefore to believe that I should not tell you of the goodness of God, when I saw at the same time that it is his will that it be known? You will see this clearly in what follows, if it be well and truly accepted. Then will you soon forget me who am a wretch, and do this, so that I am no hindrance to you, and you will contemplate Jesus, who is every man's teacher. I speak of those who will be saved, for at this time God showed me no one else; but in everything I believe as Holy Church teaches, for I beheld the whole of this blessed revelation of our Lord as unified in God's sight, and I never understood anything from it which bewilders me or keeps me from the true doctrine of Holy Church.

Julian of Norwich

Julian of Norwich, *Showings*. Classics of Western Spirituality. Tr. and introd. Edmund Colledge O S A and James Walsh S J (London, SPCK; Mahwah, NJ, Paulist Press, 1978), p. 285.

Again he said unto me, 'My beloved and my bride, love thou me! All thy life, thy eating and drinking and sleeping and all that thou dost is pleasing unto me, if only thou lovest me.' And he said, 'I will do great things through thee in the sight of all people; thou shalt be known and glorified, so that many shall praise my name in thee.'

These and other similiar things did he say unto me. Then, when I heard these words I did count over my sins and consider my faults, and how that I was not worthy of such great love. And I did begin to cast doubt upon these words, wherefore my soul said unto him who had spoken unto it: 'If thou wert truly the Holy Spirit thou wouldst not speak thus unto me, for it is neither right nor seemly, seeing how that I am weak and frail and might grow vainglorious thereat.'

He answered me, 'Reflect and see if thou couldst be vainglorious because of all these things for the which thou art now grown proud; and see if thou couldst not perceive the folly of thy words by thinking of other things.'

So then did I endeavour to grow vainglorious, that I might prove if what he said were true; and I began to gaze at the vineyards, that I might learn the folly of my words. And wheresover I looked he said unto me, 'Behold and see, this is my creation,' and thereat did I feel the most ineffable sweetness.

Angela of Foligno

Angela of Foligno in *An Anthology of Mysticism*. Ed. Paul de Jaegher SJ (London, Burns, Oates and Washbourne, 1953), p. 251.

I value the contact with God through the Sacrament more than anything in the world; but I don't believe that I think the Sacrament is confined by God to those who receive it from apostolically ordained priests. You will perhaps be sorry I feel like this; I hope not! Perhaps I am too 'protestant,' am I? But I don't want to be intolerant like the Papists, with all their defences and walls to shut other Christians out, and their refusal even to pray with them – that *can't* be Christian; what would Christ have thought of it? When we were little girls going to the daily convent school at Varazze for a time, the nuns wouldn't even let us join in prayers with the other children; we had to sit down, lest the awful sin should be committed of praying with little heretics. My mother was much vexed by this. To my mind it is anti-Christ.

Rose Macaulay

Rose Macaulay, *Letters to a Friend 1950–52* (London, Fontana Books, 1961), p. 335.

If you wish to follow your being in the way God created you, you must in noble-mindedness fear no difficulty; and so in all hardihood and pride you must neglect nothing, but you should valiantly lay hold on the best part – I mean, the great totality of God – as your own good. And so must you also give generously, according to your wealth, and make all the poor rich: for veritable charity never fails to prevail over those who began with the pride of their whole will; so that she gives truly what she wishes to give, overcomes what she wishes to overcome, and maintains what she wishes to maintain.

O dear child! I entreat you now that you will always work without grumbling, purely with your will accompanied by all the perfect virtues, in every good work small or great. And do not wish or demand any favour from God, either for your deeds or for your friends; do not ask him for spiritual joys in any sort of repose or consolation, unless this is as he himself wills. Let him come and go according to his holy will, and let him do, as his sublimity demands, all his will with you and with all those whom you long to instruct in his love.

Hadewijch of Brabant

Hadewijch, *The Complete Works.* Classics of Western Spirituality. Tr. and introd. Mother Columba Hart OSB (London, SPCK; Mahwah NJ, Paulist Press, 1980), p. 60.

The deterioration of kingship to brutal authority also holds true in the relationship of man to woman. According to the original order, she was entrusted to him as companion and helpmate. Consequently, if she is to stand by his side in lordship over the earth, she must be endowed with the same gifts – to understand, to enjoy, and to create. But, usually, she is less endowed with these gifts and consequently runs less danger of losing herself in one-sidedness. Thus she will be able to serve man in their mutual duties; she protects man from his natural one-sidedness by her own harmonious development. But the relationship of the sexes since the Fall has become a brutal relationship of master and slave. Consequently, women's natural gifts and their best possible development are no longer considered; rather, man uses her as a means to achieve his own ends in the exercise of his work or in pacifying his own lust. However, it can easily happen that the despot becomes a slave to his lust and thereby is a slave of the slave who must satisfy him.

Edith Stein

The Collected Works of Edith Stein, Sister Benedicta of the Cross, Discalced Carmelite, vol. 2. Tr. Freda Mary Oben (Washington DC, ISC Publications, 1987), pp. 70–1.

The virtuous wife and mother fares almost the worst. With the best will in the world to stay home and do her duty she finds that everything that might give her life meaning and real importance has been taken from her. She is no longer allowed to educate her children beyond the age of six except in the most desultory and supplementary way. She isn't allowed to nurse them when they are really ill, having been led to believe that anything worse than a bad cold can be treated only by so-called professionals in a hospital's cold, clinical atmosphere. She isn't allowed to bear her children or lay out her beloved dead in the warmth of her own love in her own home. Even her cooking is done for her in crisp packages.

Everything she needs is placed just beyond her reach, driving her to leave her hearth to spend hours in stores and supermarkets, and find her recreation in public places. She's no mother, but an itinerant. Needless to say, the vivifying solace of the blessed sacrament in her own home – once accorded to responsible housewives in the early Church – isn't even to be hoped for, I'm told.

The sanctuary is often miles farther than the nearest bowling alley. So is the school, yet it often happens that her little children must be chauffeured there to be prepared for their first Holy Communion, not by her or her husband, in the warmth of the home, but by outsiders in the artificial atmosphere of a classroom. Not infrequently it happens that these outsiders are simply other mothers – whose own children are being prepared in turn by mothers not their own, in other classrooms! I do find this confusing, being allowed to teach other people's children, but not mine! One must know a young child so intimately and individually to speak to him of a God who is Love. This is a matter so private, so fundamental, and, it seems to me, so little to be undertaken in public.

Well may our Pope John XXIII ask of Our Lady of Guadalupe, as Mother of America, 'May sanctity flourish in all homes – sanctity of the family in whose midst Catholic education may receive in your sight a healthy increase.'

Yet, conditioned always to run out for whatever she needs, it's no wonder the modern housewife does the same spiritually, never thinking to stay home and run in for the sustenance of her family's spiritual life, as well as her own. Forgetting the ever-present source of grace which the sacrament of matrimony supplies her at her own kitchen sink, the spiritually hungry woman as often as not engages in a chronic desultory search among pious societies, book clubs, or libraries – far from home – for what lies under her nose in her own house. Even God, it seems to her, can be reached only by car on free afternoons. (May he forgive us!)

She is given to understand, furthermore, that to hold her husband she must spend precious time in the beauty parlor, running to the gym in between visits, or he will leave her for the tavern. Is it any wonder that at the end of her frazzled day her delicate, autonomous nervous system inevitably rebels, and she finds herself hysterically unable to pay the marriage debt? Believe me, I use the word hysterical advisedly, deeply aware of its derivation from the Greek for 'womb.'

At her Saturday night confession she may well accuse herself of what she may have been led to believe (by well-meaning persons unacquainted with inexorable female rhythms) is a mortal sin: inability to react to her husband's lovemaking with the reliable responses of an automaton. Trembling at the dire consequences of her selfishness, she may well panic with guilt, become more frigid, and her state of 'sin' may become permanent.

Solange Hertz

Solange Hertz, *Searcher of Majesty* (Westminster, MD, The Newman Press, 1963), pp. 212–13.

The third essential consisted of oneness of views and tastes any ideas of lordship or ownership being lost in love. There can be no doubt that Jesus Christ intended, by making love the law of marriage, to restore woman to the position God intended her to occupy. Of course there must and will be mutual yielding whenever there is proper love, because it is a pleasure and a joy to yield our own wills to those for whom we have real affection, whenever it can be done with an approving conscience.

Neither party should attempt to force an alliance where there exists a physical repugnance. Natural instinct in this respect is usually too strong for reason, and asserts itself in after life in such a way so as to make both supremely miserable. Another resolution that I made was that I would never marry a man who was not a total abstainer, and this from conviction, and not merely to gratify me. Besides these things, which I looked upon as being absolutely essential, I had, like most people, certain preferences. The first was that the object of my choice should be a minister. Then I very much desired that he should be dark and tall, and had a special liking for the name, 'William'. Singularly enough, in adhering to my essentials, my fancies were also gratified.

Catherine Booth

Catherine Booth, *The Training of Children and Courtship and Marriage* (London, Salvationist Publishing and Supplies, 1953), pp. 14–15.

Abelard had vaulted the orchard gate without waiting to open it. Smiling and mischievous, he came across the grass, then suddenly halted, his arms resting on a branch, his eyes fixed on them. Standing there as they did, side by side, with the budding apple-boughs above their heads, their faces turned to watch him, he suddenly felt remote, walled out from their mysterious ancient understanding. It was no altarpiece that he saw; it was an older thing than Mary the mother of Our Lord, and Anne the mother of Mary. It was Demeter and Persephone, with Pluto come to claim her, the six months ended. Then Heloise came a step to meet him, and the vision broke. He came gravely towards them, put his arms about her with a quick straining of her to his side, and then stood, looking down at his sister.

'Well? Will you give us your blessing, Denise?'

Helen Waddell

Helen Waddell, *Peter Abelard* (London, Pan, 1933), p. 121.

1 O perfect Love, all human thought transcending,
   Lowly we kneel in prayer before thy throne,
  That theirs may be the love that knows no ending
   Whom thou for evermore dost join in one.

2 O perfect Life, be thou their full assurance
   Of tender charity and steadfast faith,
  Of patient hope, and quiet, brave endurance,
   With childlike trust that fears not pain nor death.

3 Grant them the joy which brightens earthly sorrow,
   Grant them the peace which calms all earthly strife;
  And to life's day the glorious unknown morrow
   That dawns upon eternal love and life.

Dorothy Frances Gurney

Dorothy Frances Gurney in *The Westminster Hymnal* (London, Burns, Oates and Washbourne, 1953), no. 216.

We, X and Y, of our own free will join ourselves for the term of our natural lives and the duration of our mutual love, on the following conditions. We firmly intend to hold our fortune communally, while reserving the right to divide it in favour of children from our own and from other attachments. We each recognize that our worldly goods belong directly to our children, legitimate or not, and that they have the right without distinction to bear the names of the fathers and mothers who have acknowledged them: we intend to forswear the law permitting the denial of one's family. We equally bind ourselves, in the event of separating, to divide our fortune, having deducted our own children's legal portion. In a perfect union, the one who died first would leave half his property to his children or, if childless, as of right to his relict, unless, that is, the deceased had disposed of his half as he saw fit.

This, approximately, is the formula of the marriage contract whose introduction I propose. I can already see sanctimonious hypocrites, prudes, clergy and all the rest of the damned rabble rising against me the minute they read it.

Olympe de Gourges

Olympe de Gourges, *The Rights of Women* (Paris, 1791). Tr. Val Stephenson (London, Pythia Press, 1989), p. 17.

If Christ lives in us, then he prays in us, and our chief concern should be to provide him a place where he can pray. We know the joy of slipping into a silent church, out of the din and roar of traffic. What joy for him to push open our swing doors and find in us a place of silence where he can pray his prayer 'that they all may be one'. How good if he can say of us 'This is my body in which I can pray, through which I can make contact with souls, into whom and through whom which channel I can pour my love, which I can even break, if need be, for the salvation of the world.' But he waits for our Fiat before taking possession.

Mother Maribel of Wantage

Sister Janet CSMV, *Mother Maribel of Wantage* (London, SPCK, 1972), p. 63.

There was a thawing then
in the hearts of the women,
and after the hard frost
of the hard years,
their unshed tears
were flowing.

They understood
how the Lord,
takes the loveliest least,
for his self-bestowing.

They would remember,
when they were baking bread,
how he had said
that his grace,
works secretly in them,
like yeast.

When they sifted the ash,
and blew the spark of the fire,
they would remember
the breath of the Spirit,
that fans the smoking flax.

Caryll Houselander

Caryll Houselander, 'The Sermon on the Mount' in *The Flowering Tree* (London, Sheed and Ward, 1945), p. 13.

Let the Lord kiss me with the kiss of his mouth,
for thy breasts are better than wine. Canticles 1.1.

I have often noticed that, as far as we can understand, the soul appears here to be speaking with one person and asking for peace from another. For she says: 'Let him kiss me with the kiss of his mouth'. And then she seems to be speaking to the person in whose presence she is – 'Thy breasts are better'. I do not understand how this can be, and I am very glad not to do so. For really, daughters, the soul should not so much meditate upon or be taught to meditate upon or reverence her God in the things which with our lowly intelligence we can apparently comprehend in this life, as in the things which are quite incomprehensible. And so, when you read some book or hear a sermon or think upon the mysteries of our sacred faith and find you cannot properly understand the subject, I strongly recommend you not to tire yourselves or strain your powers of thought by splitting hairs over it; it is something not meant for women – and many such things are not meant for men either!

When the Lord wishes to explain the matter to us, he does so without making us labour at it. I say this to women and also to such men as have not to defend the truth by their writings: those whom the Lord has chosen to expound such things to us must of course labour and they will gain greatly by so doing. But for us the task is simply to take what the Lord gives us; and not to tire ourselves out by worrying over what he does not give us, but to rejoice as we think what a great God and Lord we have, out of whose words alone may contain within itself a thousand mysteries, so that we cannot even begin to understand it. If it were written in Latin or Hebrew or Greek, this would not be surprising; but even in our own vernacular, how many things there are in the Psalms of the glorious King David which, when explained to us in Spanish, are as obscure as if they were in Latin!

Teresa of Avila

Teresa of Jesus, *The Complete Works* vol. 2. Tr. and ed. E. Allison Peers (London and New York, Sheed and Ward, 1946), p. 359.

Now give me leave to tell you the beginning of my way that the Spirit first led me into. In the first place, then, after some years that I had lived in some good degree of an illuminated knowledge, setting under the visible teachings of men, that could give no further light than that they had arrived from others, through all of which I traced as a wandering spirit that could find no rest: but something still I found within myself that did open to draw in from a more pure air, than I could meet without me: whereupon I introverted more into my own inward deep, where I did meet with that which I could not find elsewhere . . . Whence we are now free to be married unto him that is raised from the dead, and so shall become the Lamb's wife, jointured into all the lands and possessions that he hath. The eternal revenues are belonging to her, whether invisible or visible: all power in heaven and earth is committed to her . . . whether it be gifts of prophecy, or of revelation, or of manifestation, or of discerning of spirits: or that high tongue of the learned, which only speaks from Wisdom's breath.

At which opening, my spirit even failed within me, as desponding ever to get rid of my first husband . . . that first husband who so long hindered my marriage with the Lamb.

Jane Lead

Jane Lead, *A Fountain of Gardens Watered by the Rivers of Divine Pleasure and Springing up in all Varieties of Spiritual Plants* (London, 1697–1701) vol. 1, pp. 6, 68–71. Quoted in *Women of Spirit*, ed. Rosemary Radford Ruether and Eleanor McLaughlin (New York, Simon Schuster, 1979), pp. 190–1.

Ah, dear child, may God give you what my heart desires for you, and may you love him as he deserves. Still, I could never endure, dear child, that someone before me loved God as dearly as I. I believe that many loved him as fondly and dearly, yet I could hardly bear that someone would know him with such passion.

To enable the soul to attain this perfection, Christ has made his body into a staircase, with great steps. See, his feet are nailed fast to the cross; they constitute the first great step because, to begin with, the soul's desire has to be stripped of self-will, for as the feet carry the body, so desire carries the soul. Reflect that no soul will ever acquire virtue without climbing this first step. Once you have done that, you come to real, deep humility. Climb the next step without delay and you reach the open side of God's Son. Within, you will find the fathomless furnace of divine charity. Yes, on this second step of the open side, there is a little shop, full of fragrant spices. Therein you will find the God-Man; therein, too, the soul becomes so satiated and inebriated as to become oblivious of self for, like a man intoxicated with wine, it will have eyes only for the blood spilt with such burning love. With eager longing it presses on upwards and reaches the last step, the mouth, where it reposes in peace and quiet, savouring the peace of obedience. Like a man who falls asleep after drinking heavily and so is oblivious of both pain and pleasure, the bride of Christ, brimming over with love, sleeps in the peace of her bridegroom. Her own feelings are so deeply asleep that she remains unruffled when assailed by tribulations and rises above undue delight in worldly prosperity; for she stripped herself of all desire of that kind back on the first step. Here on the third she is conformed to Christ crucified and made one with him.

Catherine of Siena

I Catherine: Selected Writings of Catherine of Siena. Letter of 18 March 1376 Tr. Kenelm Foster and Mary John Ronayne (London, Collins, 1980), pp. 105–6. Quoted in *Medieval Religious Women*, vol. 2: *Peace Weavers*, ed. John A. Nichols and Lillian Thomas Shanks (Kalamazoo, MI, Cistercian Publications, 1987), p. 278.

And I saw one like a lovely maiden, her face gleaming with such radiant splendour that I could not perfectly behold her. Whiter than snow was her mantle and more shining that the stars, and her shoes were of the finest gold. In her right hand she held the sun and the moon and tenderly embraced them. On her breast was an ivory tablet in which there appeared the form of a man, the colour of sapphire; and all creation called this maiden Lady. But she spoke to the form which appeared in her bosom, saying: 'With you is the beginning in the day of your power, in the splendour of the holy ones; I bore you from the womb before the morning star.' (Ps 109.3 Vulgate)

And I heard a voice saying to me: 'This maiden whom you see is Love, who has her dwelling place in eternity. When God wished to create the world, he leaned down in the tenderest love and provided all that was needful, as a father prepares an inheritance for his son.'

Hildegard of Bingen

Hildegard of Bingen in *Ep 30*: PL 197: 192D–195 A. Quoted in *Medieval Religious Women* vol. 2: *Peace Weavers*, ed. John A. Nichols and Lillian Thomas Shanks (Kalamazoo, MI, Cistercian Publications, 1987), p. 114. Translated by Barbara Newman.

Now we have one answer to the question, Why must we be always seeking for the lost Child?

Why must we be always feeling the pain of loss?

If we did not, we should not realize that our idols are not God, are not Christ.

Bad as they are, they match our limitations; and if they could content us, we should never know the real beauty of Christ: we should not become whole.

It is one of God's great mercies that, although our vanity and our fear and other mean passions crave for satisfaction, when they are satisfied, we are not. There is an essential you, an essential me, who cannot be satisfied excepting by God: that is why the sense of loss saves us from complacency in our idols and drives us to go on seeking for the lost Child.

That is why people who seem to have got (and even to have got by their own efforts) all that life can give are so often aware of an inexplicable lack, a want in themselves.

Our conception of Christ makes us what we are, makes our effect on others what it is, influences us and influences everyone with whom we come into contact.

Our Lord said to his Apostles: 'It is expedient for you that I go away.'

It is the same for us. We know him only by continually learning him anew; we get away from false gods only by continually seeking him; we hold him only by losing him.

He goes away from us only because it is expedient for us. He goes away that we may seek him. The sense of loss, the awareness of insufficiency, makes us long for him as he is; it makes us willing to go out from ourselves and find him where he is.

He wants us to seek, because he wants to give himself to us. It is an experience like the experience of emptiness: the emptiness must be there that he may fill it; and we must be aware of it in order that we may want him to fill it.

'Why hast thou done so to us?'
And the answer is simple, after all: 'Seek and ye shall find.'
His meaning is love.

Caryll Houselander

Caryll Houselander, *The Reed of God* (London, Sheed and Ward, 1955), pp. 88–9.

8

Crowned with an honour women never knew before

The Virgin Mary is an ambiguous sign for women in the Church. On the one hand she has been sentimentalized and on the other she has been magicalized. In either case this leaves present-day women with a dilemma. How can any truth and wisdom about Mary of Nazareth be retrieved and speak to our spiritual growth as believing women nowadays? And equally how can the woman who has been so exalted be reclaimed as part of the heart of the Christian tradition?

Firstly it is worth noticing that when women write about Mary they too are guilty of deploying her as a weapon. Christine de Pisan, the medieval Frenchwoman, exhorts other women to be 'humble and patient' because of the humility with which Mary greeted the incarnation. Teresa of Avila writes in an altogether more vigorous tone when she says she wishes that 'certain learned men . . . would learn something of the humility of the most holy Virgin!'

The most enlightening of the texts I have found and selected here come either from very simple hymns or from descriptions of visions of the Virgin Mary. Where women speak of what they experience as direct revelation of her they use words like honour and glory. With the medieval mystic, Elizabeth of Schönau, they hear her say, 'You can hope for good gifts from me, and so will all receive who have faith in me.' The visions are unpredictable; the disclosure they comment upon can be naive or funny as for instance with the revelations of Birgitte, where Mary took off the swaddling clothes of the baby Jesus to show them her naked child. As Hadewijch claimed: 'She it was who tamed wild Love and gave us a lamb for a lion.'

The Catholic tradition has risked Mariolatry by exalting Mary; the Protestant tradition has not taken this risk but, by expunging Mary from its canons, its liturgy and iconography, it has defaced the image and likeness of women. A healthy redress of balance will only be restored when, with a commentator like Dorothy L. Sayers, we can say: 'Only one Jesus is to die today – one person whom you know – the truth of God and the fact of Mary.' Where we deny the fact of Mary we deny the incorporation, the bodily intervention of a woman, of Mary in our own redemption. The incarnation goes off at half cock.

The Hidden Tradition

This chapter is short; I have deliberately chosen it as the finale of the book. None of us can get round the truth of God – and the fact of women. My own desire is that the truth and the fact should somehow come together and find their focus in the lived understanding of all Christbearing women. In Mary, 'we are all crowned with an honour women never knew before'.

Whatever gifts God bestowed upon us
There was no one who could
Understand true love
Until Mary, in her goodness,
And with deep humility,
Received the gift of Love,
She it was who tamed wild Love
And gave us a lamb for a lion;
Through her a light shone in the darkness
That had endured so long.

Hadewijch of Brabant

Hadewijch of Brabant in *Beguine Spirituality* ed. Fiona Bowie (London, SPCK; New York, Crossroad, 1989), p. 125.

What a great wonder it is
That into the humble form of a woman
The King entered.
God did this,
Because humility rises above everything.
And what great fortune is contained
In this feminine form,
Because the malice that flowed from one woman,
This woman has wiped away hereafter;
She has established the sweetest odour of virtues,
And she has honoured and adorned heaven
Far more than she earlier disordered the earth.

Greetings, noble, glorious and chaste beloved.
You image of purity,
You ground of sanctity,
Pleasing to God.
Your womb contained joy
Just as the grass was infused with

176

Greenness, when the dew sank into it;
Therefore Mother everything joyful has been
Created through you.
Now let the whole Church, dawning rose-red,
  break the day in joy
And sound in harmony because of the loveliest
  Virgin
And most praiseworthy Mary, Mother of God.   Amen.

Love overflows into all things,
From out of the depths to above the highest stars;
And so Love overflows into all best beloved,
  most loving things,
Because She has given to the highest King
The Kiss of Peace.

O most radiant jewel,
Resplendent glory of the sun;
The fountain from the heart of the Father
Has streamed into you:
His own unique Word
Through which he created the primordial
  matter of the world
Which Eve overturned like a whirlwind
The Word fashioned humanity for your sake
  Father
And thus you Mary are that lucid matter
Through whom the Word breathed forth
  everything of value,
Just as it led all creatures into being out of
  primordial matter.
Therefore the consummate benediction is
In womanly form,
Beyond all creation
Since God was made human
In a Virgin most sweet and blessed.

Today
He has appeared to us
Through the gate that was hidden and locked,
Because the serpent has suffocated in a woman.
Thus the flower of the Virgin Mary
Radiates illuminated in the first red of day-break.

Because a woman instituted death;
The clear Virgin has abolished it;
Certainly a heavenly infusion
Poured into you,
Because the highest Word
In you took on flesh.

You are the radiant white lily
Whom God perceived
Prior to all creation.
You the most beautiful and loveliest;
God so delighted in you that he pressed within you
The passionate embrace of his own heat,
So that his own son was suckled by you.
Truly has your body contained joy,
Since out of you every heavenly harmony sounded,
Because, Virgin, you carried the son of God,
When your own purity became illuminated in God.

Hildegard of Bingen

Hildegard of Bingen in *Medieval Women's Visionary Literature* ed. Elizabeth
Alvilda Petroff (Oxford University Press 1986), p. 279.

At this same period, on the festival of the Assumption of our Lady, I
was in a monastery of the Order of the glorious Saint Dominic,
thinking of the many sins which in times past I had confessed in that
house and of other things concerning my wicked life, when there
came upon me a rapture so vehement that it nearly drew me forth out
of myself altogether. I sat down and I remember even now that I could
neither see the Elevation nor hear Mass being said, and later this
caused me a certain amount of scruple. While in this state, I thought I
saw myself being clothed in a garment of great whiteness and brightness. At first I could not see who was clothing me, but later I saw our
Lady on my right hand and my father Saint Joseph on my left, and it
was they who were putting that garment upon me. I was given to
understand that I was now cleansed of my sins. When the clothing was
ended, and I was experiencing the greatest joy and bliss, I thought that
our Lady suddenly took me by the hands and told me that I was giving
her great pleasure by serving the glorious Saint Joseph and that I might
be sure that all I was trying to do about the convent would be
accomplished and that both the Lord and they two would be greatly
served in it. I was not to fear that there would be any failure whatever
about this, although the nature of the obedience which it would have
to render might not be to my liking. They would keep us safe and her
Son had already promised to go with us: as a sign that that was true,
she said, she would give me this jewel. Then she seemed to throw
round my neck a very beautiful gold collar, to which was fastened a
most valuable cross. The gold and stones were so different from
earthly things of the kind that no comparison between them is
possible: their beauty is quite unlike anything that we can imagine and
the understanding cannot soar high enough to comprehend the nature

of the garment or to imagine the brightness of the vision which it was the Lord's will to send me, and by comparison with which everything on earth looks, as one might say, like a smudge of soot.

The beauty which I saw in our Lady was wonderful, though I could discern in her no particularly beautiful detail of form: it was her face as a whole that was so lovely and the whiteness and the amazing splendour of her vestments, though the light was not dazzling, but quite soft. The glorious Saint Joseph I did not see so clearly, though I could see plainly that he was there, as in the visions to which I have already referred and in which nothing is seen. Our Lady looked to me quite like a child. When they had been with me for a short time and caused me the greatest bliss and happiness – more, I believe, than I had ever before experienced, so that I wished I need never lose it – I seemed to see them ascending to heaven with a great multitude of angels. I remained quite alone, but so greatly comforted and exalted and recollected in prayer, and so full of tender devotion, that I stayed for some time where I was, without moving, and unable to speak, quite beside myself. I was left with a vehement impulse to melt away in love for God, and with other feelings of a like kind, for everything happened in such a way that I could never doubt that this was of God, however hard I tried. It left me greatly comforted and full of peace.

Teresa of Avila

Teresa of Jesus, *The Complete Works* vol. 1. Tr. and ed. E. Allison Peers (London and New York, Sheed and Ward, 1946), pp. 262–3.

Revelations 7.22
After this the Virgin Mary appeared again to me, in the same place, and said: It has been a long time since in Rome I promised you that I would show you here in Bethlehem how my offspring had been born. And although in Naples I showed you something of it, that is to say the way I was standing when I gave birth to my son, you still should know for sure that I stood and gave birth such as you have seen it now – my knees were bent and I was alone in the stable, praying; I gave birth to him with such exultation and joy of my soul that I had no difficulties when he got out of my body or any pain. Then I wrapped him in swaddling clothes that I had prepared long ago. When Joseph saw this he was astonished and full of joy and happiness, because I had given birth without any help.

Revelations 7.23
At the same place where the Virgin Mary and Joseph were adoring the boy in the cradle, I also saw the shepherds, who had been watching their flocks, coming so that they could look at the child and adore it.

When they saw the child, they first wanted to find out whether it was a male or a female, for angels had announced to them that the saviour of the world had been born, and they had not said that it was a saviour-ess. Then the Virgin Mary showed to them the nature and the male sex of the child. At once they adored him with great awe and joy. Afterward they returned, praising and glorifying God for all they had heard and seen.

Birgitte

Opera Sante Birgitte. (MS 14, 2. Nurenberg 1500.) Tr. Barbara Obrist. Quoted in *Medieval Women Writers* ed. Katharina M. Wilson (Manchester University Press 1984), p. 245.

Follow the example of your Queen, the sovereign Virgin, who, after the extraordinary honour of being chosen Mother of the Son of God was announced to her, humbled herself all the more by calling herself the handmaiden of God . . . So, my ladies, be humble and patient, and God's grace will grow in you, and praise will be given to you as well as the Kingdom of Heaven.

Christine de Pisan

Christine de Pisan, *The City of Ladies* pp. 218, 254–5. Quoted in *Women of the Medieval World* ed. Julius Kirshner and Suzanne F. Wemple (Oxford, Basil Blackwell, 1987), p. 354.

1 Ave Maria! O Maiden, O Mother,
   Fondly thy children are calling on thee,
   Thine are the graces unclaimed by another,
      Sinless and beautiful star of the sea!
         Mater amabilis, ora pro nobis!
         Pray for thy children who call upon thee;
         Ave sanctissima! Ave purissima!
         Sinless and beautiful, star of the sea.

2 Ave Maria! the night shades are falling,
      Softly our voices arise unto thee,
   Earth's lonely exiles for succour are calling,
      Sinless and beautiful, star of the sea!
         Mater amabilis, ora pro nobis!   &c.

3 Ave Maria! thou portal of heaven,
   Harbour of refuge, to thee do we flee,
   Lost in the darkness, by stormy winds driven
   Shine on our pathway, fair star of the sea!
      Mater amabilis, ora pro nobis!   &c.

Sister 'M'

Sister 'M' in *The Westminster Hymnal* (London, Burns, Oates and Washbourne, 1953), no. 183.

And at the same time as I saw this corporeal sight, our Lord showed me a spiritual sight of his familiar love. I saw that he is to us everything that is good and comforting for our help. He is our clothing, for he is that love which wraps and enfolds us, embraces us and guides us, surrounds us for his love, which is so tender that he may never desert us. And so in this sight I saw truly that he is everything which is good, as I understand.

And in this he showed me something small, no bigger than a hazelnut, lying in the palm of my hand, and I perceived that it was as round as any ball. I looked at it and thought: What can this be? And I was given this general answer: It is everything which is made. I was amazed that it could last, for I thought that it was so little that it could suddenly fall into nothing. And I was answered in my understanding: It lasts and always will, because God loves it; and thus everything has being through the love of God.

In this little thing I saw three properties. The first is that God made it, the second is that he loves it, the third is that God preserves it. But what is that to me? It is that God is the Creator and the lover and the protector. For until I am substantially united to him, I can never have love or rest or true happiness; until, that is, I am so attached to him that there can be no created thing between my God and me. And who will do this deed? Truly, he himself, by his mercy and his grace, for he has made me for this and has blessedly restored me.

In this God brought our Lady to my understanding. I saw her spiritually in her bodily likeness, a simple, humble maiden, young in years, of the stature which she had when she conceived. Also God showed me part of the wisdom and truth of her soul, and in this I understood the reverent contemplation with which she beheld her God, marvelling with great reverence that he was willing to be born of her who was a simple creature created by him. And this wisdom and truth, this knowledge of her creator's greatness and of her own created littleness, made her say meekly to the angel Gabriel: Behold me here, God's handmaiden. In this sight I saw truly that she is greater, more worthy and more fulfilled, than everything else which God has created, and which is inferior to her. Above her is no created thing, except the blessed humanity of Christ. This little thing which is created and is inferior to our Lady, St Mary – God showed it to me as if it had been a hazelnut – seemed to me as if it could have perished because it is so little.

Julian of Norwich

Julian of Norwich, *Showings*. Classics of Western Spirituality. Tr. and introd. Edmund Colledge OSA and James Walsh SJ (London, SPCK; Mahwah, NJ, Paulist Press, 1978), pp. 130–1.

On the Purification of the most glorious mother Mary, during the reading of the gospel at mass, I entered into ecstasy; and as I looked, behold, my Lady came down on a ray of light and stood at the right hand of the priest. Near her was a venerable man of great age, having a white flowing beard. 'When the sisters gave back their candles into the hands of the priest, Our Lady returned to heaven. And behold, a great host of maidens with splendid candles came to meet her. After a short pause, they returned with her to the heights, following her with joy. On the same day at vespers, when I was again in ecstasy, I saw her once more in heavenly glory. I called upon her most fervently, asking for her help. With all my love and will I pleaded, adding at the end of the prayers: 'My Lady, what shall I hope to receive from you?' And she replied: 'You can hope for good gifts from me, and so will all receive who have faith in me.'

Elizabeth of Schönau

Elizabeth of Schönau in PL 195:144. Quoted by M. Colman O'Dell in *Medieval Religious Women* vol. 2: *Peace Weavers*, ed. John A. Nichols and Lillian Thomas Shanks (Kalamazoo, MI, Cistercian Publications, 1987), pp. 89–90.

And your voice speaks:
  Sing it early in the morning watch, sing it softly, softly
  into the world's dark ear.
Sing it on your knees, sing it as though under veils, sing it as
  women sing when they are with child:
For he who is strong has become tender, the Infinite has
  become small, his power now is kindness, the Exalted
  has put on humility.
He finds room in the chamber of a maiden: his throne will

be on her lap – a cradle song will be enough praise for
him.
See, the days will not dawn for piety, and the nights are dark
with awe.
I will kindle lights, O my soul, I will kindle joy to all the
ends of your humanity:
Hail to her who carried the Lord!

Gertrude von le Fort

Gertrude von le Fort, *Hymns to the Church* (New York, Sheed and Ward, 1953),
p. 15.

O secrets of God! We can only surrender our understanding and
realize that of itself it can do nothing to fathom the greatness of God. It
is well that we should remember here how our Lady the Virgin, with
her great wisdom, submitted in this way, and how, when she asked
the angel: 'How shall this be done?' he answered: 'The Holy Ghost
shall come upon thee; the power of the Most High shall overshadow
thee.' Thereupon she was no longer concerned to argue about it;
having great faith and wisdom, she at once recognized that, in view of
this twofold intervention, there was neither any necessity for further
knowledge on her part nor any room for doubt. She was not like
certain learned men, who, not having been led in this way of prayer by
the Lord and not having the beginnings of spirituality, try so hard to
reduce everything to reason and to measure everything by their own
understanding that it looks as if all their learning is going to enable
them to succeed in comprehending all the wonders of God. If only
they would learn something of the humility of the most holy Virgin!

Teresa of Avila

Teresa of Jesus, *The Complete Works* vol. 2. Tr. and ed. E. Allison Peers (London
and New York, Sheed and Ward, 1946), pp. 392–3.

1 Lord of life and King of Glory,
   Who didst deign a child to be,
Cradled on a mother's bosom,
   Throned upon a mother's knee;
For the children thou has given
   We must answer unto thee.

2 Since the day the blessed Mother
      Thee, the world's Redeemer, bore,
   Thou hast crowned us with an honour
      Women never knew before;
   And that we may bear it meetly
      We must seek thine aid the more.

3 Grant us then pure hearts and patient,
      That in all we do or say
   Little souls our deeds may copy,
      And be never led astray;
   Little feet our steps may follow
      In a safe and narrow way.

Christian Burke

Christian Burke in *Hymns Ancient and Modern* (London, William Clowes, n.d.), no. 498.

'I, Mary, am the fact; God is the truth; but Jesus is fact and truth – he is reality. You cannot see the immortal truth till it is born in the flesh of the fact. And because all birth is a sundering of the flesh, fact and reality seem to go separate ways. But it is not really so; the feet that must walk this road were made of me. Only one Jesus is to die today – one person whom you know – the truth of God and the fact of Mary. This is reality. From the beginning of time until now, this is the only thing that has ever really happened. When you understand this you will understand all prophecies, and all history . . .'

Dorothy L. Sayers

Dorothy L. Sayers, *The Man born to be King* (London, Gollancz, 1943), p. 295. Quoted in Rosamond Kent Sprague, *A Matter of Eternity: Selections from the Writings of Dorothy L. Sayers* (London and Oxford, Mowbray, 1973), p. 49.

Biographical Notes

MADAME ACARIE (1566–1618). A mystic and respected spiritual advisor, this wealthy bourgeois French Roman Catholic laywoman was received as a Carmelite lay sister after the death of her husband.

ANGELA OF FOLIGNO (1248–1309). When her husband died she became a Franciscan tertiary and gathered a group of companions around her over whom she exercised considerable influence on account of her mystical gifts and experiences.

EMILY AYCKBOWM (1836–1900). The eminent Victorian foundress of the worldwide Anglican religious community of the Sisters of the Church.

HATTY BAKER. Freelance journalist associated with the City Temple. She was the first woman to be pastor of a Congregational Church.

BALTHILDA. Of noble Saxon stock she founded a convent at Chelles in Merovingian Gaul to which she retired once she was widowed and became Queen Dowager.

BAUDONIVIA. The nun biographer of her abbess, Radegund, a former Frankish Queen who entered the convent and gave generously to all. She collected relics on a grand scale to ensure a steady flow of pilgrims.

KATHLEEN BLISS (1908–89). One time General Secretary of the Church of England's Board of Education and lecturer in Religious Studies at Sussex University, she was also a well-known broadcaster.

KATHERINE BENNETT and MARGARET HODGE. Two American Presbyterian women who reported on 'Causes of Unrest among the Women of the Church' to the General Council of the Presbyterian Church.

CATHERINE BOOTH (1829–90). Called by God to active ministry in the pulpit, she left the Methodist Church with her husband William. They started the Christian Mission in 1865, a permanent mission to the unconverted, which became known as the Salvation Army in 1878.

EVANGELINE BOOTH (1865–1950). The daughter of Catherine and William Booth, she became the worldwide General of the Salvation Army in 1934.

FLORENCE BOOTH (1861–1957). Daughter-in-law of Catherine and William Booth and the wife of Bramwell Booth, their son, she became a prominent member of the Salvation Army and the mother of Catherine Bramwell Booth who lived to the age of 104.

BIRGITTE (1303–73). A Swedish mystic and saint who was renowned for going on pilgrimage and who founded the Brigittines.

CHRISTIAN BURKE. A hymn writer in the Anglican tradition who was born in London in 1859 and wrote *Lord of Life and King of Glory* in 1903 as a prize hymn for a Mother's Union Service.

JOSEPHINE BUTLER (1828–1906). A lifelong campaigner for women's rights and suffrage, this prominent Anglican lay woman worked for the repeal of the Contagious Diseases Acts and for the condition of prostitutes, notably in Liverpool.

CATHERINE OF SIENA (1347–80). A mystic and politician, she attempted to negotiate between warring factions when Gregory XI was pope and supported his plans for a crusade. On his death she moved to Rome as counsellor and advisor to Pope Urban VI.

ELSIE CHAMBERLAIN. A Congregational minister, she became the first woman chaplain of the British Women's Royal Air Force and National President of the Women's Council of the Free Churches. She broadcast regularly with the BBC from 1950–1967.

JANE DE CHANTAL (1572–1641). Her husband was killed in a hunting accident leaving her with four of their six children. She went on to found the Order of the Visitation which pioneered a new form of religious life for Roman Catholic women.

LUCIE CHRISTINE (1844–1908). This pseudonym was adopted by a French Roman Catholic lay woman whose spiritual journal was published in 1909. She married at the age of 21 and had five children before she was widowed at the age of 45.

CHRISTINE DE PISAN (1365–*c*.1430). Widowed at 25 with young children to raise, this Italian doctor's daughter took to writing poetry and is claimed as an early feminist in our own times.

CLARE OF ASSISI (*c.*1193–1253). A native of Assisi she was inspired by God and by the example of Francis to found monasteries of sisters in Italy, France and Germany.

ELIZABETH CLEPHANE (1830–69). The daughter of the Sheriff Principal of Fife and Kinross, she was a member of the Free Church of Scotland and known as 'Sunbeam' for her good works in Melrose.

LADY ANNE CLIFFORD, COUNTESS OF PEMBROKE, DORSET AND MONTGOMERY b.1590. The Lady Anne Clifford trail has recently been opened in the Yorkshire Dales and Eden Valley to commemorate the four hundredth anniversary of the birth of this woman who spent 26 years of her life restoring and building castles and churches.

HANNAH COGSWELL. An early nineteenth-century North American Shaker eldress.

CONSTANCE COLEMAN. A late Victorian Anglican lay woman who campaigned vigorously on behalf of women's rights and for their access to the pulpit.

ELIZABETH COLLINS (1755–1831). A young American Quaker woman whose memories of her conversion have been recorded in the North American Quaker periodical *Friendly Women.*

ELIZABETH COMSTOCK (1815–90). A member of the Society of Friends, she travelled to the United States in 1854 and Abraham Lincoln wrote of her: 'Give Mrs Comstock access to all hospitals, and to all inmates with whom she desires to hold religious services.' She worked with the negroes, the wounded of both armies during the Civil War and soldiers in army prisons.

DOROTHY DAY (1897–1980). The Roman Catholic lay woman who founded the influential Catholic Worker Movement and was indomitable in her work for peace and human rights.

DHUODA. A lay woman author of the Carolingian age who married Bernhard of Septimania in the palace of Aachen in 824.

LINA ECKENSTEIN. A late nineteenth-century Anglican scholar and historian.

MARY BAKER EDDY (1821–1910). Founder of the Christian Scientists, she believed that with the birth of Christian Science came the insight that God is Mother as well as Father.

ELIZABETH OF SCHÖNAU (1129–64). She became abbess of the double monastery of Schönau in the diocese of Trier in 1157 and there experienced 12 years of visions and ecstasies which her brother Egbert collated.

ELIZABETH OF THE TRINITY (1880–1906). A French Carmelite sister whose spiritual writings, journals and letters were published after her death.

CHARLOTTE ELLIOTT (1789–1871). The victim of a lifetime of ill health, this lay woman was the composer of over one hundred hymns.

JANET ERSKINE STUART (1857–1914). Born in the Anglican rectory at Cottesmore in Rutland, the youngest of thirteen children, she became a Roman Catholic in 1879 and a Religious of the Sacred Heart two years later. For three years she served as Superior General of her congregation and travelled widely at this time.

GERTRUDE VON LE FORT. A convert to Roman Catholicism. Her writings on the place of women had considerable force in the middle years of this century.

CAROLINE FOX (1819–71). Born in Cornwall, this distinguished Quaker woman became a friend of the Coleridges and Carlyles, John Stuart Mill and William Wordsworth. Her diary was published in 1882 and again in 1944.

ELIZABETH FRY (1780–1845). The great Quaker prison reformer was born near Norwich, one of the seven daughters of John Gurney of Earlham. Her work in the prison service took her to France and Germany but she is chiefly known for the reforms she instigated in the UK.

JOAN MARY FRY (1862–1955). This Quaker woman gave the Swarthmore lecture in 1910. She was founder of the allotment garden schemes and deeply concerned about industrial strife, poverty and unemployment among Welsh miners.

CHARLOTTE PERKINS GILMAN. An early twentieth-century North American sociologist who questioned traditional eschatology, suggesting that a female-based spirituality would centre attention on the needs of the human person within this world rather than the next.

ISABELLA GILMORE (1842–1923). Widowed at the age of forty and a trained nurse, she was asked by Bishop Thorold of Winchester to re-shape the Anglican Deaconess Order. This had been founded in 1862 as an order parallel to male clergy, to consist of independent women working in parishes, who would be answerable only to the bishop.

OLYMPE DE GOURGES (1745–93). A French woman and revolutionary Republican who worked for women's rights and was executed for her efforts.

HILDA GRAEF. A historian and scholar, she devoted many years to the study of the history of the early Church.

CAROLINE C. GRAVESON (1874–1958). This Quaker woman gave the Swarthmore lecture on 'Religion and Culture' in 1937. For thirty years she was vice-principal of Goldsmith's College, London University for the women's side and wrote educational books and children's stories.

SARAH LYNES GRUBB (1773–1842). This Quaker woman preacher was born in London, lived in Ireland and died in East Anglia after extensive travels. She preached in markets and in the streets for fifty-two years.

DOROTHY FRANCES GURNEY (1858–1932). A Victorian vicar's daughter, she converted to Roman Catholicism with her husband in 1919.

HADEWIJCH. This Beguine mystic lived in the early 13th century and wrote in the dialect of Brabant. She may have lived either in Antwerp or in Brussels.

FRANCES RIDLEY HAVERGAL (1836–79). The daughter of the vicar of Astley in Worcester, she edited his music in 1871 as well as writing her own hymns.

SOLANGE HERTZ. A twentieth-century North American Roman Catholic lay woman. In the preface to *Searcher of Majesty* she claims, 'I wrote this book mostly to cheer us women up!'

HILDEGARD OF BINGEN (1098–1179). A German woman who possessed the gift of prophecy even before entering the convent at the age of eight. Here she saw visions and wrote extensively until her death at the age of eighty.

L. VIOLET HOLDSWORTH (1869–1954). This Quaker woman gave the Swarthmore lecture on 'Silent Worship' in 1919. She travelled widely in Italy, Australia and New Zealand and wrote innumerable devotional books.

LADY HOSIE. An Anglican lay woman and ardent campaigner for women's rights in the early years of the twentieth century.

CARYLL HOUSELANDER (1901–54). A prolific Roman Catholic spiritual writer of prose and poetry, this lay woman had profound mystical experiences while still in her teens and an acute sense of the presence of Christ in others.

ELIZABETH FOX HOWARD (1873–1957). Coming from an old Quaker family she did not herself join the Society of Friends until she was thirty, when she became active in the interests of humanitarian causes. During the 1914–18 war she was visiting Quaker chaplain to conscientious objectors in prison and worked for enemy aliens.

JULIA WARD HOWE (1819–1910). Born in New York, she married the director of the Perkins Institute for the Blind in Boston and worked actively for the abolition of slavery and women's suffrage.

REBECCA JACKSON. A black nineteenth-century visionary and Shaker eldress who preached sixty-nine sermons in the summer of 1834 on a preaching tour west of Philadelphia.

JULIAN OF NORWICH (1342–*c*.1415). The English mystic's revelations are preserved for us in the *Shewings* or *Revelations of Divine Love*. She is named after the cell where she lived as a recluse, adjoining St Julian's Chapel in Norwich.

MARGERY KEMPE (1373–*c*.1438). Born in Norfolk she married John Kempe in 1393 and had fourteen children before setting out on a series of pilgrimages to Italy and the Holy Land. Her experiences are recorded for us in *The Book of Margery Kempe*. A younger contemporary of Julian of Norwich, she is known to have consulted her on occasion.

JANE LEAD (1642–1704). Widowed at 46 this English woman was an early member of the Philadelphian Society, an early form of the Theosophists.

ANN LEE (1736–84). The founder and leader in the USA of the United Society of Believers in Christ's Second Appearing or Shakers. She became identified with the second Messiah and was greatly loved and respected by her followers.

KATHLEEN LONSDALE (1903–71). She became professor of Chemistry at London University and was one of the first two women elected a Fellow of the Royal Society. She was created a Dame of the British Empire in 1956 having worked actively for peace during the Second World War and been imprisoned for refusing to register as a fire-watcher.

MOTHER MARIBEL OF WANTAGE (1887–1970). An Anglican

190

religious of the Community of Saint Mary the Virgin, she trained as an artist at the Slade before entering the convent. Her Stations of the Cross, carved in teak, and other works are at St Mary's Convent, Wantage.

MARIE DE FRANCE. The first known woman to have written poetry in her own language in all of Western Europe sometime between 1160–1215.

MARIE DE L'INCARNATION (1599–1672). Born Marie Guyard and widowed with one child at the age of twenty-one, this French Roman Catholic nun established an Ursuline mission in Quebec and worked for over thirty years among the Huron Indians and the Iroquois.

MECHTHILD OF MAGDEBURG (c.1210–82). A German Beguine, she had visions and revelations for some twenty years before becoming a Cistercian nun.

HANNAH MORE (1745–1833). An Anglican religious writer and philanthropist who set up schools in Somerset and Friendly Societies for the education of adults.

FLORENCE NIGHTINGALE (1820–1910). The English hospital reformer began training as a nurse in 1851 and served extensively abroad during the Crimean war.

CAROLINE MARIA NOEL (1817–77). The daughter of an English Anglican vicar, she wrote a few hymns in her twenties but produced her main work in her middle years.

MARGUERITE D'OINGT. Born in 1310, she entered the Carthusians and became prioress of her community at Poleteins where she was known as a mystic and writer.

MARY PENINGTON (c.1625–82). She married Isaac Penington in 1654 and became an ardent Quaker along with her husband. She is also known by her maiden name as Mary Proude.

MAUDE D. PETRE (1863–1942). This Roman Catholic lay woman was a prominent religious thinker and friend and supporter of the Modernists George Tyrrell and Friedrich von Hügel.

EDITH PICTON-TURBERVILLE. An eminent Anglican lay woman who campaigned for the rights of women in Church and state.

CHRISTINA ROSSETTI (1830–94). Poetess and invalid sister of Dante Gabriel Rossetti, she was a high Anglican by temperament and in practice and ended her life as a nun in All Saints Home, Margaret Street.

MAUDE ROYDEN (1876–1956). Educated at Cheltenham Ladies College and Lady Margaret Hall, she lectured in the Oxford University extension delegacy and devoted her energies to campaigning for women's suffrage and religious and ethical rights. She was a noted preacher at the City Temple and elsewhere.

DOROTHY L. SAYERS (1893–1957). She read modern languages at Somerville College, Oxford and went on to write detective stories and translate Dante. Her most celebrated work as a Christian apologist was *A Man born to be King*, the radio play which was broadcast by the BBC from 1941–2.

LESBIA SCOTT (1898–1986). A hymn writer who was married to a naval officer and wrote hymns for her own three children, 'not for publication, but for use in our own nursery, as an expression of the faith we were trying to give the children'.

RICHENDA SCOTT. Born in 1903, this Quaker woman was chosen to give the Swarthmore lecture on 'Tradition and Experience' in 1964. She worked on the drafting committee for *Advices and Queries* from 1961–1967 and herself wrote extensively about Quaker history, completing a biography of Elizabeth M. Cadbury in 1955.

ATHENE SEYLER. A noted actress, she was a convert to the Church of England in the middle years of this century.

MARY F. SMITH (1892–1978). A member of the Society of Friends, she joined the Episcopalian Church after the death of her first husband when she married Lionel Smith, the rector of the Edinburgh Academy.

HANNAH WHITALL SMITH (1832–1911). She was born to a Quaker family in Philadelphia. A founder member of the Women's Christian Movement and the suffrage movement in the USA, she wrote extensively and her books were widely translated.

EDITH STEIN (1891–1942). She converted to Roman Catholicism after being brought up in a devout Jewish family and became a Carmelite nun. During the war she was arrested and condemned for her Jewish origins, ending her life in the gas chamber at Auschwitz.

CAROLINE E. STEPHEN (1834–1909). Born in Cambridge, the Anglican daughter of Sir James Stephen, she became a Quaker in her middle years. In *Quaker Strongholds* and *Light Arising* she gave a striking statement of the basis of the Society of Friends.

MARY STOCKS. Born in 1891, she worked for women's suffrage and to promote the welfare state. As Principal of Westfield College she became a frequent broadcaster and was made a peeress in 1966.

BARBARA STODDART (1865–1915). She was born in Fair Isle, Shetland and moved to the Orkneys as a child where she became a member of the Salvation Army. She served in England and the United States.

EVELYN STURGE (1875–1961). A member of the Society of Friends, she organized relief work for Belgian refugees in Birmingham during the First World War and after the Second she used War Damage Compensation received for the destruction of her own home to build four flats on the site for elderly people.

TERESA OF AVILA (1515–82). The great Spanish Carmelite and mystic founded and reformed convents all over Spain and was declared a Doctor of the Church in 1970.

THÉRÈSE OF LISIEUX (1873–97). The French Carmelite nun who wrote her autobiography at the command of her prioress and whose spiritual teaching is known as the 'Little Way'.

EVELYN UNDERHILL (1875–1941). An Anglican lay woman, spiritual director and retreat conductor, she wrote extensively about mysticism and the spiritual life and appears in the liturgical calender of the Episcopal Church as 'mystic and theologian'.

HELEN WADDELL (1889–1965). An Irish Presbyterian lay woman, she was a great scholar and translator of medieval Latin and wrote the famous novel *Peter Abelard*.

MARY WARD (1585–1645). A Yorkshirewoman who founded the Institute of the Blessed Virgin Mary, the first unenclosed order for active apostolic women religious in the Roman Catholic Church.

ANNA WHITE. A late nineteenth-century Shaker who wrote on the meaning and message of Shakerism as well as on the motherhood of God.

FRANCES WILLARD. An American Methodist woman who, by her death in 1898, had been national president of the Women's Temperance Union and an early suffragette.

OLIVE WYON. An Anglican lay woman who was directed by Evelyn Underhill during the middle years of this century.

Bibliography

Ayckbowm, Mother Emily *A Valiant Victorian: The Life and Times of Mother Emily Ayckbowm 1836–1900* (London, Mowbray, 1964).

Baker, Hatty *Women in the Ministry* (London, C. W. Daniel, 1911).

Baptist Hymn Book, The (London, Psalms and Hymns Trust, 1962).

Bliss, Kathleen *The Future of Religion* (London, Pelican, 1972).

Bliss, Kathleen *The Service and Status of Women in the Churches* (London, SCM, 1952).

Booth, Bramwell *Echoes and Memories* (London, Hodder and Stoughton, 1925).

Booth, Catherine *Female Ministry; or, Woman's Right to Preach the Gospel: an Address by Mrs General Booth* (London, Salvation Army Book Department, 1909).

Booth, Catherine *Papers on Aggressive Christianity* (London, Salvation Army, 1890).

Booth, Catherine *The Training of Children and Courtship and Marriage* (London, Salvationist Publishing and Supplies, 1953).

Booth, Evangeline *Woman* (New York, Fleming H. Revell, 1930).

Booth, Florence *Mothers and the Empire* (London, Salvation Army Book Department, 1914).

Bowie, Fiona, ed. *Beguine Spirituality* (London, SPCK; New York, Crossroad, 1989).

Chantal, Jane de. *Francis de Sales, Jane de Chantal: Letters of Spiritual Direction.* Classics of Western Spirituality. Ed. and introd. Wendy M. Wright and Joseph F. Power OSFS (Mahwah, NJ, Paulist Press, 1988).

Christian Faith and Practice in the Experience of the Society of Friends (London Yearly Meeting of the Religious Society of Friends 1960).

Clare, Saint, *Francis and Clare: the Complete Works*. Classics of Western Spirituality. Tr. and Intro. Regis J. Armstrong OFM Cap and Ignatius C. Brady OFM (London, SPCK; Mahwah, NJ, Paulist Press 1982).

Corrigan, Dame Felicitas *Helen Waddell* (London, Gollancz, 1986).

Cropper, Margaret *Sparks among the Stubble* (London, Longmans, 1955).

Day, Dorothy *On Pilgrimage: The Sixties* (New York, Curtis Books, 1972).

Dronke, Peter *Women Writers of the Middle Ages: A Critical Study of Texts from Perpetua to Marguerite Porete* (Cambridge University Press 1984).

Eckenstein, Lina *Women under Monasticism* (Cambridge University Press 1896).

Elizabeth of the Trinity, *Spiritual Writings*. Ed. M. M. Philipon OP (London, Geoffrey Chapman, 1962).

English Hymnal, The (London, Mowbray, 1975).

Fletcher, Sheila *Maude Royden: A Life* (Oxford, Basil Blackwell, 1989).

Friendly Women, vol. 9, no. 3.

Fry, Elizabeth *Observations on the Visiting, Superintending and Government of Female Prisoners* (London, 1827).

Fry, Joan Mary *The Communion of Life*. Swarthmore Lecture 1910 (London, Headley Brothers, 1910).

Gourges, Olympe de *The Rights of Woman – Paris, 1791*. Tr. Val Stevenson (London, Pythia Press, 1989).

Graef, Hilda *The Light and the Rainbow* (London, Longmans, 1959).

Grierson, Janet *Isabella Gilmore* (London, SPCK, 1962).

Hadewijch, *The Complete Works*. Classics of Western Spirituality Tr. and introd. Mother Columba Hart OSB (London, SPCK; Mahwah, NJ, Paulist Press, 1980).

Heeny, Brian *The Women's Movement in the Church of England* (Oxford, Clarendon Press, 1988).

Hertz, Solange *Searcher of Majesty* (Westminster, MD, The Newman Press, 1963).

Houselander, Caryll *The Comforting of Christ* (London, Sheed and Ward, 1947).

Houselander, Caryll *The Flowering Tree* (London, Sheed and Ward, 1945).

Houselander, Caryll *The Reed of God* (London, Sheed and Ward, 1955).

Bibliography

Hymns Ancient and Modern (London, William Clowes n.d.).

Janet, Sister, C S M V *Mother Maribel of Wantage* (London, SPCK, 1972).

Jaegher, Paul de, S J, ed. *An Anthology of Mysticism* (Burns, Oates and Washbourne 1935).

Julian of Norwich, *Showings*. Classics of Western Spirituality Tr. and introd. Edmund Colledge O S A and James Walsh S J (London, SPCK; Mahwah, NJ, Paulist Press, 1978).

Kirshner, Julius and Suzanne F. Wemple, ed., *Women of the Medieval World* (Oxford, Basil Blackwell, 1987).

Lonsdale, Kathleen, *I Believe* (Cambridge University Press 1964).

Menzies, Lucy, ed. *Collected Papers of Evelyn Underhill* (London, Longmans, 1946).

Ministry of Women, The. A report by a committee appointed by His Grace the Lord Archbishop of Canterbury (London, SPCK, 1919).

Monahan, Maud *Life and Letters of Janet Erskine Stuart* (London, Longmans, 1923).

Monk, Wendy, ed. *The Journals of Caroline Fox 1835–1871* (London, Elek, 1972).

Morgan, Dewi, ed. *They became Anglicans* (London, Mowbray, 1959).

Nichols, John A. and Lillian Thomas Shanks, ed. *Medieval Religious Women vol. 2: Peace Weavers* (Kalamazoo, MI, Cistercian Publications, 1987).

O'Faolain, Julia and Lauro Martines, ed. *Not in God's Image* (London, Fontana, 1973).

Orchard, M. Emmanuel, I B V M ed. *Till God Will: Mary Ward through her Writings* (London, Darton, Longman and Todd, 1985).

Petre, Maude D. 'Devotional Essays' in *The Method of Theology* (London, Catholic Truth Society, 1902).

Petroff, Elizabeth Alvilda, ed. *Medieval Women's Visionary Literature* (Oxford and New York, Oxford University Press, 1986).

Reufer, Linda Hill, ed., *Daily Readings from Quaker Writings Ancient and Modern* (Oregon, Serenity Press, 1988).

Richardson, Mrs Aubrey, *Women of the Church of England* (London, Chapman and Hall, 1908).

Royden, Maude in *The Ethics of Birth Control* (London, Macmillan, 1926).

Royden, Maude 'War and the Woman's Movement' in *Towards a Lasting*

Settlement ed. Charles Roden Buxton (London, George Allen and Unwin, 1915).

Ruether, Rosemary Radford, *Womanguides* (Boston, Beacon Press, 1985).

Ruether, Rosemary Radford and Eleanor McLaughlin, ed. *Women of Spirit* (New York, Simon & Schuster, 1979).

Sayers, Dorothy L. *A Matter of Eternity: selections from the writings of Dorothy L. Sayers,* ed. Rosamond Kent Sprague (London and Oxford, Mowbray, 1973).

Sayers, Dorothy L. *Are Women Human?* (Grand Rapids, MI, Eerdmans, 1971).

Song Book of the Salvation Army, The (1986 edition).

Stein, Edith, *The Collected Works of Edith Stein, Sister Benedicta of the Cross, Discalced Carmelite,* vol. 2. Tr. Freda Mary Oben (Washington DC, ISC Publications, 1987).

Scott, Richenda C. *Tradition and Experience.* Swarthmore Lecture 1964. (London, George Allen and Unwin, 1964).

Stocks, Mary *My Commonplace Book* (London, Peter Davies, 1970).

Teresa of Avila, Saint *The Complete Works of Saint Teresa of Jesus,* 3 vols, ed. E. Allison Peers (London and New York, Sheed and Ward, 1946).

Teresa of Avila, Saint *The Letters of Saint Teresa of Jesus,* 2 vols, Tr. E. Allison Peers (London, Sheed and Ward, 1980).

Thérèse of Lisieux, St *Autobiography of a Saint* (London, Collins, 1958).

Thérèse of Lisieux, St *Collected Letters* (London, Sheed and Ward, 1949).

Thompson, D. P., ed. *Women in the Pulpit* (London, James Clarke, n.d.).

Turberville, Edith Picton *Woman and the Church* (London, T. Fisher Unwin, 1917).

Underhill, Evelyn *Concerning the Inner Life with the House of the Soul* (London, Methuen, 1947).

Waddell, Helen, *Peter Abelard* (London, Pan, 1933).

Westminster Hymnal, The (London, Burns, Oates and Washbourne, 1953).

Whitson, Robley Edward, ed. *The Shakers: Two Centuries of Spiritual Reflection* (Mahwah, NJ, Paulist Press, 1984).

Williamson, Joseph *Josephine Butler – the Forgotten Saint* (Leighton Buzzard, The Faith Press, 1977).

Wilson, Katharina M., ed. *Medieval Women Writers* (Manchester University Press; University of Georgia Press, 1984).

Wyon, Olive, *Prayer* (London, Fontana, 1962).